HANDLEY PAGE HALIFAX

HANDLEY PAGE HALIFAX

SECOND WORLD WAR STRATEGIC BOMBER

PHILIP BIRTLES

First published in Great Britain in 2026 by
Fonthill
An imprint of
Pen & Sword Books Ltd
Yorkshire – Philadelphia
www.fonthill.media

Copyright © Philip Birtles, 2026

ISBN 978-1-78155-927-7

The right of Philip Birtles to be identified as
Author of this work has been asserted by him in accordance
with the Copyright, Designs and Patents Act 1988.

A CIP catalogue record for this book
is available from the British Library.

All rights reserved. No part of this book may be reproduced, transmitted, downloaded, decompiled or reverse engineered in any form or by any means, electronic or mechanical including photocopying, recording or by any information storage and retrieval system, without permission from the Publisher in writing. NO AI TRAINING: Without in any way limiting the Author's and Publisher's exclusive rights under copyright, any use of this publication to "train" generative artificial intelligence (AI) technologies to generate text is expressly prohibited. The Author and Publisher reserve all rights to license uses of this work for generative AI training and development of machine learning language models.

Typeset in SabonLTStd 10/13 by
SJmagic DESIGN SERVICES, India.
Printed and bound in the UK by CPI Group (UK) Ltd, Croydon, CR0 4YY

The Publisher's authorised representative in the EU for product
safety is Authorised Rep Compliance Ltd., Ground Floor,
71 Lower Baggot Street, Dublin D02 P593, Ireland.
www.arccompliance.com

For a complete list of Pen & Sword titles please contact
PEN & SWORD BOOKS LIMITED
George House, Units 12 & 13, Beevor Street, Off Pontefract Road,
Barnsley, South Yorkshire, S71 1HN, England
E-mail: enquiries@pen-and-sword.co.uk
Website: www.pen-and-sword.co.uk

or

PEN AND SWORD BOOKS
1950 Lawrence Rd, Havertown, PA 19083, USA
E-mail: uspen-and-sword@casematepublishers.com
Website: www.penandswordbooks.com

Dedication

In Memory of Douglas Newham 13 November 1921 – 14 March 2022

Doug was a Second World War RAF Bomber Command navigator who flew in Wellingtons and Halifaxes. He joined the RAF as volunteer aircrew on 4 August 1941, completing his training as an Air Observer (Navigation) ready to join 156 Squadron at Warboys on 5 September 1942 with Wellington IIIs, concentrating on target marking using Gee. This squadron became part of the PFF (Path Finder Force), with less experienced crew members, like Doug, posted elsewhere. Doug and his crew joined 150 Squadron at Kirmington on 23 October 1942, by which time he had been promoted to sergeant, and flew on his first operational mission on 15 November—a gardening sortie to Rochelle. After two more combat operations, Doug was part of a 150 Squadron detachment sent to North Africa, departing Perranporth on 9 December, based in Algeria.

Doug completed his first tour of thirty bombing operations with Wellington Mk IIIs against German targets in Tunisia, Sardinia and Sicily, and experienced a significantly reduced loss rate than if he had stayed in Britain. He maintained this was the first major piece of luck in his career. Out of thirty-nine navigators training with him at Jurby, only three survived, representing a loss rate of 92 per cent.

Doug returned to Britain by troop ship in May 1943 and then was posted to a Staff Navigator's course, gaining promotion to Flying Officer in November 1944. After a year on instruction duties, he was offered the post of Navigation Leader on 10 Squadron at Melbourne on 10 November 1944 with the rank of Flight Lieutenant, flying in H2S-equipped Halifax Mk IIIs. His first of twelve combat operations with 10 Squadron was to Essen on 12 December, with Doug's crew being the lead aircraft of the whole attack on Kamen on 24 February 1945, and the final operation to Osnabruck on 25 March. Doug's combat experiences are covered in greater detail in Chapter 12.

On 7 May 1945, 10 Squadron transferred to Transport Command with conversion to Dakotas where Doug continued as Squadron Navigation Leader, the squadron then training for para-trooping, glider towing and supply dropping ready for a move to Asia. VJ Day was declared on 15 August 1945, and 10 Squadron was sent to India on general transport duties and low-level supply dropping. Doug was sent home in May 1946, and after a short ATCO course in preparation for being employed by BOAC, he left the RAF on 21 August 1946 with the rank of Flight Lieutenant and the award of the Distinguished Flying Cross.

After the war Doug joined BOAC, later British Airways, as senior operations manager which included planning flights for members of the Royal Family. He and his wife Julienne retired to Cumbria when Doug became chairman of the Cockermouth branch of the RAFA, where he encouraged the local air cadets. Even in his mid-90s, Doug was an active fundraiser and supported local charities. He used to give regular talks and attended reunions, sometimes being flown in light aircraft all over Britain. He was skiing in the Alps until he was 95, when he had to stop as he couldn't get insurance. I once told Doug he was my role model.

Contents

	Dedication	5
	Introduction	9
1	Halifax Design and Development	29
2	Halifax Production	63
3	Initial RAF Halifax Bomber Operations	92
4	Merlin Halifax Operations	102
5	Support Operations by Merlin-Powered Halifaxes	144
6	Mediterranean Operations with Merlin Halifaxes	183
7	The Hercules-Powered Halifax Bomber Development and Operations	195
8	Signals Intelligence	233
9	Maritime Operations	240
10	Training	258
11	Cargo Halifax and Halton	267
12	Flight Lieutenant Douglas F. Newham DFC	288
13	*Friday the 13th* Restoration	301
	Appendix I: Halifax Production	309
	Appendix II: Halifax Units	312
	Appendix III: Halifax Specification	319
	Appendix IV: Preserved Halifaxes	322
	Further Reading	328

Introduction

In the Second World War, like the Hurricane was overshadowed by the Spitfire, the Halifax was also considered second to the Lancaster. With its large bomb-bay the Lancaster could carry a wide range of bomb loads, but the Halifax was a more versatile platform, performing a wide range of duties, including troop carrying, glider towing and it became an effective post-war airliner as the Halton. It was part of the traditional Handley Page long line of heavy bombers from the First World War O/100 to the Victor V-bomber in the Cold War.

The Halifax was not the only Second World War RAF heavy bomber to suffer development challenges. The Lancaster was considered superior, but it was developed from the very inferior Manchester, which was plagued with two unreliable, but very large Rolls-Royce Vulture engines. As a result, Roy Chadwick went back to his Avro drawing board and developed the excellent Lancaster, powered by four of the more advanced and reliable Rolls-Royce Merlin engines. The Short Stirling was restricted by its specification, which kept the wingspan short enough for the aircraft to fit into particular RAF hangars. This was totally unnecessary with the hangars built on RAF Bomber Command airfields in the RAF Expansion Scheme and during the war. This lack of wingspan limited its high-altitude performance. The Halifax was very robust, and while the Lancaster only operated as a heavy bomber in the European theatre, Halifaxes served with not only Bomber Command, but also Coastal and Transport Commands, from Britain, North Africa, the Middle East and Asia.

Halifaxes in Bomber Command service dropped only a total 23.5 per cent bomb tonnage, compared with the Lancaster at 63.7 per cent. With the exception of the Lancaster, Halifaxes dropped more tonnage in the bomber offensive than the rest of the Second World War RAF bombers combined. It was also deployed on duties when the Lancaster was not. The Halifax was the only British four-engine bomber to operate from overseas bases. Although Air Vice-Marshal D. C. T. Bennett, commander of the Path Finder Force (PFF), admitted the Halifax was not as good as the Lancaster, it nevertheless did sound work. Air Chief Marshall 'Bomber' Harris disliked the Halifax, which may be the reason for the lack of publicity of the aircraft's operations and achievements

Handley Page Ltd. was registered on 17 June 1909 by Frederick Handley Page, with the aim of undertaking aeronautical engineering, the first such company to be registered in Britain. He made the first successful flight in an aeroplane of his own design and construction on 26 May 1910 with a few hops, but his lack of piloting skills forced him to concentrate on his engineering talents. In September 1911, Frederick moved from his sheds at Barking to larger premises at 110 Cricklewood Lane, within easy reach of Hendon, where a flight shed was made available on the airfield by George Holt Thomas of Airco. The main reason for the move to larger premises was to be able to build the Geoffrey de Havilland designed BE.2a biplanes for the RFC (Royal Flying Corps), although only two were completed due to problems with raw materials.

The company had been in business for five years when the First World War started on 4 August 1914, having produced just eight aeroplanes of its own design, compared with 100 produced by Short Brothers, 200 by Bristol and increasing output by Sopwith and Vickers. Handley Page therefore offered his aircraft manufacturing factory to both the War Office and Admiralty, the latter showing an interest, with plans to produce bombers and coastal patrol aircraft. Of the greatest interest was a long-range bomber capable of attacking the German fleet at Kiel before it was put to sea, as well as the growing number of Zeppelin airship sheds under rapid construction. The resulting design was the Type O/100, with a wingspan of 100 feet, the Admiralty ordering four prototypes in February 1915. Despite having only twelve employees,

The Handley Page specialisation in heavy bombers started with the First World War O/100 and finished with the Cold War Victor V-Bomber. Powered by two Rolls-Royce 250hp Eagle II engines the prototype was first flown from Hendon on 17 December 1915. This aircraft, 3117, was powered by four 200hp Hispano-Suiza engines for trials at Farnborough in October 1917. (*Handley Page Association*)

working 9.5 hours a day, seven days a week, progress was so good the order was increased to twelve, with soon after a further twenty-eight aircraft, resulting in a subsequent increase in the workforce, increasing to 150 by the end of November. Power came from two R-R (Rolls-Royce) Eagle engines developing initially 250hp, but later increasing to 320hp. Having been moved down the Edgware Road to Hendon, the first flight was made on 17 December 1915. First deliveries were made to the RNAS (Royal Naval Air Service) training squadron at Manston in October 1916, with the first regular unit, 7 Squadron equipped in April 1917, used mainly for night bombing, with more squadrons following.

Meanwhile Handley Page was developing an improved O/400 bomber with reduced drag nacelles housing 360hp R-R Eagle VIII engines. It had increased fuel capacity and could carry more bombs. As a result, increased manufacturing space was required and a new factory was built on eleven acres by Somerton Road in Cricklewood. There was a drawing office fronting Claremont Road and a 160-acre airfield adjoining on the Clutterhouse Farm site. The prototype 3138 initially was powered by two 275 Sunbeam Maori engines having been progressively modified from an O/100. The first production aircraft, C3487, was assembled at the Royal Aircraft Factory in March 1918 from components built at Cricklewood. With development concentrating on the new bomber, an initial contract was placed on 14 August 1917 for 100 O/400s, while other quite different projects were also studied. With German Gotha night attacks on London in September 1917, a further 150 O/400s were ordered from Handley Page with another 150 from subcontractors, the first twenty delivered for service in April 1918, with over 200 delivered by August 1918. O/400s entered service at Villeseneux

The HP O/400 was a similar airframe to the O/100, but was powered by two R-R Eagle VIIIs, two Sunbeam Maori, or two Liberty engines, increasing cruising speed from 76mph to 97mph. The prototype 3138 was first flown with 320hp Eagle IVs from Martlesham Heath in September 1917. O/400s served in the USA with 'Gallopin Goose' compared with a Martin MB-1 at Kelly Field, Texas in 1921. (*Handley Page Association*)

with 16 Squadron RNAS in March 1918, which became 216 Squadron when the RAF was formed on 1 April.

The Company was encouraged to study a new requirement for a long-range heavy night bomber capable of reaching German strategic targets, including Berlin from bases in East Anglia. Known as the HP.15 Type V/1500, it was powered by four R-R Eagle VIII engines mounted in pairs between the wings with two to a nacelle, the forward in the tractor configuration and the rear driving a pusher propeller. It was an enlarged development of the O/400 at twice the weight, and carrying more than double the weapons load and fuel, including twenty-eight 112lb bombs suspended vertically. Strict security surrounded the project, resulting in design work and prototype construction to take place in Belfast at Harland & Wolff—many of the workforce normally employed on interior fittings of luxury ocean liners. An initial order was placed on 27 January 1918 with Harland & Wolff for twenty V/1500s with further orders to follow, while the Handley Page factory at Cricklewood was fully occupied with O/400 production. The first flight of O/400 B9463 was from Clutterhouse Farm airfield on 22 May 1918, with further flight testing following. The volume required meant using additional production space with William Beardmore at Dalmuir as well as Harland & Wolff in Belfast. 86th Wing Independent Force was

The next major bomber development was the HP O/1500 powered by four R-R Eagle VIII engines mounted in pairs between the wings. The prototype, B9463 was first flown from Martlesham Heath on 22 May 1918 after initial assembly at Cricklewood. The prototype was returned to Cricklewood, where it was pushed out for a test flight in August 1918. (*Handley Page Association*)

formed in great secrecy at Bircham Newton in Norfolk where two units, 166 and 167 Squadrons were formed to introduce the V/1500s into RAF service. No. 166 Squadron was reformed on 13 June 1918, taking delivery of the first V/1500s in October, but was disbanded on 31 May 1919. No. 167 Squadron was formed on 18 November 1918 with V/1500s and disbanded on 21 May 1919. The Three V/1500s delivered to 166 Squadron suffered various teething troubles, but were ready for combat on 9 November with bomb loads of 1,000lb each, the target being Berlin. The raid was cancelled due to bad weather and was ready to go 48 hours later when the Armistice was agreed.

By the end of the First World War, over half of the 794 O/400s ordered had been completed and 60 out of 210 V/1500s, mostly being delivered into storage. A number were converted for civil use at very low cost with Handley Page Transport, which was formed on 14 June 1919. Initial tasks for the converted O/400s included newspaper distribution and carrying passengers. During the First World War, the Cricklewood factory had employed 5,000 people, but after the Armistice the workforce was reduced to less than 100, with subcontractors also drastically reduced. Handley Page did benefit from the development of slotted wings, which as a safety feature reduced accidents, avoiding stall and spinning during take-offs and landings.

An early commercial development was the W.8 G-EAPJ, powered by a pair of 450hp Napier Lions engines and was first flown on 2 December 1919. Structurally, it was similar to the O/1500. The W.8 had a cruising speed of 115mph and could carry twelve passengers, later increasing to fourteen. (*Handley Page Association*)

From the O/400 the W.8 airliner was developed, making its first flight in December 1919, from which was developed a military version known as the W.8d Hyderabad adopted by 99 Squadron. The Hyderabad was designed as a DH 10 and Vickers Virginia replacement as a lighter alternative to the Vickers Virginia, with a crew of four and capable of carrying two 550lb bombs, or similar weight of smaller bombs. Self-defence was from four Scarff ring mounted Lewis guns. Power came from two Napier Lion IIB engines. The prototype J6994 was first flown in October 1923 from Cricklewood, and a production order was placed for fifteen aircraft, which entered service with 99 Squadron at Bircham Newton in December 1925, remaining with them until January 1931. No. 10 Squadron was reformed at Upper Heyford on 3 January 1928 with Hyderabads which it retained until November 1931.

A version of the civil W.10 airliner was developed as the Hinaidi bomber, with initially a wooden structure, but later used an all metal construction; it remained in RAF service with four squadrons until 1936. The prototype J7745 was converted from a Hyderabad and was first flown from Martlesham Heath on 26 March 1927. In its production version, it was powered by a pair of Bristol Jupiter VIII engines and taken on tropical trials in Egypt and India, where the wooden structure stood up very well. Following these trials, the type replaced Hyderabads with 10 and 99 Squadrons

The Hyderabad prototype J6994 was first flown from Cricklewood in October 1923 as a long range bomber for the RAF capable of carrying two 550lb bombs. A total of forty-five production bombers were built, including J8810, as well as commercial versions. (*Handley Page Association*)

The next bomber development for the RAF was the Hinaidi the prototype of which was converted from Hyderabad J7745, which was powered by two Gnome-Rhone Jupiter engines, and flown for the first time from Martlesham Heath on 26 March 1927. The wooden construction was replaced with all metal in the Hinaidi II prototype J9478 which was first flown from Cricklewood on 8 February 1929 by Major Cordes. (*Handley Page Association*)

The massive HP.42, of which four were built for Imperial Airways, was powered by four Bristol Jupiter engines and could carry up to twenty-four passengers over a range of 500 miles. The first flight was with G-AAGX 'Hannibal' from Radlett was on 14 November 1930 and was delivered on 5 March 1931 . This aircraft crashed on 1 March 1940 in the Gulf of Oman. (*Handley Page Association*)

as Hinaidi Is. The Hinaidi II all metal prototype J9478 was produced to Spec. B.13/29 and first flown from Cricklewood on 8 February 1929 with an order placed for thirty-three metal Hinaidis in 1929 for 10 and 99 Squadrons. Their Hyderabads were issued to 502 (Ulster) Squadron at Aldergrove and 503 (County of Lincoln) Squadron at Waddington, who replaced them with Hinaidis in October 1933, until withdrawn by 503 Squadron in November 1935. Meanwhile 10 Squadron operated Hinaidis from December 1930 until September 1932 and 99 Squadron Hinaidis from October 1929 until December 1933.

Following the financial crisis of 1921, the development of large airliners began, resulting in the impressive HP.42 airliner which served with Imperial Airways from 1932 until after the start of the Second World War, keeping the expertise in design and development of large aircraft.

In an effort to improve on the earlier obsolete aerodynamic bomber configurations, Specification B.19/27 was issued on 17 August 1927 for a new generation of night bombers with improved performance. Among the requirements was steady approach for bomb aiming, adequate self-defence, ease of maintenance, good controllability (even with one engine out), and freedom from pilot fatigue. Two easily maintained engines were required with enough fuel for a 920-mile flight, cruising at 115mph, with a service ceiling of 17,000 feet and landing speed of 55mph. Handley Page offered

Designed to match an advanced Specification B.19/27 as night bomber, the Heyford had its streamlined fuselage and Kestrel IIIs engines attached to below the upper wing. The prototype J9130 was first flown from Radlett on 12 June 1930 and later served with 99 Squadron. A production order later followed for fifteen aircraft and the aircraft served with both 10 and 99 Squadrons. (*Handley Page Association*)

their answer to the specification on 16 November 1927 with the original layout HP.38, which was to become the Heyford. It had a 75-foot wingspan with the fuselage attached to the underside of the top wing and the first prototype, J9130, was first flown on 12 June 1930 from Radlett with the Vickers Type 50, the main rival. Following successful service trials at Martlesham Heath, and with RAF squadrons, a production contract was received for what had become the HP.50 covering fifteen Heyford Mk.Is powered by a pair of 575hp R-R Kestrel engines. The first production example, K3489, was flown from Radlett on 21 June 1933, with deliveries to 99 Squadron at Upper Heyford starting on 14 November 1933 replacing Hinaidis. Heyfords remained with 99 Squadron until replaced by Vickers Wellingtons from October 1938. On 9 December, a further contract was placed for twenty-three more Heyfords to equip 10 Squadron. These later aircraft incorporated a number of improvements, resulting in being designated Mk.IA, with many of the earlier aircraft modified to the same standard. Heyford IAs were delivered to 10 Squadron at Boscombe Down and replaced with Mk.IIIs from November 1935 until June 1937.

Meanwhile Handley Page continued to improve the Heyford with Mk.II K4029 powered by two Kestrel VI engines to Specification B.28/34 with an order placed for sixteen aircraft. Further improvements used on K4029 included enclosed pilots' cockpit which was evaluated at Martlesham Heath in May 1935. Further improvements resulted in Heyford Mk.III to Spec. B.27/35 of which twenty were ordered in July 1935, extended to an additional fifty aircraft, before the biplane configuration gave way to a more modern monoplane layout. First Mk.III deliveries were made to 166 Squadron which reformed at Boscombe Down on 1 November 1936, which kept them in service until September 1939. A total of eleven RAF squadrons flew Heyfords as front-line bombers from 1933 until 1939, including 7, IX, 38, 97, 102, 78, 149 and 148 Squadrons, with none taking part in active operations during the Second World War.

As aircraft development progressed, there was a need to replace the original space-frame construction with metal-stressed skin structures. This would reduce drag while increasing performance, with the addition of retractable undercarriage and supercharged engines driving variable pitch propellers. The first stage in this process was the HP.47 in a small scale as a single engine mailplane, leading to the HP.51, a twin Pegasus high wing bomber with a fixed undercarriage, which first flew on 10 October 1936 and was later developed into the Harrow. This was followed by the smaller HP.52 Hampden, which was one of the first RAF bombers to enter combat in the Second World War in 1939.

While flying an Avro Avian modified for auto-slot development, one of the test pilots, J. L. Cordes had to make a precautionary landing due to poor weather in March 1928. He chose a field between the main railway line and Watling Street, south of St Albans, and just north of Radlett. The farmer helped to park the aircraft for the night, continued the next day to Cricklewood. Cordes reported the landing field may make a good site for a future airfield. Although nothing was done for a while, six months later Cricklewood was becoming limited for flying for larger and faster aircraft. By June 1929, the new site was already being used for test flying, with construction of an assembly and flight test hangar soon after. With the sale of the airfield at Cricklewood, helped by grants from the local councils, the site was closed to flying on 8 November 1929, with the new Radlett Aerodrome opened by HRH Prince George on 7 July 1930.

Hannibal made its first flight from Radlett on 11 November 1930, the eight HP.42s were followed by 124 Heyfords, 100 Harrows and an initial batch of 500 Hampdens. When the RAF Expansion Programme was established in 1935, RAF bomber units were increased from forty-one squadrons to sixty-eight over the next two years. By this time, Germany had replaced France as our potential enemy. There was also the belief that the bomber would always get through, and the new high-performance monoplanes would replace the antiquate biplanes then in service.

The first monoplane bomber produced by Handley Page was the Harrow to Spec. B.1/35 which originally had been designed as a transport, but was now required to carry a bomb load of 3,000lb, although it still had to retain the capability of carrying twenty fully equipped troops. In August 1935, a single order was placed for 100 aircraft for rapid production to follow the last Heyfords. The first Harrow, K6933, was first flown from Radlett on 10 October 1936 powered by two Bristol Pegasus

The Harrow was Handley Page's answer to Spec. B.1/35 for an advanced twin Bristol Pegasus engine-powered bomber for the RAF with the first prototype, K6933 flying for the first time on 10 October 1936 from Radlett. Initial deliveries were to 214 Squadron at Scampton in January 1937. A total of 100 Harrows were built by Handley Page. (*Handley Page Association*)

X engines as the Mk.I. K6934. The first fully equipped Mk.II was powered by two Pegasus XX engines. It followed the first aircraft to Martlesham Heath and was fitted with nose and tail gun turrets. Difficulties with the armament resulted in the first fifty entering service without turrets; the first delivery, K6935, went to 214 Squadron at Scampton on 13 January 1937, followed by 37 Squadron at Feltwell in March and April. All were powered by Pegasus Is and therefore designated Mk.Is. As Pegasus XXs-powered Mk.IIs became available, some joined 214 and 37 Squadrons before others went to 115 Squadron at Marham, and 215 and 75 Squadrons both at Driffield. Production ended with K7032 in December 1937, remaining in service as night bombers until 1939, when they were replaced by Wellingtons; the Harrows did not see combat during the war.

Although not a heavy bomber, the twin-engine Hampden continued the Handley Page bomber tradition. The new twin-engine aircraft was to be of stressed-metal construction with a retractable undercarriage to Spec. B.9/32. Top speed was expected to be 190mph and a ceiling of 22,000 feet designated the HP.52. Power was from two supercharged Pegasus XVIIIs. The forward narrow fuselage was flat-sided and the tail mounted on a slim boom. The prototype K4240 was first flown on 21 June 1936.

The HP.52, later to become the Hampden, was designed from 1932 to update the RAF bomber capability, which had been in serious decline since the end of the First World War. Power came from two Bristol Pegasus engines for the prototype K4240, which flew for the first time on 21 June 1936. (*Handley Page Association*)

At the mock-up conference at Cricklewood on 25 September an order was confirmed for 180 production Hampdens, with a further 100 from Short & Harland in Belfast.

When re-engined with a pair of Napier Dagger engines, L7271 became the Hereford making its first flight on 6 October 1938, and in due course the Daggers were replaced by the favoured Pegasus XXs. The main difference between Hampden and Hereford was some structural changes affecting interchangeability. A production order was placed for 100 Herefords from Belfast with the first, L6002, making its first flight on 17 May 1939. The first Radlett-built Hampden, L4032, was first flown on 21 June 1938. On 6 August, a contract was placed with English Electric for seventy-five Hampdens. The first delivery to the RAF was 49 Squadron at Scampton on 20 September 1938.

As production became established, deliveries to the RAF increased rapidly with 83 Squadron joining 49 Squadron at Scampton and 50 Squadron at Waddington. Further production contracts were placed in Canada for delivery to Britain, and production at Cricklewood and Radlett increased with a total of 500 delivered by June 1940. In 1939, 44 Squadron joined 50 Squadron at Waddington, followed by 61 and 144 Squadrons at Hemswell, with all these squadrons operational by September 1939. By the outbreak of war, 212 Hampdens had been delivered to

Production Hampdens had a transparent nose for bomb aiming by day or night, but the low drag fuselage was too slim to have a standard gun turret, so single Vickers guns were mounted in the nose and each of the lower and upper rear gunner's positions. Five hundred Hampdens were built by Handley Page, 770 by English Electric and 160 from Canada. (*Handley Page Association*)

the RAF. The Dagger-powered Herefords tended to overheat and were restricted to crew training. Initially allocated to day operations, the first armed reconnaissance was on 29 September 1939 when 144 Squadron was sent to Heligoland Bight and attacked enemy shipping, although five Hampdens were shot down by fighters, sadly demonstrating their vulnerability. Following this, Hampden squadrons were switched to night operations. With its withdrawal as a night bomber by the spring of 1942, Hampdens were allocated to other duties, including torpedo bombers with Coastal Command on convoy protection, with replacement by Beaufighters in 1943. Two examples of Hampdens are the subject of demanding restoration programmes, one at RAF Museum Cosford and the other at East Kirkby.

When Specification P.13/36 was issued, Handley Page tendered the twin R-R Vulture-powered HP.56, but the new engine suffered serious development problems, Handley Page selected four R-R Merlins to power what became the HP.57 Halifax, of which there will be more later, as the subject of this book.

Meanwhile, production continued when war was declared in September 1939 using the Government Shadow Factory Scheme with Hampdens already in production at English Electric at Preston, and Herefords being built by Short & Harland in Belfast, allowing Handley Page to build up Halifax volume production at Cricklewood and

With the approach of the Second World War, Handley Page commenced design of the Halifax heavy bomber, of which more details to follow. This example is HP-built B.Mk.I L9530 MP-L of 76 Squadron in August 1941. (*Air Historical Branch*)

Radlett. By the end of the Second World War, Halifax production was running down and replaced by the passenger and cargo transport Halton, a similar airframe and engines, with the armament removed. Haltons served with BOAC and cargo Halifaxes also took part in the Berlin Airlift until replaced by the next type from Handley Page, the Hastings military transport of which 152 were built for the RAF and RNZAF using the wing and powerplants of the Halifax fitted with a new tailwheel fuselage, with a large cargo door and capable of dropping paratroops.

Studies were being discussed in mid-1943 for a possible military transport to replace the Halton. In April 1944, the Air Ministry issued Spec. C.3/44 for a multi-purpose RAF transport, and the Handley Page proposal accepted for two HP.67 Hastings C.1 prototypes TE580 and TE583, the civil version of which would be the Hermes. With great urgency to get the Hermes G-AGSS flying as soon as possible because of competition from other manufacturers, the maiden flight was made from Radlett on 2 December 1945, but control could not be maintained, and it crashed fatally 3 miles from take-off. However, production of the Hastings prototypes with a production order for 100 aircraft was accelerated powered by four Bristol Hercules radial engines, while the investigation into the crash continued. With the runway at Radlett considered too short, the Hastings prototype TE580 was taken to RAF Wittering where final assembly was undertaken on 7 May 1946. It then returned to Radlett, where it was formally named Hastings on 4 September 1946. The second prototype was flown from Radlett on 30 December, both aircraft going to Boscombe Down for service trials. Meanwhile production of the first 100 aircraft had started at Cricklewood, with final assembly at Radlett, and the first production aircraft, TG499, flew on 25 April 1947. Following completion of trials and clearance for service, the first deliveries were to 47 Squadron at Dishforth in October ready for service in the Berlin Air Lift.

A second Hastings unit was 297 Squadron, also allocated to the Berlin Airlift, with 53 Squadron coming in near the end, the operation finishing on 6 October 1949. Following the first 100 Hastings, a follow-on order was placed for sixty-five Hastings C.2s to Spec. C.19/49, although the number was later reduced to twenty-five. The C.2 was in effect the standard production standard incorporating all the earlier improvements with all up weight increased to 80,000lb and additional fuel capacity. The last six aircraft on the production line, plus four others were converted to Met.1s for operation by 202 Squadron based at Aldergrove for weather reconnaissance over the North Atlantic. When the Hastings C.2 entered service, the increased fuel tankage proved helpful, with fifty of the earlier versions brought up to the same standard as C.1As, with underwing external fuel tanks added. Abingdon was the base for 24 and 47 Squadrons as tactical transports, while Lyneham was the base for 53, 99 and 511 Squadrons tasked with long-range strategic routes to Asia. Other units were 36, 59, 114 and 116 Squadrons, while 70 Squadron was based in Cyprus for Middle East local transport and 48 Squadron was based in Singapore for local operations in Asia. Before production ceased, another twenty-four Hastings were ordered in 1951, including three more VIP C.4s to add to the one already in service. The C.4s were allocated to the VIP Flight with 24 Squadron. Three Hastings were ordered for the RNZAF, with a final RAF batch of seventeen aircraft, completed in October 1952.

The Hastings post-war transport was based on the Halifax wing, engines and undercarriage, with a new fuselage added. Two prototypes were initially ordered, TE580 and TE583, followed by 100 aircraft ordered for the RAF. The first prototype was flown from Wittering on 7 May 1946 and the first unit to be equipped with Hastings was 47 Squadron to participate in the Berlin Air Lift. A further twenty-five Hastings C.2s were later ordered for the RAF. Hastings C.1 TG536 was used by the SCBS for crew training and was at the Chivenor air show on 23 August 1969. (*Philip Birtles*)

The Hastings was finally withdrawn from squadron service on 5 January 1958. In addition ten Hastings were modified as T.5s for training V-Bomber air electronics officers based at Lindholme with the Bomber Command (later Strike Command) Bombing School, and unofficially referred to as 1066 Squadron in honour of the Battle of Hastings. The Hastings was finally retired with 230 OCU at Scampton on 30 June 1977, and three have been preserved, one each at IWM Duxford, RAF Museum at Cosford and the Newark Air Museum.

The civil version of the Hastings was the nose-wheel Hermes, which was ordered by BOAC, but with strong American competition it was not a commercial success. Following the loss of the first prototype Hermes on 2 December 1945, work initially stopped on the second prototype, G-AGUB, but when restarted the fuselage was extended by 160 inches as the Hermes II, but still with a tailwheel configuration. However the Hermes IV with nosewheel was offered to BOAC in September 1946. A production batch of twenty-five Hermes IVs was authorised on 19 March 1947 with power from Bristol Hercules engines. The maiden flight of the first Hermes IV, G-AKFP, was made from Radlett on 5 September 1948, as a pre-production aircraft. The first of twenty-four Hermes for BOAC was G-ALDA, but because it was overweight, together with the next three, was not accepted by the airline, their first being G-ALDE accepted on 22 February 1950, with the last, G-ALDY to BOAC on 16 January 1951. The Hermes with BOAC could carry forty first class passengers and commercial services started from London Airport on 6 August 1950. In October 1953, all surviving nineteen Hermes were withdrawn by BOAC and after a period of storage, were acquired by British independent airlines, with only G-ALDO unsold and scrapped in March 1959. Most of the independently operated Hermes were used on trooping flights as well as leased to other airlines to fulfil capacity shortages. The last Hermes was finally scrapped at Pershore in 1969, and the only surviving relic is the fuselage of G-ALDG which was for many years used for cabin crew training at Gatwick and is now preserved at Duxford.

In 1946, Handley Page continued its long tradition of producing bombers for the RAF by responding to Specification B.35/46 for a high subsonic speed V-Bomber. This resulted in the HP.80 Victor jet bomber which for ten years was part of Britain's nuclear deterrent. In June 1945, with considerable foresight, Sir Frederick requested an investigation of two classes of bomber, powered by four turbojets and a wing swept back 40 degrees with the designation HP.80, without any defined RAF requirement. By November 1946, the Air Staff were beginning to look for an Avro Lincoln replacement with a four-jet-powered bomber capable of delivering a 10,000lb nuclear weapon at 500mph from 45,000 feet with a range of 3,500 miles. This was later increased to

The commercial version of the Hastings was the Hermes, which later featured a nose wheel undercarriage as the Hermes IV, the prototype, G-AKFP made its first flight from Radlett on 5 September 1948. Twenty-five Hermes were ordered by BOAC, but the first four were not accepted. (*Handley Page Association*)

5,000 miles at 50,000 feet, for Operational Requirement (OR) 230. A revised Spec. B.35/46 was issued in March 1947 with cruising speed raised to 575mph and all up weight increased to 100,000lb to achieve 3,500 miles range. Competitive tenders were required and out of six manufacturers, Handley Page and Avro were selected for prototype construction in July 1947.

The Handley Page aircraft was to be powered by four 7,500lb thrust Metrovick F.9 turbojets, later to be developed into the 9,000lb thrust Armstrong Siddeley Sapphire. Instead of having a traditional swept back wing, the wing planform was in the shape of a crescent with three progressively swept back sections and a span of 100 feet. The rudders were at the wing tips with an all-moving tailplane at the rear. The crew was to be five, consisting of two pilots, two navigator/bomb aimers/radar operators and an ECM/radio operator, all ideally located in a jettisonable pressure cabin, the latter concept being abandoned in 1950. In January 1948, the wing tip rudders were deleted, with a central fin and rudder on the rear fuselage.

On 26 April 1948, a contract was awarded to Handley Page for two HP.80 prototypes, WB771 and WB775, with construction beginning at Cricklewood and the new experimental department at Park Street early in 1951. In June 1952, production orders for twenty-five of each of the Victor and Vulcan were awarded, and WB771 was completed at Park Street and on 24 May was made ready for transport by road to Boscombe Down for its first flight. Following re-assembly and adjustments to the centre of gravity (C of G), the first flight was made on Christmas Eve 1952, and on 25 February the prototype returned to Radlett, where it landed on the newly extended main runway. In the event only the two pilots were equipped with ejection seats, the other three crew members sitting in rearward facing seats with escape in an emergency through the normal entry door. On 14 July 1954, during low-level calibration flights at Cranfield, the tailplane separated from the top of the fin and WB771 crashed on the runway, killing the four crew, the reason being fatigue cracks in the tailplane attachment bolts. The second prototype, WB775, joined the flight test programme with a first flight on 11 September 1954 from Radlett. At its initial production standard, the Victor B.1 had a normal take-off weight of 160,000lb, a cruising speed of 500kt and at a maximum altitude over target of 50,800 feet with a 10,000lb bomb had a still air range of 4,360nm. The Victor's bomb-bay was nearly twice the size of the Vulcan, giving it a superior load carrying capability.

In October 1955, a further order was placed for eight Victor B.1s powered by Sapphire 7s and the next twenty-four as Phase 2 with Sapphire 9s. The first production B.1, XA917, was flown from Radlett on 1 February 1956 and a new assembly hall was constructed at Colney Street which was formally opened on 26 March and located at the southern end of the Aerodrome. In March 1956, with the cancellation of the Sapphire 9 development, the second contract was revised with the first twenty-five completed as B.1s and the last eight completed as Victor B.2s powered by four R-R 17,250lb thrust Conway by-pass turbojets, the first example being XH668. In January 1956, a follow-on contract was placed for eighteen Victor B.2s. During testing, John Allam inadvertently exceeded the speed of sound in B.1 XA917 on 1 June 1957, when a sonic bang was heard from Banbury to Watford.

On 28 November 1957, 'A' Squadron 232 OCU reformed at Gaydon with the delivery of B.1 XA931 to start the RAF training programme, with additional aircraft soon added to the fleet. The first front-line RAF unit to equip with Victor B.1s was 10 Squadron, which reformed at Cottesmore on 1 April 1958, the first three aircraft arriving on 9 April. The second unit was 15 Squadron also at Cottesmore on 1 September 1958 with nine B.1s, and the third was 57 Squadron at Honington which formed on 1 January 1959, and among others included the last B.1. During bombing trials, B.1 XA921 dropped thirty-five 1,000lb bombs in one go, which was fourteen more than the Vulcan could carry. Meanwhile, XA930 was allocated to flight refuelling trials as a receiver, and the same aircraft was fitted with jettisonable de Havilland Spectre rocket packs and took off from Hatfield.

The first Victor B.2 XH668 flew from Radlett on 20 February 1959 but was lost over Cardigan Bay in mysterious circumstances on 20 August when being flown by a Boscombe Down crew. The second B.2 XH669 then took over the bulk of the flight development programme. In January 1956, a further order was placed for eighteen B.2s, and another contract was agreed for twenty-seven more B.2s—on condition Handley Page merged with either Hawker Siddeley Aviation (HSA) or British Aircraft Corporation. While Sir Frederick was prepared to merge with HSA, he died before negotiations could be completed, resulting in the cancellation of twenty-two B.2s in

The Victor V-bomber continued the HP Bomber tradition with the RAF when the prototype WB771 was first flown from Boscombe Down on 24 December 1952. Twenty-five Victor B.Mk.1s were delivered to the RAF, followed by thirty-four B.Mk.2s. Victor B.2 XM717 from the Wittering Wing carrying a Blue Steel was at Weathersfield on 1 June 1968. The type was finally retired from RAF tanker duties in October 1993. (*Philip Birtles*)

the final batch, with the last aircraft, XM718, delivered to the RAF on 2 May 1963. Victor B.2s entered service with 139 (Jamaica) Squadron at Wittering starting on 1 February 1962, the second unit being 100 Squadron also at Wittering from 1 May 1962. These aircraft were modified to carry the Blue Steel stand-off missile recessed in the bomb-bay as part of Britain's nuclear deterrent, shared with Vulcan B.2s. Nine Victor SR.2s also served with 543 Squadron from January 1966, based at Wyton in the strategic reconnaissance role.

With the premature withdrawal of the Valiants from the strategic tanker role in December 1964 due to structural failure, the Victor B.1s were withdrawn from the bomber role, and urgently converted at Radlett into flight refuelling tankers with one unit under the rear fuselage and another two under each wing. Victor B.1s were sourced from 10 and 15 Squadrons, which were disbanded in March and October 1964. The first conversions were issued to 55 Squadron at Marham from May 1965, initially equipped with wing mounted two-point flight refuelling pods, with 57 Squadron receiving three-point tankers on 1 June 1966, followed by 214 Squadron on 1 October 1966, all based at Marham.

The final Handley Page aircraft was the Jetstream, which was first flown from Radlett on 18 August designed for commuter services and executive transport. Among the American operators was Piedmont with N165PC airborne from Washington Dulles Airport in June 1986. Handley Page finally went into liquidation in June 1970, and Jetstream development became the responsibility of Scottish Aviation. (*Philip Birtles*)

With Britain's nuclear deterrent taken over by Polaris nuclear submarines, 100 Squadron was disbanded on 1 October 1968, followed by 139 Squadron on 31 December, the Victors being flown to Radlett for storage pending conversion to the tanker role. The Victor SR.2s continued in service with 543 Squadron. With Handley Page Ltd. going into liquidation on 27 February 1970, the tanker conversion contract for B.2s was placed with HSA with twenty-one Victors ferried to Woodford for conversion, followed by seven 543 Squadron SR.2s. The first conversion K.2, XL233, was delivered to 232 OCU on 8 May 1974. As conversions were completed, Victor K.2s were issued to both 55 and 57 Squadrons at Marham, playing a vital part in the first Gulf War and later in the success of the Falklands Campaign, using up much of their fatigue life. Victor K.2s were finally retired from RAF service on 15 October 1993 with the disbandment of 55 Squadron, and their role taken over by VC-10s of 10 Squadron. This completed seventy-six years of continual service by Handley Page aircraft with the RAF and its predecessors.

Handley Page resisted the government-inspired mergers within Britain's aerospace companies in 1962, hoping to remain independent, but Sir Frederick died on 21 April 1962. Under the chairmanship of George Russell, the decision was made to remain independent by developing the HP.137 Jetstream, a small versatile twin turboprop transport for both commercial and military roles. Although initial orders and options totalled 182 aircraft, the cost of development rocketed and was approaching £13 million, which would require break-even of 1,000 aircraft, instead of the planned 400. Despite rescue attempts, on 2 March 1970 all employees were sent home and the company ceased to exist on 1 June 1970.

1

Halifax Design and Development

The RAF possessed the most powerful air force in the world at the end of the First World War, including a major independent strategic bomber force, outside the control of the Royal Navy and Army. This great strength was soon reduced rapidly, with rapid disarmament and for a number of years little government investment in aircraft development. What little defence funding was available tended to be invested in the established services, with the young RAF trailing behind. The situation was not helped by the continuing efforts of the League of Nations disarmament commission, which severely restricted progress, with restrictions from 1925, and a stipulation there should be no increase in armaments during its existence. The RAF Expansion Scheme had started in 1927, mainly with improvements to bomber stations, but with bombers themselves hardly advanced at all from war vintage. By 1934, it had become obvious to the British Government that significant improvements needed to be made to aircraft capability, which had been left far behind other European nations, including a growing threat from Germany. As well as RAF aircraft being well below international standards, lack of research funding resulting in poor navigation capabilities, which caused poor target identification and destruction during the first three years of the Second World War.

With the start of a rapid expansion period large numbers of aircraft were produced, but many were unsuitable for modern combat, with little advance in technology from 1914 to 1918. However, more advanced projects were on the drawing boards, or still in the imagination of the designers. As more advanced fighters were produced by a potential enemy, it was realised bomber performance would have to improve, not just speed but also range, making the existing light and medium bombers totally ineffective as long-range strategic bombers. In 1936, the downward trend tended to be reversed when the Air Ministry issues Specification B.12/36 called for a four-engine heavy bomber resulting in the Short Stirling with an all-up weight (AUW) in the region of 55,000lb. Another medium/heavy bomber powered by two new Rolls-Royce Vulture engines developing nearly 1,700hp, with an approximate AUW of 45,000lb was called for in Spec. P.13/36. This specification was similar to B.1/35, which was in the design stage in September 1936. In January 1937, the Air Ministry cancelled the HP version of B.1/35 in favour of P.13/36, and in the following month suggested two prototypes should be built to P.13/36, one for flight trials and the other fully equipped to study armament, equipment layout and production requirements, powered by Bristol Hercules engines.

The Vulture were a high-risk development with twenty-four cylinders arranged in and X layout with four Kestrel size banks all driving one highly stressed crankshaft. Design of the Vulture started by R-R in September 1935 as a rapid means of development of a 2,000hp engine. It was ready for type testing in August 1939, achieving 1,800hp with production starting in January 1941, power gradually increasing to 2,010hp by March 1941. Unfortunately, during further testing, serious problems were experienced including connecting rod failures and some installation difficulties. These only added to production difficulties for R-R producing both Vultures and Merlins from three factories. With a greater development potential for the Merlin, and 50 per cent greater man hours to produce the Vulture, a deciding factor was the selection of four Merlins for the HP.56. It was also evident there would not be sufficient Vultures to power both the HP.56 and competing Avro 679, later to become the unsuccessful Manchester.

On 20 July 1937, HP sent general arrangement drawings to the Air Ministry (AM) showing both the twin-engine and four-engine versions, the four engine layout calling for four Hercules, or alternative Taurus engines. It was pointed out that neither four engine design would comply with P.13/36, with additional weight for extra fuel tanks, engine installation and controls, which favoured HP continuing with the twin-engine configuration. However, with the Vulture engine problems this was overruled, and the four-engine configuration adopted. The heavier aircraft had an empty weight of 23,000lb with an AUW of 55,000lb, and design changes resulted in a six-month delay to the project.

Airframe construction was all metal as a mid-wing cantilever monoplane, with a wingspan of no more than 100 feet to fit into existing RAF hangars. In addition to strategic night bombing, this aircraft had to be capable of dive-bombing and carriage of torpedoes in the anti-shipping role. The aircraft was to have a high cruising speed to reduce time over hostile territory, adequate self-defence from nose and tail power operated gun turrets. It needed the latest navigation and bomb aiming aids, and should be capable of maintenance when required in the open. A crew of four would be carried consisting of two pilots with one also responsible for navigation, bomb-aiming and nose gunner, plus a wireless operator and tail gunner. The fully stressed skin wing was to have integral fuel tanks. Defensive armament was a nose turret with two 0.303-inch Browning machine guns with at least 1,000 rounds per gun and a tail turret with four Browning machine guns also with 1,000 rounds per gun. Weapons load was four 2,000lb or sixteen 500lb/250lb bombs. The crew were to be supplied with oxygen for high altitude operations, flight deck heating, full radio and blind landing equipment, and an alternative weapon load of two 18-inch torpedoes.

Handley Page (HP) submitted their HP.56 for Spec. P.13/36 in March 1937 which was successful in gaining a development contract on 30 April 1937 for two prototypes, L7244 and L7245, both still powered by Vulture engines. During a mock-up conference on 15 July, a warning was given that the Vulture development programme was suffering a probable delay, with Bristol Hercules engines as an insurance. On 19 July, Air Marshal Sir Wilfred Freeman, the Air Member for Research and Development, asked for comparative GAs of the Twin Vulture layout compared with a four Taurus version, which did increase the wing area and AUW. Fortunately, the torpedo requirement was cancelled on 30 July. Further investigation revealed that four Merlins would provide better take-off power over the Taurus, while carrying 8,000lb of bombs over 2,000 miles. By September, the four-Merlin configuration was agreed and also the dive-bombing requirement was deleted. With four Merlins the wingspan was increased from 88 feet to 99 feet, still in compliance with the RAF requirements, and on 3 September, the contract was amended replacing the two Vultures with four Merlins and the designation of HP.57. Both prototypes were hand-built, with the first as a shell for aerodynamic development, and the second fully equipped for service trials. Traditional HP construction methods were used for the fuselage structure, tailplane and control surfaces, but the wing integral fuel tanks with a combined flat sheet/corrugated stressed skin were a new development for the design team. Only the prototypes had integral fuel tanks, as it was a requirement for the production aircraft to have self-sealing tanks as an operational necessity, resulting in the newly developed integral wing structure not being adopted unto the later Victor V-Bomber. Another innovation was a sliding bomb door installation, reducing drag on the approach to target. A single main-wheel undercarriage with a cast leg was supplied by Messier.

With the initial requirement for a 70-degree dive-bombing attack, dive brakes were required, especially with experience of possible elevator failure while diving. Slotted flaps were considered, but in June 1937, the specification was altered to reduce the dive angle to 25 degrees, and to simplify stowage, load was reduced from sixteen to fifteen bombs. At a mock-up conference in July 1937, where a preliminary flight deck mock-up was shown, Major Cordes, the chief test pilot, criticised the rudder bar which was not parallel to the aircraft centre line and too narrow. He was also unhappy with the undercarriage and flap control, which was mounted horizontally, instead of vertically, where the levers should move in the same sense as the flaps and undercarriage.

By November, R-R had provided information on the Merlin installation, allowing design to progress with engine mountings. This was followed by an order being placed on R-R for one aircraft set only, due to a high demand for the engine with many other RAF aircraft. Unlike other manufacturers, such as Avro, HP decided to retain design authority for the engine installation, only accepting advice from R-R. It was a great relief for the design team, when the Air Ministry dropped the requirement to carry torpedoes, and also removed provision for catapult take-off assistance. When performance with four Merlins was studied, a take-off with four engines at 2,850rpm, the take-off clearance to clear a 50-foot imaginary screen would be 760 yards, improving to 710 yards with the expected 3,000rpm, which was more than adequate. Then came the cancellation of the dive-bombing requirement, and the catapulting requirement, relieving the high structural demands and reducing weight. Despite the original specification from the Air Ministry, HP was able to produce a new generation of strategic bomber, meeting all the new requirements over a period of just 38 months. Despite there being no official requirement for fuel jettison, HP made provision, as a heavily loaded bomber would be unable to make an emergency landing for 2 to 3 hours after take-off, resulting in the development of a flush fitting jettison valve under the two outer wing tanks.

At this stage, the HP.57 was becoming a conventional mid-wing monoplane powered by four Merlins in mid slung nacelles. The fuselage had flat sides for ease of production and where the wings of the HP.56 had a swept wing leading edge planform, the HP.57 was equal tapered with straight wing spars. Performance figures were also compared with power from four Napier Daggers, Bristol Taurus or Hercules, but Daggers and Taurus resulted in inferior performance and were rejected. The Hercules power-plant was heavier than the Merlin by 1,500lb with 1,500bhp in level flight at 15,000 feet, and would also require some airframe strengthening with increased weight. Overall range would be less with Hercules, but both maximum and cruising speed would be higher. While the Hercules was an air-cooled radial layout, Merlins were liquid-cooled and suffered from radiator failures, leaking coolant and poor exhaust flame damping. Handley Page designers were unhappy with working with Rolls-Royce on the Merlin, with every part of the cooling system requiring multiple changes, and much duplication of work. The double curvature cowlings were more costly to produce, and benefits were not achieved over radial installations. Liquid-cooled engines were more vulnerable to combat damage, which was of concern to the crews, and more demanding to maintain in the field for the hard worked ground crew.

In October 1939, a further engine study was made based on available American engines which included the Wright Cyclone and Pratt & Whitney Wasps. However, the design team was already studying Bristol Hercules in detail, which developed 1,330bhp at 2,800rpm for take-off, compared with 1,075bhp at 3,000rpm with the Merlin. In addition, wind tunnel tests were carried out on the favoured Boulton & Paul turrets to check drag, trim changes and structural loadings. There were satisfactory results from nose and tail turrets, although HP preferred mid-upper and mid-ventral turrets in place of the tail turret insisted on by the Air Ministry. A tail turret certainly added structure and weight on the aft C of G (Centre of Gravity), but was probably considered a more effective defence.

With Avro given priority over Handley Page for Vulture engines and also the choice of gun turrets with Frazer Nash given priority to Avro, HP were faced with the less than ideal, at the time Merlins, and looked at alternative engines. There was also insufficient production capacity for Frazer Nash turrets to be fitted to both types.

Going back a year, detail design progress was going well with the HP.57 and by October 1938, with drawings for the integral wing fuel tanks complete and design completed on the wing section between the inner and outer engines. Integral fuel tanks were located between the spars, but later to be deleted for operational reasons.

On 9 January 1938, the first production order was placed for 100 B.Mk.Is for what was to become the Halifax. Prototype assembly began at Cricklewood in March 1938. Under Air Ministry Scheme K in April 1938, 250 Halifaxes were to be produced by April 1942, but in October 1938 following the Munich crisis, the numbers were doubled under Scheme L. Even with the programme of subcontracting major assemblies, the numbers of aircraft required were well beyond the capabilities of Handley Page resulting in English Electric at Preston replacing Hampdens with Halifaxes from early August. To facilitate quantity production and ease maintenance, many design changes were made.

Work had started on building the first prototype at Cricklewood and by January 1939, the issue of production drawings had started with orders placed for raw materials, and Merlin X power plants had been approved after flight trials in a Whitley. The Messier hydraulic system had been approved for use in the Halifax, but had not yet entered production.

The first prototype was ready at Cricklewood at the start of the war, without gun turrets, as they were not available. The Merlin Xs were fitted with de Havilland two position variable pitch duralumin blade propellers. Temporary fuel tanks were installed in the bomb-bay allowing the integral tanks between the engines to be used for water ballast during full load and overload tests. As Radlett was not considered ideal for a new prototype initial flight, the grass airfield at 13 OTU at Bicester was chosen as the nearest non-operational RAF airfield with adequate hangars for assembly and room for flight testing. As the main fuel tanks were integral structure, with any effects of flexing to be determined, for the first flight fuel tanks were fitted in the bomb-bay. After assembly, initial ground runs were made on 15 October, ready for taxiing tests on 20 October. Following some delay while a brake problem was corrected, Halifax L7244 was flown for the first time by Major Jim Cordes on 25 October 1938, at a weight of 34,500lb with the undercarriage locked down. The second flight was made

The first Halifax L7244 was a basic aerodynamic prototype without any armament or military equipment to test the flying characters of the aircraft. (*RAF Museum*)

on 3 November and following satisfactory preliminary handling flights the aircraft was returned to Radlett for a comprehensive flight development programme. During early flight trials fuselage oscillation was experienced, which took some time to cure following many adjustments.

The prototype was delivered to the A&AEE at Boscombe Down on 22 November 1939, but the incorporation of final modifications delayed flight testing until May 1940, with take-off performance and stalling at a weight of 45,000lb, was found to be 95mph clean and 79mph with undercarriage and flaps lowered. Ground testing demonstrated the capability of carrying 11,000lb bombs in a combination of up to 2,000lb. The aircraft remained at the A&AEE until August 1940 when the prototype was brought up to date for use by HP to test production modifications. Among powerplant problems experienced during early testing was inadequate operation of dzus fasteners on the cowlings, the propeller had to be taken off to remove the oil header tank, and the spark plugs were deteriorating causing piston damage. At the final production conference on 19 September 1940, major points were raised concerning the engine installation and the strong possibility was raised of replacing Merlin Xs with Merlin XXs. The new engine incorporated an improved supercharger and other improvements. L7244 was damaged at Boscombe Down and used for engineering training as 3299M until struck of charge.

The Halifax prototype L7244 was flown at the A&AEE Boscombe Down for initial service trials during the autumn of 1940. (*Air Historical Branch*)

The decision to install Merlin XXs in the Halifax was made on 21 October 1940, which involved replacing the oil cooler and changing the radiator configuration. The new Merlins were to power the 201st aircraft onwards, and the all-up weight was increased from 55,000 to 59,000lb. In the event Merlin XXs were installed from the 101st aircraft, which was L9515, the first Mk.II, which was first flown on 27 June 1941. The provision of Merlin XXs would allow operations above 15,000 feet and with two minor structural modifications on the 56th Halifax and subsequent aircraft, all-up weight was increased to 60,000lb which gave a range of 1,900 miles with a 11,000lb bomb load.

Major James Cordes had joined HP in 1928 as assistant test pilot, after distinguished service in the First World War. He was known as the 'debonair Major' as he usually flew wearing white overalls and wore a monocle. As deputy to Tom England, Cordes made the maiden flight of the Heyford in June 1930, and shared the first flight of the HP 42 on 14 November 1930, followed by flying the HP 43 in June 1932. With the departure of Tom England on 31 August 1934, Jim Cordes was appointed chief test pilot, making the maiden flights of the HP 51 in May 1935, the Hampden on 21 June and Harrow on 10 October, both in 1936. Major Cordes led the flight testing of the Halifax prototype, and as chief test pilot was responsible for high standard of flight controls and handling. By June 1940, flight testing of L7244 had confirmed the rudders as satisfactory, with improvements being made to elevator leading edge shape, and aileron tab area increased. Jim Cordes left Handley Page on 31 July 1941 to become chief pilot at 7 AAU (Aircraft Assembly Unit) at Hooton Park where Canadian built Hampdens were assembled, and where Hoverfly helicopters were delivered. Jim retired from test flying at the end of the Second World War, and died in 1980 at the age of 85.

Flight Lieutenant James Talbot joined Handley Page in 1941 and on 17 July the same year was flight testing Halifax Mk.I L9490 when there was a fuel transfer problem. As a result, he had to make a forced landing near North Mimms, Hertfordshire, with only slight injuries to those on board. Two weeks later he was appointed chief test pilot with the departure of Major Cordes. His main task was leading the continuing Halifax production and development test flying. This work included the first flight of Hercules-powered Mk.III R9534 on 12 October 1942, followed by the first production Mk.III, HX226, in August 1943. During his time at Radlett, he made the first brief flight of the experimental tailless Manx prototype on 25 June 1943, but was sadly killed when the prototype Hermes G-AGSS crashed on its first flight on 2 December 1945 due to being uncontrollable.

Flight testing at Handley Page was shared between two teams, one at Radlett responsible for production testing and the other at Park Street concerned with fight development, much of the work being routine production or gradually investigating performance boundaries to their limits. New modifications were tested, usually with just a pilot and flight test observer on board. Throughout most of the Second World War, the HP test pilot team consisted of J. Talbot, T. V. Mitchell, J. Marsh and W. G. Sanders, who in addition to flying from Radlett also supported YARD at York and made liaison visits to RAF squadrons.

Service trials were the responsibility of the Aeroplane and Armament Establishment (A&AEE) at Boscombe Down, both prototypes and modified production Halifaxes, to ensure they not only met the specification, but were safe and easy to operate by relatively inexperienced aircrew. The bulk of early service testing at the A&AEE was shared by the more representative second prototype L7245 and first production aircraft L9485, which were delivered to Boscombe in September and October 1940, respectively. Overall handling was found to be good; ailerons and elevators became heavy at over 250mph. With a take-off weight of 55,000lb at full fuel and half bomb load, range was estimated to be 1,860 miles. Guns were fired successfully in dives up to 320mph. Criticism were mainly poor performance due to low-powered and unreliable Merlin engines and serious rudder overbalance, both of which were mainly overcome at the A&AEE. Rudder overbalance was more serious in asymmetric flight. Following repairs to L7245 after an undercarriage collapse on take-off, repairs included structural strengthening to increase take-off weight to 60,000lb. However, take-off distance increased by 50 per cent over the 55,000lb weight and climb was sluggish and an altitude of 20,000 feet was unobtainable. With Halifaxes entering service, this performance was disappointing. Speed was reduced by around 20 per cent due to drag and gun turret weight. Range with full fuel of 1,392 gallons and a bomb load of 8,000lb, at a take-off weight of 58,000lb was reduced from the initial estimate of 1,860 miles to 1,700 miles.

Halifax B.I L7245 was the fully equipped second prototype and used for full service trials at Boscombe Down from 7 September 1940. It was used by No. 25 Halifax Conversion Flight from 17 November 1941. (*Handley Page Association*)

Above: The Radlett-built first production Halifax B.I L9485 was also used by the A&AEE for operational trials from 6 August 1941. It was powered by four Merlin Xs and was without the mid upper turret, but with beam gun positions. It was retired to No. 4 School of Technical Training on 15 September 1942. (*Air Historical Branch*)

Below: The nose gun turret and bomb aiming position on Halifax B.I, with four Merlin X engines. (*Handley Page Association*)

Also tested was the hundredth Halifax of each production line to ensure no deterioration in performance or handling during production. All pilots at A&AEE were RAF, supported by civilian observers, and while at Boscombe Down, in addition to flying characteristics, maintainability was also evaluated. The A&AEE test crews were often responsible for the simulation extreme flying conditions, going to the boundaries of safety to ensure the average crew would be able to operate the aircraft safely. Boscombe Down was also the home of the Handling Squadron, with responsibility of compiling pilot's notes defining control limits, use of controls not just for service pilots, but also ATA pilots used for deliveries to squadrons.

In addition to the second Halifax prototype, L7245, by the end of 1940, Boscombe Down was evaluating first production Halifax, L9485, testing the aircraft to its planned AUW of 53,000lb. During take-off at full power there was a slight tendency to swing to the left, but it was easily corrected by the use of rudder until 40mph had been reached. Stalling was checked with satisfactory behavior and no wing drop. The controls were overall effective, and landings were straightforward with the control column brought back on finals to achieve a three-point landing. In addition to handling tests, effectiveness of armament was also tested, including guns and bomb release. Perhaps the most demanding testing was to cure rudder overbalance, which made control difficult in a sideslip.

The first production aircraft undertook most of the initial armament trials, including Boulton Paul turrets and the two beam guns. The ventral Type R turret had a restricted view though a periscope and was overall ineffective with slow rotation and elevation of

The Halifax tail gun turret was a Boulton Paul Type E version with four 0.303-inch guns. (*Handley Page Association*)

the two guns resulting in it being removed in service. The mid-upper two-gun Type C turret had good rotation and elevation speeds and was acceptable once the depression angle had been reduced to stop shooting the flaps. The Type C nose turret suffered a reduction in rotation at speeds above 260mph until airflow deflectors allowed operation at an acceptable speed of 310mph. Ammunition feed to the four-gun Type E tail turret proved difficult until servo feed assisters were fitted in late 1941. Bombing trials were completed by 1942 with bombs up to 8,000lb cleared for service use.

Following the use of the fully equipped second prototype L7245 for preliminary armament trials at A&AEE, it was loaned to 35 Squadron for initial handling experience. When A&AEE testing was completed, the aircraft was allocated to ground instruction as 4204M until withdrawn. The first production Halifax, L9485, was retained as a trials aircraft with AUW increased to 53,000lb and 4,000lb bomb development. It was flown by A&AEE crews on armament trials after which it was allocated to ground instruction as 3362M.

Among other establishments involved with Halifax operational development was the Airborne Forces Experimental Establishment (AFEE) at Beaulieu. The Royal Aircraft Establishment (RAE) at Farnborough was mainly a research organization but was also responsible for accident investigations. In September 1941, a theoretical report

In addition to service trials at Boscombe Down, the second prototype L7245 was used for crew training by 35 Squadron before being withdrawn from use. (*Handley Page Association*)

was issued by the RAE with a study of performance for the three major four-engine heavy bombers to aerial tow the large Hamilcar military glider. The report estimated the performance of all three types, including take-off, climb and cruise, with assistance of rockets on the bombers. When a practical trial was made with a Lancaster with an AUW of 49,500lb towing a Hamilcar at an AUW of 36,000lb, take-off performance was critical, and the concept abandoned as impractical. By 1943, the RAE were experimenting with the concept of twin tugs using two Halifax, which resulted in the Hercules-powered Halifaxes being cleared by AFEE, and selected by 38 Group for towing Hamilcars singly as well as Horsas and two Hadrians. Halifax was also cleared to drop by parachute a Jeep and 6lb anti-tank gun as a combination. For this, the aircraft AUW was 60,000lb with a minimum drop height of 1,000 feet at speeds up to 130mph. It was also capable of carrying six 400lb containers, with ten fully equipped paratroops. The Halifax became accepted as the Airborne Support aircraft until replaced in RAF service by the Handley Page Hastings in the 1950s.

The Halifax was also used by the Telecommunications Research Establishment (TRE) which was originally located at Worth Matravers near Swanage with the aircraft based at Hurn. However, to avoid a possible enemy paratroop drop to

The first production Halifax B.I L9485 was used for a range of trials before being withdrawn from use and used for ground instruction. (*RAF Museum*)

either capture or sabotage the highly classified equipment, the facility was moved to Malvern, with the aircraft based at Defford. The TRE were responsible for the development of Klystron and Magnetron valves for the ground mapping H2S radar. The Halifax was ideal for the test installations, as the roomy fuselage provided a wide choice of scanner positions. The first experimental installation was in Halifax V9977 with work starting in January 1942 at Radlett, and delivery to Hurn on 27 March, where the H2S system was installed by TRE personnel. The first flight was made on 16 April from Hurn until transfer to Defford. The aircraft suffered an engine failure on 7 June followed by a fire, the resulting crash killing the pilot and five engineers on board. Fortunately, the second Halifax W7711 was able to join the programme in June, and Halifaxes W7808 and W7823 were also allocated to TRE; W7808 was allocated to service trials with the production standard H2S.

One of the senior members of the HP design team was a German national, Dr G. Lachmann, who had never applied for British citizenship. When war was declared, Dr Lachmann, like many other foreigners, was interned under Defence Regulation 18B. Despite many requests from 'HP' appealing for his release, there was no success, although he was permitted to work on basic and structural problems for Handley Page, through his assistant, G. Lee. There was no good reason to keep Dr Lachmann interned, as the regulations were intended to be guidelines, not rigid law.

The second prototype was close to completion fully fitted with equipment and armament, which was flown from Radlett by Major Cordes on 17 August 1940. It was soon delivered to the A&AEE at Boscombe Down where it was joined by the first production aircraft, L9485, which first flew on 11 October. It went to the A&AEE two days later to avoid risk of bombing in the London area, and preparation for testing was completed at Boscombe Down. By then, the Halifax was involved in a wide range of service testing. Handling at the stall was good with no tendency of wing drop during take-off or landing, and at a weight of 50,000lb flying characteristics were so good the leading slots could be deleted in production. Although there was a tendency to swing to the left during take-off, it was easily controlled by a light touch on the brakes and full rudder until 40mph had been reached. The second production Halifax, L9486, was delivered to Boscombe Down in December and was allocated to early crew familiarisation. It was found the aircraft handled so well it could be landed with hands off the control column, using only the fore and aft trim.

Considering the major advance in technology over previous heavy bombers, with a monoplane configuration, four engines and metal stressed skin construction, difficulties during the flight testing were almost to be expected, but capable of being solved. Aileron control had to be improved, and initially rudder response at low speeds was unresponsive. Stalling was straightforward with no wing drop tendency, and elevator control was effective. Nose gun turret operation could be restricted by airflow when in a dive but this was corrected by fitting balance flaps. Overshoot after an abandoned landing was straightforward at full power, with undercarriage retracted as soon as possible, and flaps remaining selected until as safe height had been achieved. Landings were normally in a three-point attitude, while braking without any swing. Overall crew communications were considered satisfactory, but communications between the navigator's position and the astrodome for sextant position sightings could be difficult when crawling under the second pilot's position in full flying kit. Gun operation was good at all speeds, although they were harder to move above the normal cruising speed of 260mph, but steady aim was still possible. It was found performance was unaffected by leading edge slats, resulting in the early aircraft slats being locked shut, and from the sixtieth aircraft they were deleted altogether in a new wing design.

There were delays while British Messier put the main undercarriage into quantity production, and Dowty were asked to provide an alternative source, as they had factory capacity to spare. They planned to adapt the Manchester unit for the Halifax, prompting the possibility that with the same engines as the new Lancaster, and the same undercarriage, it might be suggested the same structure would simplify the current material shortages. In fact, the change to a Dowty undercarriage would require a complete change of the hydraulic system, as well as suitable shock absorbers not being available, and could not be justified financially or the production delays.

With continued product development being studied, also included the carriage of two 4,000lb or one 8,000lb bombs in the existing bomb-bay. A performance estimate for the Halifax Mk.I with a total weight of 55,000lb gave a maximum cruising speed of 263mph and range with 8,000lb bomb load of 1,970 miles, although increased drag reduced the actual performance, mainly due to the configuration of the engine nacelles.

By August 1941, work was underway for the introduction of Bristol Hercules engines as the Mk.III with a wingspan of 104 feet, and was otherwise very similar to the earlier marks, favouring the new version for later production. As production built up, improvements were being incorporated in batches. The first fifty aircraft were Mk.I Series 1 with a maximum AUW of 55,000lb and no mid-upper or beam guns. The next twenty-five aircraft were Mk.I Series II with AUW increased to 60,000lb and Vickers 'K' guns in beam hatches. The Mk.I Series III started with L9600 with fuel capacity increased to 1,636 gallons. Each Series featured improvements with the installation of 24-volt generators. Following the Mk.I Series III down the production lines was the Mk.II powered by more reliable Merlin XX or 22s, and although the AUW was still 60,000lb, fuel capacity was increased to 1,882 gallons. By this time, the beam guns had been replaced by a mid-upper turret. The prototype B.Mk.II was converted from B.Mk.I L9515, powered by Merlin XXs was delivered to Boscombe Down in July 1941. It was found that despite the increased power and without the ventral and mid-upper turrets, there was little improvement in performance. Fuel consumption and range were investigated at a take-off weight of 60,000lb gave a practical range of 1,330 miles, and when fully equipped performance was estimated to be 7 per cent worse. For the maritime role HR815/G was flown from St Eval in June 1943 with a fuel load of 2,746 gallons. From the 14.5-hour flight a range of 2,150 miles was established. Reports were also coming from squadrons in combat of a major loss of performance, which the A&AEE and Handley Page worked together to achieve improvements.

During 1942, efforts continued to investigate a cure to the rudder over balance problems, which may have been the cause of a number of unexplained accidents and combat losses. The worst situation was the loss of power from both port

Radlett-built Halifax B.I L9515 at Boscombe Down on 17 April 1942 later became the B.II Prototype powered by four Merlin XXs. It was retired to No. 4 School of Technical Training on 12 October 1943. (*RAF Museum*)

engines, with starboard engines at full take-of power. In late 1941, rudder trim movement was restricted which resulted in high foot loads, until reducing speed to 160mph when the rudders violently overbalanced, with the loss of control only recovered by reducing power on the starboard engines. By modifying the rudders with bulbous nose shapes, known as noseings, allowed control to 140mph with a 10-degree bank avoiding overbalancing, but still with high foot loads on the rudder. By mid-1942, further changes were made to the balance tab and rudder tab which reduced foot loads to acceptable levels, but there was still a low tendency for rudder overbalance.

To check the effectiveness of the latest modifications, in December 1942, B.Mk. II W7917 was delivered to Boscombe Down from 102 Squadron, but on its first test flight to assess handling on 4 February 1943, it crashed due to loss of control, killing the crew. It was found the top half of one rudder had detached in flight, causing a violent overbalance and loss of control. Testing continued with HR679 with all the aerodynamic modifications, including similar rudders to W7917, designated Series IA. With a gradual reduction in airspeed, during steady sideslips, overbalance was not experienced until 120mph, when the rudders moved to full travel. Control was regained at 150mph after dropping 4,000 feet in a spiral dive. As a result of the full investigation, larger fins cured the problem, and rudder restrictors were fitted to squadron aircraft. Service pilots were also briefed on the rudder overbalance problem.

Above: Radlett-built Halifax B.II Srs 1A HR861 with the original fin/rudder configuration and armed with a mid-upper gun turret. It was delivered to 32 MU on 10 June 1943, issued to 10 Squadron on 16 June and was declared missing on 11 August 1943. (*RAF Museum*)

Opposite above: Pilot's controls in a Halifax B.II. (*RAF Museum*)

Opposite below: Bomb aimer position in nose of Halifax B.II. (*RAF Museum*)

The next major task was to investigate the Halifax lack of expected performance. Four B.Mk.IIs were tested at Boscombe Down between August and October 1942. W1008 was an early development aircraft without a dorsal turret or air filters; W7801 was a new aircraft with large flame damping exhaust shrouds, a night black overall finish and partly closed bomb door around a 4,000lb bomb; DG221 was a service aircraft in poor condition after only ten operations; and W7776 which had been both nose and dorsal turrets removed. The worst aircraft was DG221 which showed poor workmanship and maintenance, with a rough surface finish. The handling was so bad, the trials were abandoned due to doubts about airworthiness. Naturally, W7776 was the best, allowing the identification of a suitable standard of equipment and good

Halifax Design and Development

FIG. 1 — INSTRUMENT PANEL

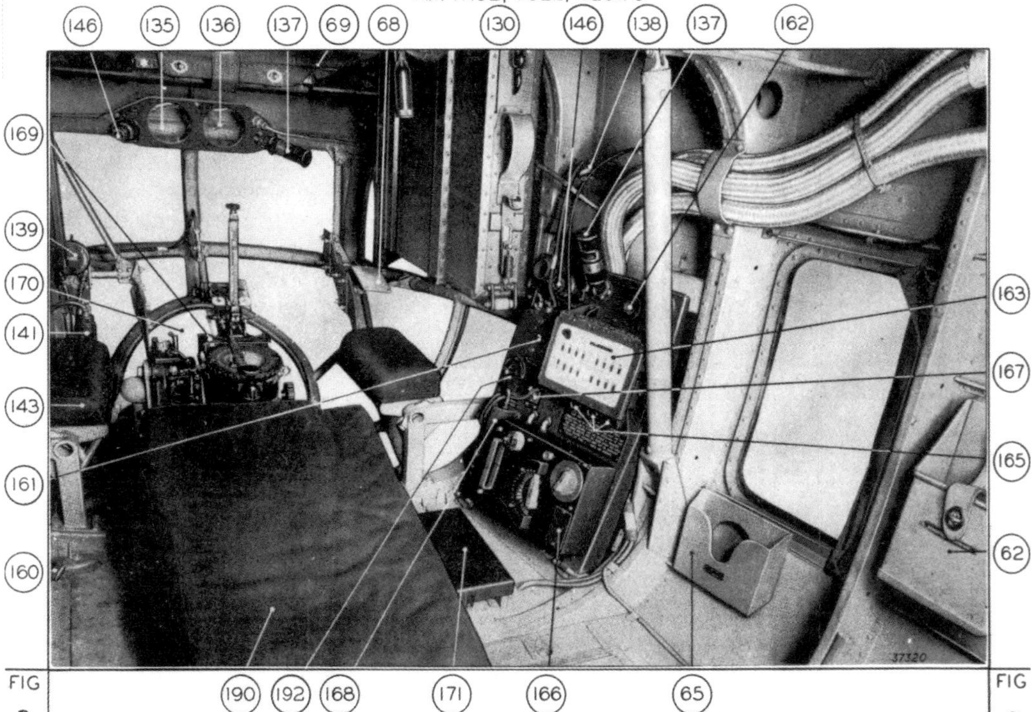

FIG. 2 — BOMB AIMER'S STATION – STARBOARD SIDE

A.P. 1719B, VOL. I, SECT. 3

Flight engineer's panel on starboard side of Halifax B.II flight deck. (*RAF Museum*)

surface finish. To confirm success of the trials, L9515 was modified to a low drag configuration, resulting in a top speed of 275mph.

The first fully modified reduced-drag aircraft, HR679, designated B.Mk.II Series I (Special), was fitted with a low-profile Type A dorsal turret and was delivered to Boscombe Down in January 1943. A 'cleaned up' Series I (Special), W7922, with 78 Squadron also achieved improved performance. Probably the greatest performance benefit was the increase in maximum cruising height at a cruising speed of 155mph. An additional successful modification was the fitting of Merlin 24s to V9985 in late 1943, improving take-off distances by between 30 and 40 per cent. A final improvement in late 1943 was a 5-foot increase in wingspan.

Armament trials started in early 1942, with nine B.Mk.IIs allocated. W1009 was used to assess maximum speed at which the Type C nose turret could be rotated, which was 325mph. Mk.II R9375 with Type E tail turret had an improved ammunition feed approved in mid-1942. A Type A mid-upper turret with extended vertical movement was successfully tested in mid-1943. In late 1942, R9436 was tested satisfactorily with a two 0.5-inch Browning Boulton Paul mid-upper turret. In early 1943, DT728 was used to approve the installation of a Mk.VIII Type A turret as a drag reducing effort. Unsuccessful tests were found with fitting of radar to the rear turrets of W1008 and R9436, where turret control was unacceptable due to excess torque experienced. A trial installation of rocket projectiles (RP) was made to JD212 to investigate ground attack, but ground firing tests damaged the front fuselage and air firings were abandoned. Triple flare chutes in DT728 were considered unsafe with little improvement to modified chutes in JD254.

Halifax B.II Srs I armed with three gun turrets and exhaust flame dampers. (*Handley Page Association*)

Above and below: Leavesden-built Halifax B.II JP228 fitted with the much-improved fin and rudder profile and with an H2S radome under the fuselage. This aircraft was delivered to 45 MU on 3 February 1944, issued to 30 APU on 23 February 1944 and 1 FTU on 12 March 1944. (*RAF Museum*)

Above: Frederick Handley Page welcoming a Russian delegation to Radlett in front of a Halifax B.II. (*Handley Page Association*)

Below: A poor image of a Samlesbury-built Halifax B.II JD212 used for unsuccessful RP trials at A&AEE carried under the inner wing, which when fired, damaged the aircraft. This aircraft went on to operate with 429 Squadron from 20 January 1944, but two days later was issued to 419 Squadron. It finally went to 1666 HCU on 21 April 1944 and was struck off charge (SOC) 17 July 1944. (*RAF Museum*)

Progress was being made on design of the Hercules-powered Mk.III and a Mk.IV was in project design with a stronger fuselage and floor, and increased bomb load. Power could be from Hercules, or the in-development R-R Griffons, the new project being designated Mk.IV. To investigate some of the Mk.IV features, Mk.II HR756 was allocated as the HP.60 Mk.IV prototype, with lowered Merlin engine nacelles, followed by the Mk.V powered by Merlin 22s and fitted with a Dowty main undercarriage and hydraulics. By November, the Ministry of Aircraft production (MAP) was requesting as many as available Mk.IV improvements to be incorporated in existing Halifax production as soon as possible.

Five Halifax B.Mk.Vs were tested at the A&AEE, the first being DG235 in January 1943 for the evaluation of fishtail exhausts at night. Visibility was significantly reduced with shrouds fitted to DG281 in May, but the drag reduced speed by 5 to 7mph, and a reduction in operating altitude of 2,000 feet. The exhaust glow was further reduced by fitting close fitting shrouds to DK256 and using a special paint. The first Merlin engine Halifax to be fitted with D Type fins of a 30 per cent increase in area was DK145, which completely overcame the rudder overbalance problem.

When flown in combat the Mk.II Series I, it was found the front and mid-upper turrets were rarely used. With one engine failed, a return on three engines required

Merlin XX-powered Speke-built Halifax B.V DG235 in September 1942 at Boscombe Down. It was issued to 408 Squadron on 11 October 1942, then Rolls-Royce on 31 December 1942. It passed to 1667 HCU on 23 September 1944 and was SOC at 48 MU on 1 November 1945. (*RAF Museum*)

Halifax B.IIIs at Radlett in January 1944 with the improved fin and rudder shape and armed with a mid-upper turret and carrying H2S radar below the fuselage behind the bomb bay. (*Handley Page Association*)

all loose equipment to be jettisoned because of excess weight of the mid-upper Type C turret. 'HP' was keen to reduce defensive armament in night bombers and pointed out to the MAP night bombers did not require the same number of defensive guns as day bombers. By removing both the nose and mid-upper turret overall weight would be reduced by 1,450lb, giving an increase in speed of 16mph.

In early 1942, the Special Operations Executive (SOE) stated a requirement for fast long-range penetration aircraft for the supply of resistance workers and agents in France, for which five Halifax Mk.IIs were modified. The front and mid-upper turrets were removed and apertures faired over, long-range fuel tanks were installed, and a paratroop cover and fairings fitted for issue to 138 Squadron at Tempsford, with the designation Mk.II Series 1 (Special). When the improved performance of the aircraft became known there was great enthusiasm within 4 Group to have both turrets removed and faired over. The work was carried out by Tollerton Aircraft Services for 138 Squadron, when it was known as the Tollerton or 'Z' Nose.

As the programme progressed, the Air Ministry continued to increase fixed equipment and protection items, adding to the overall weight of the aircraft. From

1941 to 1942, the weight of fixed equipment increased from 2,851lb to 3,599lb, with protection equipment growing from 1,739lb to 2,574lb. HP pointed out if increase in equipment and modifications continued at the same rate, by the end of 1942, the Halifax would be unable to carry an effective bomb load. These modifications and trial installations included target towing, paratroop installation, armour plating around the power plants, a ventral gun turret installation, a landing arrester gear, and rocket assisted take-off. The Air Staff considered the aircraft suitable for a number of roles with the corresponding equipment fit, while HP were continually attempting to improve performance and achieve more power from the engines, for it to be more effective as a night bomber. The need for arrester gear was removed in May 1942, with probably many other modifications not required operationally.

The thirty-first production Halifax Mk.I, L9515 was allocated to development for increasing both range and performance. As part of this programme No. 6 fuel tanks were added and cowlings were modified to reduce frontal area, with power from Merlin 10s. In 1942, a metal mock-up low drag nose replaced the gun turret, and the engines were changed to Merlin 22. With successful completion of the tests, a Perspex nose cone was fitted. The inboard nacelles were modified to reduce drag and a type A Mk.8 turret was fitted. This was followed by HR679 which was modified to become the first Mk.II Series IA with a lengthened nose and Perspex cone, and power from Merlin 22s. B.II HR756 was being upgraded with Merlin 22s and designated as the Mk.II Series II to follow the Series IA. However, it was pointed out that there was little enthusiasm for producing a small batch of series IAs, before having to tool up for the Series II. It was therefore suggested the Series II be abandoned in favour of the Mk.IV powered by Merlin 61s. The Series IA was therefore authorised for production.

One of the major problems with the Merlin-powered Halifaxes was exhaust flame damping, which had been the subject of studies by the A&AEE, R-R and HP for some time, although the problem was possibly over emphasised, even after powering with Hercules engines. Flame damping trials were made with W1008 powered by Merlin 22s in 1942, but only a small glow was detected directly behind and from the side at 175 yards. The aircraft was fitted with ram's horn type exhausts with anti-glow shrouds, while other aircraft had saxophone type exhausts with flame dampers, and were considered satisfactory by the A&AEE.

There was an increase in accidents in 1942 due to pilots losing control in excessive sideslip when using violent rudder. Routine Halifax flight trials by HP and A&AEE had found rudder control good during normal flight as sideslips and engine cutting at low speeds was not part of the flight testing. During further testing, the rudder showed little response below 120mph, and at speeds below 150mph the rudder tended to overbalance. Then crews complained of rudder overbalance when carrying evasive manoeuvres, or engine cut at low speed. With a number of aircraft reduced to wreckage and the crews killed it was difficult to determine the cause, but where control was lost at higher altitudes giving the pilot a chance to recover, the cause was found to be insufficient fin area, causing overbalance. Both HP and A&AEE carried out flight testing, eventually establishing a 'D' fin and rudder as standard.

In early 1942, there were complaints from some squadrons regarding a lack of performance, and a 10 Squadron Mk.II DG221 was allocated to flight testing for an official investigation. It was found that additional drag was caused by a rough finish camouflage, some of the small additional items of equipment fitted and poor workmanship. The A&AEE were also carrying out tests on L9515 to ascertain fuel consumption and range for the Mk.II. It was found overall easy to operate, except some difficulties were experienced when heavily overloaded. Fuel consumption varied little over a wide range of cruising speeds, as well as in the climb. The only reduction was found with the use of hot air intakes, which reduced range by 16 per cent. The original bomb doors could only be fully closed when carrying 2,000lb bombs, but had to be left partly open when loaded with 4,000lb and 8,000lb bombs, and although there was no deterioration in take-off performance, the extra drag did reduce range. As a result, Phillips and Powis were contracted to design and assembly what were known as Type B doors, but after trials with V9985 were found unacceptable. For the Halifax, Mk.III Type C doors were designed and produced by Evans Bellhouse, but did not fit Mk.IIs and Mk.Vs.

Additional work in 1942 included the commencement of work on the Hercules 6-powered Halifax Mk.III in the experimental department. The Halifaxes for SOE operations were being converted, including H2S ground mapping radar in a radome under the fuselage with W7823 used for trials. For glider towing duties, W7801 was modified and delivered to Netheravon for operational trials and tests were still continuing on the fin/rudder configurations. While work on the Mk.IV was delayed, there was an interest in converting the Mk.IIIs for Coastal Command service. The latter requirement was to combat the German U-boats in the North Atlantic, which were able to operate beyond the range of existing land-based maritime patrol aircraft. The Mk.III appeared to be the solution and during November, a group of Coastal Command officers discussed the new variant, insisting on Hercules 7 or 17 engines, due to the reported Merlin unreliability. The war load was to be either four 18-inch, or two 21-inch torpedoes, plus six depth charges.

With assurances from Bristol for the Hercules engines, the specification offered allowed for 1,882 gallons of fuel giving an endurance of 10.3 hours and a range of 1,600 nautical miles. When carrying a war load of 8,220lb, operational endurance became 8.5 hours over a range of 1,280 nautical miles. The torpedoes were located in the main fuselage bomb-bay with depth charges in the wing bomb cells. The 0.303-inch Vickers gun in the nose was replaced by a 0.50-inch Browning or 20mm cannon. By December, Coastal Command defined their general requirement, with out of the two alternatives considered, a scheme favoured using the Mk.II fuselage with new bomb door hinges to allow them to close around the two torpedoes. The General Arrangement (GA) of the Mk.III modified for torpedo carriage followed a few days later, when it was pointed out the quickest delivery for Coastal Command would be to adopt the Mk.II Series IA, as it was in current production. This was adapted for maritime use and entered service with Mk.V Series 1As, although both were eventually replaced by Mk.IIIs.

The main Halifax advantages over the Lancaster was its roomier fuselage interior and it had a better ditching record. It was believed Merlin engines operated poorly at low speeds for long duration flights, but when tested by the A&AEE a Mk.II flown by a Coastal Command crew covered 2,132 nautical miles over 14.5 hours without

Number 3 and 4 Hercules engines on test in a Halifax B.III with another Halifax in the background. (*RAF Museum*)

any problems. In operational flying, sorties were being completed lasting 13 hours regularly without any failures. To assist detecting U-boats ASV (Air to Surface) Mk.III radar was fitted, with depth charges carried in the wing cells, and endurance increased by fitting three 230-gallon fuel tanks in the bomb-bay.

Additional achievements in 1942 were the first release of an 8,000lb bomb by 76 Squadron in April on Essen and the fitting of H2S ground mapping radar and bombing aid to two Halifaxes by the Telecommunications Research Establishment (TRE). The H2S was fitted under the fuselage aft of the bomb-bay under a streamlined radome, but as already mentioned, unfortunately the first aircraft crashed killing all onboard, including some of the radar experts, and destroyed the first experimental magnetron valve. Priority was given to the second partially modified Halifax which was delivered to the Bombing Development Unit at Boscombe Down by the end of 1942. With Hampden production coming to an end in Canada, there were plans to produce the Mk.Vs there. However, the Mk.V featured a Dowty lever suspension main undercarriage with a revised hydraulic system. Unfortunately, there were stress failures in the castings used to replace the forgings, restricting maximum landing weight to 40,000lb, and production plans in Canada did not go ahead. By the end of 1943, Mk.V UK production was completed, and most were used by Coastal Command and other non-heavy bombing duties. With Merlin engine failures still a concern, a meeting was held at MAP in January 1943 to devise a cure, one step being to ensure all parts, such as radiators and header tanks should be mounted on flexible mountings to reduce vibration. The faults were not the responsibility of HP, as the failures were of R-R equipment.

To overcome continuing Merlin problems with the Halifax, Bristol Hercules air-cooled radial engines were specified for Halifax Mk.IIIs, the first being a conversion of Mk.II, R9534, which made its first flight in October 1942. Initial trials showed inadequate directional control with the Hercules engines, requiring additional rudder area, to avoid rudder overbalance. Further modifications were introduced over 1942 and 1943 which improved directional stability. The final rudder configuration with a 50 per cent increase in area was adopted for the Mk.III, and fitted retrospectively to Halifax Mk.IIs and Mk.Vs, with limitations of maintaining airspeed of over 120mph with one or more engine out, and to avoid excessive yaw at slow speeds.

The Halifax Mk.III was planned as an interim version, with the Mk.IV powered by the high-altitude Hercules, but this engine suffered development problems, never achieving a satisfactory reliability, resulting in Mk.IV development being abandoned. This meant that the Mk.III became the most produced version of the Halifax, which incorporated a number of the aerodynamic and structural improvements planned for the Mk.IV. In addition, the aircraft was to be capable of tropical operations, making the Halifax second to none, while further development made it superior to all other heavy bombers. Hercules engine development resulted in no more Merlin versions being produced, the Hercules-powered developments undertaking many additional roles in the European theatre and overseas.

Radlett-built Halifax B.III prototype R9534 powered by four Hercules VI engines in November 1942 with the nose gun turret faired over. This was a conversion of a B.II. This aircraft was delivered to A&AEE on 13 September 1943, then RAE Farnborough 13 May 1944 and retired to No. 4 School of Technical Training on 14 June 1944. (*Air Historical Branch*)

Above: Fitted with three gun turrets, production Halifax B.III and carrying H2S ground mapping radar in January 1945, probably at Boscombe Down. (*RAF Museum*)

Below: Radlett-built Halifax B.III LV857 in 1944. This aircraft was delivered to 35 Squadron on 10 February 1944, then 10 Squadron on 12 March 1944, before going to 51 Squadron on 19 March 1944; it went missing on 31 March 1944. (*Handley Page Association*)

The first production Mk.III was flown from Radlett on 29 August 1943 with further projects in development, including the Mk.VI powered by Hercules 10 SM engines. Among the projects was the HP 64, a transport development, using all the Bomber flying surfaces and engines, attached to a new circular section pressurised fuselage. With HP committed to bomber development, the transport fuselage design was transferred to Flight Refuelling, where there was spare design and manufacturing resource available. The HP 65 was a logical improvement of the existing airframe, increasing the bomb load, longer range, better operational ceiling, and a higher cruising speed. It was on this version HP planned to pioneer the use of laminar flow wing drag reducing section. This version used the standard Mk.III fuselage modified to take the loads of a stronger bomb carrying beam with larger bomb doors. This was fitted to a NACA 66 series laminar flow aerofoil wing section, with a span of 113 feet. The aspect ratio was 11:1 with leading and trailing edges tapering equally, and built around a single 40 per cent wing chord single wing spar. Wing leading edge de-icing was by hot air from the engines, which were Hercules 38s still under development. The main undercarriage was planned to be a twin wheel single leg type which would be fully enclosed in the nacelle when retracted, reducing drag. The fuel capacity of 2,500 gallons would give a range of 3,170 miles cruising at 20,000 feet at 240mph. The maximum speed was 350mph at 27,000 feet.

Sir Frederick Handley Page ('HP') and his senior staff maintained a close relationship with the squadrons flying the Halifax on operations, to ensure the performance and operation were meeting the requirements. Feedback from both 4 and 6 Groups was

Unidentified Hercules-powered Halifax B.VI at A&AEE Boscombe Down. (*RAF Museum*)

Radlett-built Halifax Mk.VI LV838 fitted with a cargo pannier below the bomb-bay. It was delivered to A&AEE on 5 February 1944, then sent to 29 MU on 2 January 1946, where it was SOC on 28 November 1946. (*Handley Page Association*)

satisfactory, particularly with reference to the robustness and strength of the aircraft. An improvement in overall handling was requested. Neither Bomber Command nor the Air Staff wanted the mid-upper upper-gun turret deleted, although HP wanted it to be removed to reduce drag. As a result of the AOC 4 Group giving orders for it to be removed, and it became approved, when performance improvements more than justifying its removal.

The new Hercules 38s were tested in Halifax R9534 in March 1943, but in their current form were not considered ready for production status in the near future. Also production difficulties with building the high-tolerance laminar flow wing structure caused abandonment of the HP 65, and concentrating on a conventional two spar wing, while retaining the 55-foot centre section on which the engines were mounted.

On 27 November, after discussions, a new project HP 66 was launched to cover Spec. B.27/43. Two prototypes were ordered powered by Hercules 100 engines as well as a third prototype powered by Hercules HE 15MT designated HP 69. The Air Staff specified the fitting of standard bomb doors, as there was no requirement for the carriage of 4,000 or 8,000lb bombs. It was planned to move the H2S scanner forward to under the nose.

With series production of the Mk.III under way, the wing was strengthened to allow an AUW of 65,000lb, which also included sliding tubes in the main undercarriage and strengthened tail wheel assembly, which were introduced early in production. This allowed the fitting of stronger wings, which were tested on R9534 and HR845, the skin thickness increasing from 22 to 24 gauge and new wingtips fitted, both of which increased weight by 60lb. With the undercarriage strengthening included, weight increase was 110lb. The Halifax Mk.III featured all the proven features of earlier models, to which were added new equipment and aerodynamic refinements. There were more Mk.IIIs produced than any other Halifax version, and HX227 was used by the A&AEE for assessment on maintenance and reliability over 150-hour intensive flight trials in September and October 1943. Any part or system which had failed or become defective was acted upon by HP and modified to prevent any occurrence. Extended wingtips for later production Mk.IIIs increased the rate of climb by 70 to 120 feet per minute, and service ceiling was improved by 800 feet.

With the established entry into service of the Mk.III, a further development with the designation HP 61 was being finalised. As with the Mk.III, it was tropicalised from the start, and the main feature was power from four Hercules 100 engines supplied in a self-contained power plant with fuel injection. To maintain performance in tropical climates, the fuel system was pressurised, which was also added to the Mk.IIIs in production. Fuel capacity was increased to 2,190 gallons with a new wingspan of 103 feet 8 inches. This new version became the Mk.VI, with production starting in November. With gains in Mk.VI airframe production, the supply of Hercules 100 was at a lower rate, some Mk.VIs were powered by 1,580hp Hercules 16s, with the designation Halifax Mk.VII, the last of the bomber versions. The majority were delivered to Free French squadrons in 4 Group and RCAF squadrons in 6 Group. Both the Mk.VI and VII were similar in all improvements, and only differed in engines and all up weight.

At the end of 1943, the Air Staff concentrated on Hercules-powered Halifaxes and 1,470hp Merlin 24-powered Lancasters, with Stirlings phased out of Bomber Command. The performance of both types was very similar, although the Halifax had made the greatest gains from inception, probably due to Avro's initial commitment to the Vulture-powered Manchester. Because of its larger bomb-bay, Lancasters were later developed to carry Barnes Wallis developed 12,000lb 'Tallboy' and 22,000lb 'earthquake' bombs, while the Halifax by then was not required to carry bombs larger than 4,000lb.

In 1943, the modification of Halifaxes for Coastal Command operations was started by Cuncliffe-Owen at Eastleigh, in preparation for maritime reconnaissance and meteorological (MET.) duties. In addition to bombing and maritime duties, Halifax were also used by 38 Group for glider towing, the dropping of SOE (Special Operatives Executive) agents in support of the French resistance, and airborne support. No. 100 Group used Halifax for radio/radar frequency surveillance and countermeasures. Transport Command used Halifax for high-speed transport of troops and equipment. In January 1944, modification 1020 was the conversion for Met. operations tested on Halifax LL186 and adopted for manufacture of kits by Cuncliffe-Owen. The aircraft had a separate Met. observers' position and were equipped with Gee and Loran navigation aids, as well as a radio altimeter after work by Cuncliffe-Owen ASV, Mk. V was fitted at St Athan. The converted Mk.Vs were still powered by the unreliable Merlins, which did not generally operate well over long-range low speed sorties, resulting in frequent engine failures.

Although the Halifax was overall easy to handle, a geared rudder tab was fitted to the Mk.VIs to counteract a violent swing on take-off in the event of an engine failure. The first prototype was a converted Mk.III, LV776, which was first flown on 19 December 1943, powered by Hercules 100s. Due to delay in producing engines, the first production Mk.V, NP715, did not fly until 10 October 1944, giving a performance improvement better than any other Halifax or Lancaster. The maximum AUW was 68,000lb, maximum speed 312mph, service ceiling 24,000 feet and with a maximum bomb load of 14,000lb, it could fly 1,260 miles. The Lancaster excelled as a bomber, while the Halifax was a better all-round aircraft.

Design of the transport Halifax version began in 1943 as a paratroop carrier and large military glider tug. All offensive and defensive equipment was removed, with a number of Mk.IIIs modified, but retaining the rear gun turret. A pannier was fitted in the bomb-bay, the aircraft being redesignated Mk.C.III. This would allow, at the end of the war, for many Halifaxes to be converted as transports for personnel and freight. As a progression, the Mk.C.VIII was developed with the rear turret replaced by a cone fairing. With the formation of the Airborne Forces ready for the invasions of enemy territory, retired Halifax and Stirling bombers were used to tow the larger troop-carrying gliders, such as the Airspeed Horsa, and the even larger Hamilcar was towed by an improved Halifax, initially as the A.Mk.V, and later the A.Mk.VII.

Unidentified Halifax B.VI with nose gun removed. (*Handley Page Association*)

The Airborne Support squadrons needed a fast long-range penetration aircraft for SOE support, the glider towing version being to a similar specification. The only defence was the rear turret. A total of 12 paratroops could be carried and exited through a cone, and a glider towing hook was fitted just aft of the tail wheel. The first Halifax A.Mk.Vs joined 295 Squadron in February 1943. The Halifax was superior as a glider tug in every respect to the Lancaster. The Airborne Forces Halifaxes had the H2S radar removed, but were equipped with Gee and Rebecca navigation aids. The ultimate Airborne Forces Halifax was the HP 71, with the designation A.IX, fitted with a rear turret mounting two 0.5-inch Browning guns and a fuel capacity of 2,070 gallons, and 145 aircraft built. They did not enter service until 1946 when 47 and 113 Squadrons were equipped. A further development known as A.X, powered by Hercules 100 engines, did not go into production.

In November 1943, to provide support for Bomber Command, 100 Group was formed for electronic intelligence gathering and spoof raids using 'window' (aluminium foil) strips to confuse enemy radars. In addition to collecting data on enemy radar and radio frequencies to allow counter interference, the Halifaxes were able to divert enemy night fighters away from the main bomber formations. By March 1945, 100 Group had standardised on a mixture of Halifax and Boeing B.17s. The capacity of the Halifax Mk.IIIs fuselage was used to advantage, with its better performance and ready availability, and classified equipment installed at RAF Maintenance Units (MUs).

The converted Halifax C.VIII PP285 at Radlett with the cargo pannier part lowered and showing one of the wing cell bomb doors open. This aircraft was retained by HP and declared Cat.E write off at 58 MU on 30 March 1948. (*RAF Museum*)

In early 1945, Halifax Mk.III HX229 undertook flight trials to determine the effects of cargo pannier on performance in preparation for its soon-to-be expected entry into in civil operations. By June 1945, three Halifax C.VIIIs were on loan to BOAC for use on flights from London to Lagos.

Although when Spec. B.1/39 was originally issued, a requirement for flight refuelling capability was included, no interest was shown by the RAF until the approach of VE Day, when long-range bomber operations were being considered in Asia against the Japanese. Even then, no further action was taken until 1946 when Coastal Command considered flight refuelling Halifax Met.VIs, with discussions taking place between HP, Flight Refuelling and the MOS. A proposal was made to increase the fuel capacity of Halifax GR.VIs from 2,880 to 3,840 gallons, but this did not answer the Coastal Command requirement. The interior capacity of the fuselage was in full use with equipment and three 230 bomb-bay tanks. It was eventually agreed to make provision for the flight refuelling the bomb-bay tanks and, if possible, the No. 2 tanks. The tail turret was to be replaced by a fairing, and small windows in the fuselage for the operator, as the refuelling hose was pulled in by hydraulic winch towards the receiver aircraft. At a meeting on 2 April 1946, the conversion of ten Halifax 'receiver' aircraft was approved, and three Lancaster bombers should be converted to 'tankers' to support Coastal Command Met. duties. The initial trial installation Halifax was available at Staverton, where it was being converted by Flight Refuelling to be ready by November. Further conversions would await satisfactory test results, but during these trials, Coastal Command lost interest, as new, more suitable aircraft were in development.

Samlesbury produced Halifax B.VI RG820 at Hatfield on 5 April 1948 for icing tests on the No. 3 engine propeller. It was delivered to the RAF on 28 November 1951 and became 6903M training airframe. (*Philip Birtles*)

2

Halifax Production

Halifax production was a major undertaking for both Handley Page at Cricklewood and Radlett, complemented by the operation of government built shadow factories. Whereas France had been seen as our natural enemy in the 1920s, by 1933 the threat was obviously coming from emerging Nazi Germany, leaving little time to create a modern bomber force, with no foundations already existing. The defence Requirements Sub-Committee (DRC) as part of the Committee of Imperial Defence (CID) produced a report in March 1934 concluding that long-term defence needed to be prepared against Germany as the potential belligerent. A second report issued in July 1935 decreed it was impossible to guarantee no hostilities beyond January 1939, a prediction which was to prove accurate. The DRC was therefore tasked with producing a defence programme to achieve a practical state of readiness for the fiscal year 1938-39. To achieve these goals Air Staff (AS) Schemes were progressively released with C issued in 1935 calling for sixty-eight RAF bomber squadrons. This was replaced in February 1936 by Scheme F, still calling for the same number of squadrons, but specifying larger aircraft carrying twice the bomb load.

In 1936, Specifications B.12/36 and P.13/36 were issued, as mentioned previously, the latter being amended in September 1937 to fit the HP 57 project, powered by four R-R Merlins. This allowed HP at Cricklewood to begin the task of planning setting up of the production processes and estimating costs of jigs and tools. The two HP 57 prototypes were to be built as soon as possible for flight trials with no delays for checking jigs, solving urgently any problems found. HP 57 design started in August 1937, with the issue of production drawings from December 1938. This allowed for jig and tool design, and production to start soon after. The criteria for the aircraft was not just based on performance, as it needed to be built quickly, easily and be cost effective. It must also be easy to maintain in service, often in the most basic of conditions.

Handley Page pioneered effective production processes, using split production, where the major assemblies had a high level of interchangeability and were mainly pre-equipped. The fuselage centre-section with stub wings containing the inner engines was the foundation, to which was added the front fuselage and nose, rear fuselage with turret bolted on the end. The centre-section wing was extended by an intermediate wing section, to which was added outer wings with outboard engine nacelles, and finally the tail assembly. These assemblies could be produced alongside the car mass production process using semi-skilled and often unskilled labour. When completed by a supplier, the sections were transported to the main production lines and rapidly assembled, with the addition of engines and undercarriage. Another innovation was lofting, where full-scale drawings were transferred photographically on to metal and could be circulated around the production sites for installation on the jigs.

Delays were experienced due to the changing Air Ministry requirements for RAF expansion. Insufficient funding slowed bomber force production and constrained development. Britain was faced with the development of an effective fighter force to defend against enemy attacks, while requiring a strategic force to protect supply convoys and project air power into occupied Europe. The Air Ministry proposals were Scheme L in early 1937, which called for a front-line force of 2,500 aircraft including 1,659 bombers to be available by April 1939. This was replaced by Scheme J, increasing Bomber Command to ninety squadrons with 1,442 aircraft, including heavy bombers to be available by early 1943. In late 1937, Scheme K increased fighter strength, but reduced front-line bomber strength and reserves. Scheme L allowed a rapid expansion to 12,000 aircraft over two years, with emphasis on fighters and no increase in bombers.

This fragmented approach did not allow effective detailed planning for large scale production, either by the Air Ministry or industry. The only way to build aircraft at low cost was to plan long production runs with modern aircraft equipping sufficient RAF squadrons. Complementing aircraft production were engines, systems and equipment development, with Boulton & Paul gun turrets and Messier undercarriage. Hydraulics causing bottle necks, and raw material shortages were experienced. All of this the manufacturers had to cope with, to meet the delivery of what had become the Halifax to the first squadron in mid-1940.

With production capacity limited at Cricklewood and Radlett, English Electric at Preston were already producing Hampdens, and with the completion of those contracts were able to start tooling up for Halifax bombers. Scheme L doubled the target for Halifax production, in addition to calling for 1,500 each of Manchesters and Stirlings. This allowed new production lines to be established and subcontractors to be set up for jigs, tools, equipment and parts. A request was made to HP in March 1938 for an increase in Halifax production, which would double the number of machine tools and require 2,000 more semi-skilled workers. By October 1938 'HP' stated that for production of 1,000 Halifax, a peak delivery rate of fifty to sixty aircraft a month would be necessary. This required increased manufacturing facilities, with a cost of £750,000 for jigs. It was essential that a high production rate was achieved, not only to equip RAF squadrons, but ensure the aircraft were not becoming obsolete when entering service late. As a reserve, 'HP' proposed higher jig manufacture, to be kept in reserve for the time when manufacture would increase.

Finally, a production contract was placed on 7 January 1938 for 100 Halifax bombers, stimulating the need for more jigs and an increased workforce to prepare for a long, sustained production run. Although the bomb load was still restricted to 8,000lb, the crew was now increased to five members and power was from four Merlins. At a rate of fifty to sixty aircraft a month, jigs would cost between £1 million and £1.25 million. In the first six months of 1939, master assembly jigs were under construction, increasing with textile machine makers work force in the second part of the year, allowing Halifax production to become established throughout 1940.

Above: Halifax detail front fuselage assembly at Cricklewood. (*Handley Page Association*)

Below: A fully equipped and painted Halifax fuselage centre fuselage assembly delivered to the Radlett production line. (*Handley Page Association*)

A Halifax B.II Merlin power plant ready to be offered up to the number 4 position on the wing. (*Handley Page Association*)

The substantial increase in demand for additional Halifax was beyond the capabilities of just the HP factories, resulting in the first delivery of B.Mk.II V9976, which was ground run on 15 August 1940 from English Electric. Production by English Electric was to a very high standard and within six weeks of starting, it was planned to be producing one aircraft a day. A full set of jigs were sent to Preston, where a valuable level of co-operation had been achieved following the completion of Hampdens. Plans from the Air Ministry in November 1939 were to provide tooling for a batch of 500 Halifax at a rate of twenty-two a month, which would be produced jointly between HP and English Electric. At this time, HP were experiencing delays in raw material supply, which the government were unable to rectify. With plans to build 100 aircraft per month, a new shadow factory at Speke, Liverpool operated by Rootes Securities was to be constructed. By November 1939, over 80 per cent of the prototype jigs were complete and 60 per cent of production jigs were ready. To increase manufacturing space, HP took over the old Nieuport factory at Cricklewood, adding an additional 70,000 square feet of floor space.

Above: Halifax B.IIIs LV859 and LV865 on Radlett Aerodrome awaiting delivery to the RAF on 28 January 1944. LV859 was delivered to 25 Squadron on 9 February 1944, soon passing to 10 Squadron on 12 March, before going missing on 27 March 1944. Meanwhile, LV865 was delivered to 35 Squadron on 9 February 1944 and soon moved to 51 Squadron on 15 March. It was written off on 17 September 1944, probably from an accident. This demonstrates the short service life of the Halifaxes and their crews. (*Handley Page Association*)

Below: Halifax nose production at English Electric, Preston. (*Handley Page Association*)

Above: Halifax final assembly at Samlesbury. (*BAE Systems Systems*)

Below: Halifax B.III almost ready for roll-out at Samlesbury. (*BAE Systems*)

Above: A pair of Halifax B.IIs on the apron outside the factory at Samlesbury. (*BAE Systems*)

Below: Halifax B.IIs outside No. 1 Shed at Samlesbury including W1173 of 405 Squadron. (*BAE Systems*)

Above: Halifax GR.III at Samlesbury ready for delivery to Coastal Command. (*BAE Systems*)

Below: Halifax B.II W1005 departing Samlesbury on its delivery flight to RAF Bomber Command. It was delivered to 102 Squadron at Dalton on 26 January 1942, and moved to 1652 HCU on 12 December 1942, with whom it was written off on 15 February 1944. (*RAF Museum*)

Halifax Production

With the outbreak of war, the government expanded the shadow factory scheme to cope with the increasing requirements for Halifax. In addition to Rootes Securities, London Aircraft Production Group (LAPG) and Fairey Aviation at Manchester Ringway were commissioned. The LAPG consisted of London Passenger Transport Board (LPTB) with extensive manufacturing facilities at Aldenham near Watford, Duple Bodies and Motors, Park Royal Coachworks, Chrysler Motors and Express Motor & Body Works. Overall management was by LPTB and HP providing the necessary information and drawings to the individual companies.

With the first flight of the prototype on 24 October 1939 and subsequent flight development programme, anticipated modifications were expected. This affected production by subcontractors, but planning was already in place to cope with these changes. Shortages during the expansion years continued during the first two years of the war with many delays. These were made worse by management having to organise and supply subcontractors with information, and the overall training of new personnel working in the expanding production base, often with little experience. The worst shortages were with extrusions, forgings and high strength castings. The government ministries were constantly changing priorities, and as the flight testing progressed, modifications had to be incorporated in existing aircraft, and those on the production lines.

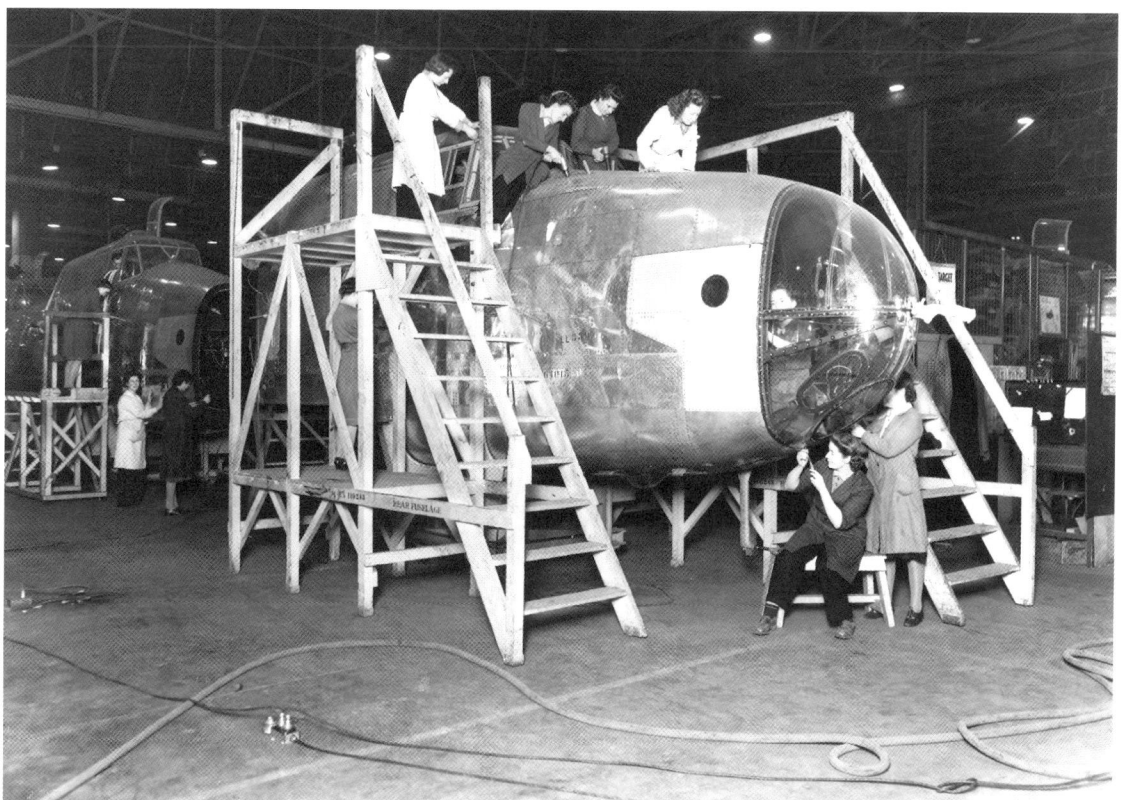

Halifax nose assembly at Rootes Securities, Speke using female workers. (*Handley Page Association*)

Above: The massive shadow factory at Speke with Halifax under fuselage assembly in foreground on 28 February 1945. (*Handley Page Association*)

Below: Halifax wing/fuselage centre section assembly at Speke with male and female workers. (*Handley Page Association*)

Above: Halifax wing centre section assembly ready for aircraft final assembly at Speke. (*Handley Page Association*)

Below: Halifax fuselage interior looking aft at Speke. (*Handley Page Association*)

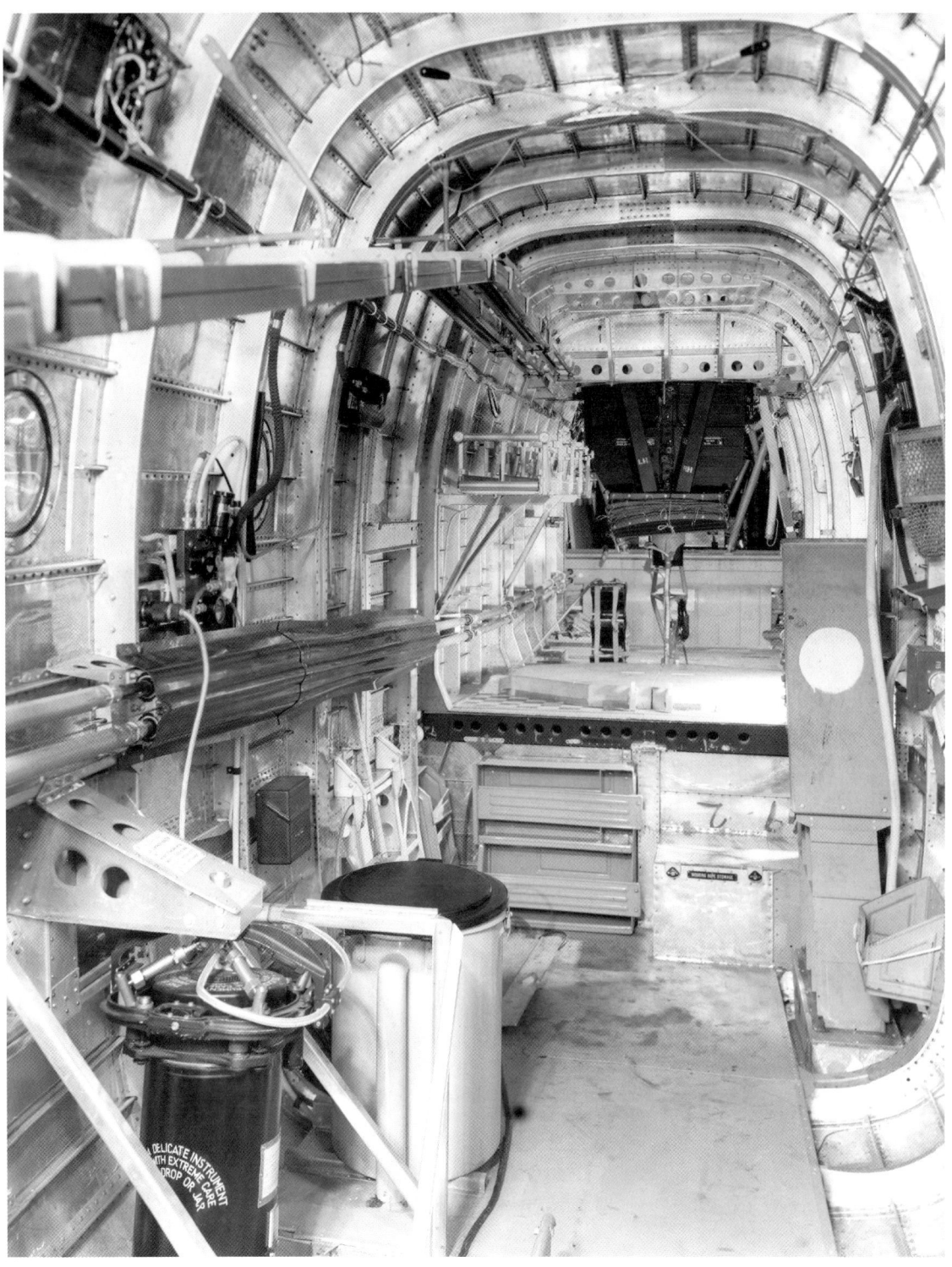

Halifax fuselage interior looking forward over the wing centre section at Speke, where there is much more clearance than inside Lancasters. (*Handley Page Association*)

Interior of aft fuselage showing rear turret access, at Speke. (*Handley Page Association*)

Rear of pilot's instrument panel, showing complexity and wiring, at Speke. (*Handley Page Association*)

Halifax Production

Above: Female workers assembling parts inside fuselage.

Below: Blind workers part numbering at Speke. Blind workers were also able to sort rivets. (*Handley Page Association*)

Above: Final assembly of Halifax B.II at Speke, ready for painting. (*Handley Page Association*)

Below: Halifax pilot's instruments and controls at Speke on 28 February 1945. (*Handley Page Association*)

Halifax flight deck and access to bomb aimers position in the nose, at Speke. (*Handley Page Association*)

Above: Completed Halifax B.II ready for paint shop, with many others at Speke awaiting delivery to RAF Bomber Command. (*Handley Page Association*)

Below: Halifax B.V DG235 at Speke ready for delivery to 408 Squadron. (*Air Historical Branch*)

Part of the vast Rootes Securities shadow factory at Speke. (*Handley Page Association*)

In 1940, the priority was for fighters and bombers in current production, which included Hurricanes, Spitfires for vital air defence and Blenheims, Wellingtons, and Whitleys for tactical bombing, with all priority going into manufacture; this was to the detriment of future developments. It was not until the end of 1941 that government support was given to the heavy strategic bomber programmes. In the interim, the contract was issued for the construction of 100 Halifax bombers to Spec. 32/37 for Mk.1 aircraft represented by the prototype L7245 powered by Merlin engines.

With fighter production having high priority for materials, in January 1940, the Air Council was considering giving Halifax production an equal status, with the increased orders. A further 100 Halifax had been ordered from HP, plus 300 from the new Speke factory and another 100 from English Electric. However, shortages of extrusions and forgings were still delaying production, putting at risk the formation of the first RAF squadron by mid-1940, a target which had always been unattainable. In February, the shortage of aluminium parts resulted in no overtime being worked at Cricklewood, with many of the new tools not being used.

Production of the first aircraft parts began in January, followed by detail assemblies, with plans to start assembly in August. The Outside Production Office was set up in January to arrange key worker training, supply of drawings and technical information, and supply templates and sample parts. They also advised subcontractors with selection of tools, provided advice and guidance and allocation of spares when required. A Co-ordination Committee was chaired by Thurstan James, the Director-General of Halifax production at the MAP, with representatives from HP at Radlett and English Electric to co-ordinate supplies for the production lines, meeting once a month. A Group Materials Committee with representation from each factory also met monthly to highlight material shortages.

The first production Halifax, L9485 flew on 11 October 1940, which like the prototypes, still had wing leading edge slots and was evaluated at Boscombe Down. The five companies in the overall Halifax group were referred to as 'daughter' firms, with the individual factories having 'dominion' identity. This gave an equal status for the daughter companies, with problems in common for material supply and overall administration. Handley Page meanwhile had overall responsibility for the supply of drawings, technical advice and approval of jigs. A high standard of interchangeability was achieved by checking components in alternative jigs, and one aircraft in every 100 was flown to Radlett to be flight tested to check compliance. Any corrections required were fed back to the factory responsible.

Among modifications embodied by mid-1940, was the extension of the inner engine nacelles to the flap trailing edges as a drag reduction, from the tenth aircraft onwards. Although it was decided to delete wing leading edge slots, they were locked in with the first seventy-five aircraft, from then on, a wing was designed with a new fixed wing leading edge. By this time, production expansion was moved into a number of companies, including Kenneth Hill Sandblasting in Letchworth, Daimler Company at Hendon, Elstree Film Studios and Godfrey Davis in NW London. MGM Studios in Boreham Wood was taken over and rubber press tools installed. Meanwhile, the Cricklewood factory had been extended with the takeover of Armstrong Siddeley Cars and Smiths Crisps. The London Transport Board car sheds at Aldenham were completed for the LAPG to use for aircraft assembly.

In late 1940, the MAP was planning on creation of an organisation in the York area for repair and overhaul of Halifax bombers. This was established in a shadow factory at Clifton airfield with HP responsible for its management and technical support. In late 1939, a full set of jigs and tools were supplied for each main assembly, being built by HP and the main subcontractors, with small component tools made in the factories producing the parts. By mid-1941, there were three sets of assembly jigs at Cricklewood with one set at each of the dispersed sites. As each dispersed site, jig achieved full working capacity, a further set of jigs would be supplied from Cricklewood. The MAP also suggested visits between Handley Page and English Electric should be arranged to compare production capabilities, and any improvements to be common across both sites, particularly with the use of unskilled labour.

The production build up was very slow initially, mostly due to shortage of some materials, and modifications highlighted by flight testing. V9976, the first of an initial 200 English Electric Halifax Mk.IIs, was flown from Samlesbury airfield on 15 August 1941, followed by HP's first Mk.II, L9609, in September. LAPG received R9540 as a pattern aircraft in preparation for production of 200 Mk. IIs beginning at the start of 1942, with the first (BB189) of an eventual total of 450 delivered on 10 January. Halifaxes produced by the LAPG were assembled at Leavesden near Watford, which was shared by de Havilland with Mosquito fighter assembly, also using major sections from Aldenham. Rear fuselages were built by Chrysler Motors at Kew; outer wings, nacelles and cowlings by Park Royal at White City; tail units, flaps and intermediate wing section by Express Motors at Enfield; front fuselage shells by Duple Bodies & Motors at Hendon; and LPTB produced centre fuselage assemblies and power units fully equipped before delivery to Leavesden. With such diverse production sources, it can be seen why interchangeability, combined with mass production skills of the motor industry was so vital. Initially, each unit was tasked with fitting out assemblies, but this was changed to full fitting out at Aldenham. The new shadow factory at Speke began Halifax production in 1942 with the first Mk.II, DG219, delivered on 1 April. Only twelve of this mark were produced by Rootes until it changed to Mk.5s, the first of which, DG321, was delivered on 1 August. Fairey Aviation at Stockport concentrated on Mk.Vs, with the first of 246, DJ980, delivered on 27 October 1942. The factory later produced Mk.IIIs.

Part of LPTB, Halifax rear fuselages being manufactured at White City, London. (*RAF Museum*)

Above: As part of LPTB, Halifax tailplane details being manufactured at Express & Motor Bodies in London. (*RAF Museum*)

Below: Female labour at EN&B fabric covering Halifax control surfaces as part of LPTB. (*RAF Museum*)

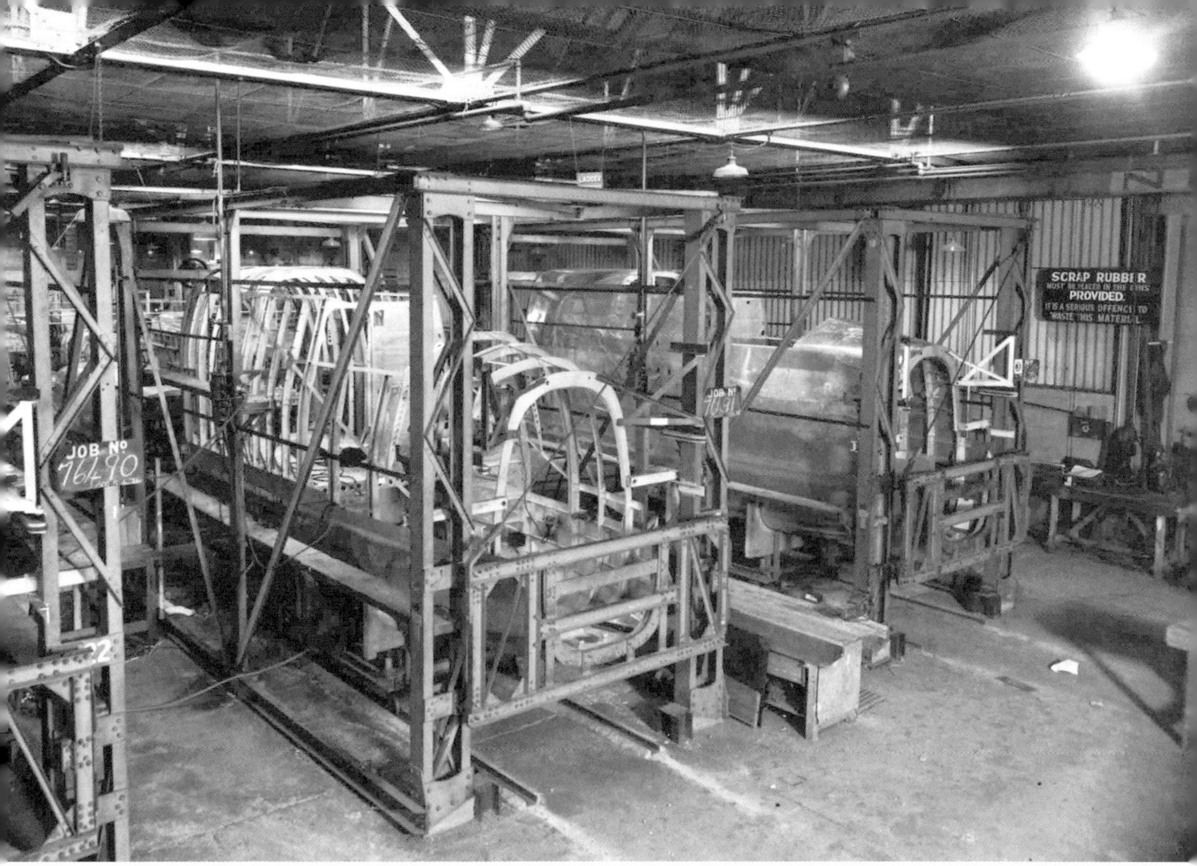

Above: Halifax forward fuselages in the jigs at Duple Bodies, as part of LPTB. (*RAF Museum*)

Below: The LPTB Aldenham bus works assembling and equipping Halifax wing and fuselage centre sections. (*RAF Museum*)

Left: Halifax final assembly with female labour at Leavesden. (*RAF Museum*)

Below: Starboard wing assembly at LPTB Leavesden. (*RAF Museum*)

Above: Halifax B.II in final assembly at Leavesden. (*RAF Museum*)

Below: Halifax B.II fully assembled at Leavesden being prepared for flight. (*RAF Museum*)

Above: Halifax B.II Srs 1A JP228 at Leavesden ready for delivery to 45 MU. (*Air Historical Branch*)

Below: Halifax B.III PN460, the last of 710 Halifaxes built by LPTB at Leavesden in April 1945 and named *London Pride*. This aircraft was delivered to 32 MU on 16 April, then 44 MU on 30 May, before issue to 517 Squadron on 3 November. It was struck off charge on 1 November 1946. (*RAF Museum*)

The total Halifax production organisation consisted of forty-one manufacturing and dispersed units supported by 600 subcontractors and 51,000 employees. The group was able to produce a Halifax every working hour of the day and night using 30,000 components. Each working hour 256,000 airframe parts were made, fitted and inspected; two thirds of an acre or seven tons of aluminium sheet was cut, formed and fitted using 70,000 rivets. There were nearly 4 miles of electric cable, 1 mile of hydraulic and pneumatic piping was installed and 3 miles of sheet metal were formed into sections.

In 1941, HP were experiencing production delays caused by late delivery of Merlin XXs and 22s, and shortages of Messier undercarriages. Merlin shortages were caused by the capabilities of just three factories at Derby, Crewe and Glasgow, which had supplied engines for Hurricanes and Spitfires during the Battle of Britain, as well as busy with urgent development of the new Griffon engine to replace some Merlins, and continuing work on Vulture engines. In the same year, Parliament voted to increase support for the heavy bomber programme, when it became obvious R-R would not be able to cope with the increased Merlin production. With the Lancaster replacing the Manchester, priority was given to Avro for Merlins. Equally, Hercules development was delayed with priority given to its development for the night fighter Beaufighter, leaving HP no alternative but to continue the use of Merlin XX and 22s. When Hercules problems were finally cleared, it was adopted for the Halifax, providing increased power and better suitability for operations in hot climates.

When ready for delivery, Halifax aircraft were flown to Maintenance Units (MUs), usually by ATA (Air Transport Auxiliary) male or female pilots, when military equipment was installed and the aircraft held until allocated to a squadron. They were then delivered by ATA pilots, often flying solo. Overseas deliveries were usually delivered by operational crews on their way to a posting, but this later became the responsibility of Ferry Command which delivered aircraft world-wide. During peak production, a Halifax was being produced every working hour, with total production reaching 6,176 aircraft when the last was delivered to the RAF in 1946. More could have been produced if modifications were not required for its different roles, all of which it operated with success.

Crews tended to prefer Halifaxes manufactured by English Electric, as they appeared to perform better, were easier to handle and had a lower empty weight. This preference was closely followed by aircraft built by HP. The LAPG aircraft were not overall to the same standards, but some did have a lower empty weight than the HP produced aircraft. As a result 'HP' requested an investigation to ensure standards were maintained, giving good handling characteristics and avoiding heavier aircraft. Although not a major producer of Halifax, Cuncliffe Owen at Eastleigh were responsible for a number of major modification and conversion programmes which the major mass production units were unable to complete. Cuncliffe Owen converted Mk.IIIs for operations with Coastal Command, ready for ASV radar to be fitted at 19 MU St Athan. They also made conversion kits for the meteorological Halifax, as well as producing fins for the main production units. Fortunately enemy action was not a major problem for Halifax factories, although air raid warnings did cause some delays. Duple Bodies within LAPG was badly damaged by bombing in addition to a number of near misses. With production rates increasing at all factories, night shifts were introduced and the new labour forces using semi-skilled and unskilled labour, both male and female. As experience was gained, teams were formed working under the guidance of skilled operatives, with unsuitable people redeployed. Female operatives were able to undertake a wide variety of tasks, and there were many that were able to achieve better than their male colleagues.

In mid-1943, the MAP published a programme for aircraft production for the second six months of the year. As a result, a third of all Halifax production was to be equipped with H2S radar with standard bomb doors, while the remainder were to be fitted with larger bomb doors and no H2S fitted, although production of large bomb doors was delayed. There were still shortages of specialist items as steel and aluminium forgings, and aluminium stampings. The completion of Halifax production was from Cricklewood and Radlett where the last of 145 Mk.A9s were completed in 1946. The Halifax had earned the reputation as a well-produced and strong aircraft, and for the crews who operated the aircraft in its many roles, it was second to none.

With the majority of Bomber Command Halifaxes allocated to 4 and 6 Groups at airfields in Yorkshire, the Ministry of Aircraft Production decided in February 1941 to set up a repair and overhaul organisation near York. The site chosen was Clifton/Rawcliffe airfield north of the city, and late in the year, a shadow factory was constructed, under the management of Handley Page, where 2,500 civilians, and many female workers were employed. The organisation was under the title of York Aircraft Repair Depot (YARD). Three runways were constructed, with initially four hangars erected on the northwest side of the site, with a fifth one added later. By the end of 1942, the third runway was completed and a second repair depot, known as Water Lane, was also built, taking the total to sixteen hangars. With most of the initial workforce recruited from the York-based LNER carriage works, the start of repair work was slow, building up as experience was gained. The first Halifax completed was L9510, which, after checking by a full RAF crew, was delivered to the RAF by an ATA pilot.

When Halifaxes were Category A damaged, they could generally be repaired by ground crew at squadron level on an RAF airfield. However, if an aircraft was designated Category B, it would have to be depot repaired. The most common causes of damage were wheels up landings, or undershooting on approach, when under fuselage structure was damaged. The aircraft would be dismantled and recovered by the RAF salvage 60 MU and delivered to YARD. Also repaired by YARD were aircraft with severe battle damage from anti-aircraft guns or enemy fighters, where the main structure was affected. In addition, Halifaxes based with Middle East squadrons were flown in for major inspections, or if they had been subject to violent evasive action.

Originally, aircraft taken to YARD were repaired and reassembled as completed original airframes, and fitted with new engines and propellers. But because of the high standards of interchangeability, it was possible to mix and match aircraft, where some may have damage to the fuselage and another to the wings, combining into one more rapidly repaired Halifax. This dramatically increased the numbers of repaired Halifaxes being returned to service, often to crew training duties. Technical problems were often caused by different modification standards of each aircraft, with some

2,000 design changes made over the period of 1941 to 1943. This required detailed surveys of each aircraft, before major assembles could be substituted from another damaged Halifax. Assemblies damaged too badly for repair were stripped of useful parts, which were overhauled ready to be used again. On completion of repairs and following reassembly, the aircraft was subjected to a full production line inspection process.

Before delivery to YARD, the aircraft would be inspected for damage assessment at the location of the incident. The scope of damage would be given to the planning department to allow a list of all replacement parts to be created. During 1944, an average of fifteen Halifax each month were completed, ready for return to service. Production flight testing was the responsibility of the HP test pilots at Radlett, who spent a month each on secondment, with flight test observers resident at Clifton; each aircraft usually being cleared after one flight. The flight test schedule used was the same as for a new production aircraft off the production lines, and usually took around 45 minutes. By the end of the war, some 2,000 Halifax bombers were returned to service by YARD, which finally closed in 1948, having made a major contribution to the war effort.

When production was completed in all five final assembly lines, a total of 6,176 Halifaxes had been built with the highest number of 2,145 coming from English Electric at Samlesbury. Handley Page completed 1,589 aircraft from Radlett, and third was Rootes Securities from Speke with 1,070 aircraft. LAPG assembled 710 Halifax from a very busy Leavesden and Fairey completed 662 at Ringway. The most plentiful version was Mk.3s with 2,091 completed, followed by 1,976 Mk.2s.

Halifax A.IX RT938, the last Halifax to be built at Radlett. It was delivered to YARD on 26 November 1946, then 48 MU on 2 January 1947, before sale to Aviation Traders on 18 August 1949. (*Philip Birtles*)

3

Initial RAF Halifax Bomber Operations

The first squadron to be equipped with Halifaxes was 35 Squadron attached to A&AEE Boscombe Down on 5 November 1940 starting crew training. With no previous experience of operating four engine heavy bombers, training was a challenge for the crews building their experience. Fortunately, most of the early crews were led by operational pilots who had experienced combat. Their first operational aircraft was L9486 collected by Flying Officer Henry from Radlett and flown to Boscombe Down on 13 November. The squadron moved to Leeming on 20 November 1940 as part of 4 Group, when due to a shortage of aircraft, prototype L7244 fitted with dual controls was loaned to the squadron from 23 November. The squadron then moved to its permanent base at Linton-on-Ouse on 5 December, where full crew training began with a slow addition of crew members. Additional aircraft began to arrive with the delivery of L9487 from 24 MU on 4 January 1941, allowing six crews to be trained which when converted to type, supported operational trials. These included checking fuel consumption, operational ceiling, handling at the 50,000lb AUW, W/T procedures, autopilot tests and use of blind approach equipment. A fourth Halifax, L9489, arrived on 12 January, but within 24 hours L9487 crashed fatally in flames on Homefield Farm, reducing the compliment to three aircraft again. The aircraft was flying a fuel test up to 12,000 feet, when a port engine failed causing a gradual descent, with fire coming from the wing. At 2,000 feet the pilot lowered the flaps and undercarriage, when the whole wing burst into flames, burning away the flying controls, causing the aircraft to dive into the ground killing all on board.

Training was then hampered for the next five weeks by bad weather. Delays to training were also caused by technical problems, when, in mid-January the aircraft were grounded due to difficulties with the hydraulic system, followed by similar problems in February. At the same time, aircraft deliveries continued at a very slow rate, with only five more being delivered in the time. By early March, more aircraft had been received with fifteen crews under training, six of whom were cleared for operations. There were serviceability problems with some deliveries by early July. Of seventeen aircraft delivered to Middleton St George, only four were operational, the remainder suffering from hydraulic problems. At Linton-on-Ouse only nine out of twenty-two aircraft were serviceable.

By this time, Bomber Command had been designated a strategic force, with enemy synthetic oil production being the prime targets, the destruction of which would

Halifax B.I L9503 TL-R 35 Squadron from Linton-on-Ouse visited Northolt on 21 July 1941. It was lost over Hamburg on the night of 15/16 September 1941. (*Air Historical Branch*)

cause disruption of German industry overall, as well as operational difficulties. As alternatives, a long list of secondary targets was created, but on 9 March, U-boat bases and production facilities were given priority due to heavy losses of Allied supply shipping, with oil production still being attacked. This delayed the realisation that Bomber Command suffered from poor accuracy, which caused difficulty locating specific targets due poor navigation aids existing. This resulted in the adoption of area bombing, where specific targets were chosen which were located in large cities to cause maximum disruption to the local population.

Orders were received on 10 March for the first night operation by 35 Squadron to Le Havre that night, with seven Halifax dispatched to attack docks and shipping, with Boulogne as an alternative. With good weather in Britain, the first aircraft, L9486, flown by Wing Commander Collings departed at 19.00hrs, followed by five more aircraft. Collings successfully dropped twelve 500lb armour piercing bombs from 13,000 feet, with hits observed along the edge of the main docks. The second aircraft, L9496, was unable to bomb Le Havre or Boulogne due to thick cloud, so Dieppe was bombed from 13,000 feet with no result observed. The third Halifax, L9498, located the target and bombed from 11,800 feet, but without observed results. This aircraft was mistaken for an enemy aircraft and shot down in error by a RAF home defence night fighter over Surrey, with only Squadron Leader Gilchrist and his flight engineer able to bale out. The fourth aircraft, L9493, made a successful attack from

11,000 feet, but was damaged by flak wounding the navigator and resulting in the loss of an engine, followed by a hydraulic failure causing the port main undercarriage to lower, although the aircraft was able to return to base safely. The fifth Halifax, L9490, bombed Le Havre from 10,000 feet through thick cloud with no results recorded. The sixth aircraft, L9488, was unable to bomb the primary target due to thick cloud, and with a shortage of fuel was unable to proceed to the secondary target, jettisoning its bombs in the Channel on the way home. A seventh Halifax was unable to go due to the familiar hydraulic failure.

The following night a force of eighty-eight bombers, including three 35 Squadron Halifaxes were sent to Hamburg to attack the Blohm and Voss U-boat factories, two of the Halifax being successful, but the third aborted due to gun turrets being unserviceable. With the main office building and two U-boat slipways damaged, the attack was considered a success. It was the first time Halifaxes and Manchesters had attacked a target in Germany, and all aircraft returned to base safely. A return was made to the same target the next night with 139 bombers, including two of 35 Squadron Halifaxes, where although there was no immediate result of destruction, a large fire was left burning in the centre of Hamburg and seven aircraft were lost, but none were from 35 Squadron. The squadron then concentrated with flying training to improve the operational capability. On 23 March, L9486 was flown to the AFDU at Duxford for tactical trials, but made a belly landing caused by hydraulic failure, a problem which took a long time to cure.

The priority for Bomber Command in March 1941 was to have been oil production and storage installations, but bad weather and the growing threat of U-boats to the

Halifax B.I L9506 TL-X of 35 Squadron crash landed at Bircham Newton on 16 June 1941 after being damaged on a night raid to Hannover by a German night fighter. (*Air Historical Branch*)

vital supply convoys to Britain, resulted in the Air Staff to call for U-boat assembly and associated industries to be attacked, initially by Whitley squadrons in 4 Group, until sufficient Halifax units had been formed. By April, it was possible to equip 76 Squadron at Linton-on-Ouse, which was reformed on 1 May 1941 from C Flight of 35 Squadron with Halifax B.Is, moving to Middleton St George on 4 June. On 15 April, three 35 Squadron Halifaxes were part of an attack on Kiel, where the U-boat yards were successfully hit. One of the aircraft, L9493, was hit by flak, damaging the hydraulics, causing the undercarriage and flaps to drop. At a drastically reduced speed, the aircraft was delayed from landing due to an enemy intruder in the circuit. While circling in preparation for landing, both starboard engines failed due to lack of fuel, but while attempting to switch tanks, the flight engineer mistakenly shut off fuel to the port side, causing them to stop. In the attempted crash-landing, the aircraft was destroyed, but apart from slight injuries to the navigator and tail gunner, the crew were safe.

By 12 June, 76 Squadron were ready to start operations with chemical works at Huls as the target. Three of 76 Squadron shared the raid with eight Halifaxes from 35 Squadron and seven 7 Squadron Stirlings. The attack was largely unsuccessful due

Halifax B.I of 35 Squadron with the air and ground crew and Flight Lieutenant Cheshire, brother of Leonard Cheshire in the centre. (*RAF Museum*)

Halifax B.I Srs.1 L9530 MP-L 76 Squadron at Middleton St George in August 1941, being prepared for the next operation. (*Air Historical Branch*)

to poor visibility, with only one 35 Squadron aircraft reporting hitting the target. One of the 76 Squadron bombed the alternative of Essen, with the other two Halifaxes returning early due to engine problems.

During early operations, problems continued with the main undercarriage hydraulic system resulting in only one main wheel coming down, and the tailwheel often suffered from severe shimmy causing failure of the unit. Until a cure was found, the tailwheels were locked down. During May, 35 Squadron again became inactive due to consistent hydraulic problems with the main undercarriages and were withdrawn from operations for two months to embody modifications to the hydraulic systems.

During this period of inactivity, on the night of 11/12 August enemy bombs hit the Linton-on-Ouse 35 Squadron hangars starting fires with incendiaries which were rapidly brought under control. Three airmen were killed and seven badly injured, as well as the Station Commander Group Captain Garraway killed while helping with firefighting. Damage to the aircraft was slight. With some reduction in combat activity, the squadron was used for promotional flights, including inspection by Winston Churchill at West Raynham and a royal presentation for King George VI, Queen Elizabeth and the two princesses at Abingdon.

Operations restarted on 11 June, with nine Halifaxes in a force of eighty bombers attacking Duisburg. Cloud cover over the target of 8/10^{ths} reduced accuracy. Six of the Halifaxes dropped their bombs from altitudes between 7,000 and 13,000 feet, but despite much of the target being obscured by cloud, they were able to locate the target through some clear gaps. One of the other Halifaxes bombed an alternative target and the other was unable to bomb because of an electrical failure. The only damage was to one aircraft which had a coolant leak in the No. 4 engine due to flak damage.

On the night of 16 June, three Halifaxes were sent to bomb Cologne as part of a larger formation, and 35 Squadron despatched three of their Halifaxes to Hanover, but continuing bad weather resulted in alternate targets of Dortmund and Vechta airfield being bombed. The two squadrons flew together on the first of a series of raids against Kiel on the night of 20 June in a combined force of Wellingtons, Hampdens, Whitleys and Stirlings the main target being *Tirpitz*, but bad weather caused the attempt to be abandoned. A further attempt was made on 23 June with a force including ten Halifaxes again with poor results on the target, and the 76 Squadron suffered its first operational loss when L9492 was shot down by an enemy night fighter with the loss of the crew. On 26 June another force was sent back to Kiel including one 76 Squadron aircraft and six from 35 Squadron, with all but one 35 Squadron Halifax bombing the target. Two nights later, two 76 Squadron Halifaxes were part of a larger force to Hamburg, before a change of operations was tried.

Although early in the War, daylight bombing attacks had caused unacceptable losses, but with the introduction of heavily defended bombers, consideration was being investigated to try daylight attacks to improve results. Despite some fierce opposition, a practical test was planned to check the feasibility. The first test was against Kiel in

Halifax B.I Srs.1 L9530 MP-T 76 Squadron. It was lost on a raid to Magdeburg on 15 August 1941. (*Air Historical Branch*)

daylight on 30 June, with excellent visibility forecast. Six 35 Squadron Halifaxes went in two V formations and bombed successfully from between 17,000 and 18,000 feet with target strikes in the docks with fires started. There was heavy accurate flak from the ground and the second formation was attacked by Bf 110 fighters. One of the fighters was shot down by Halifax L9499. Halifax L9501 was then aggressively attacked by the Bf 110s and badly damaged with one of the gunners killed, although the aircraft returned to base, the pilot Flying Officer Owen being awarded the DFC. The Chief of the Air Staff sent his congratulations to the crews and Squadron Leader J. B. Tait, the leader of the raid was awarded the DSO, as results were good enough to plan further daylight bombing raids.

A new directive was received by Bomber Command on 9 July, with the main aims of the dislocation of the enemy transport system, and a reduction in civilian population morale. With the supply crisis at sea reduced, and Hitler having attacked his former ally in Russia, there was limited success against oil production, and so reducing morale with the enemy workforce became a priority. Attacking enemy transportation systems became a priority, in particular, railway centres and inland waterways. With the benefit of clear moonlit nights railway targets were attacked in Hamm, Osnabruck, Soest, Schwerte, Cologne, Dusseldorf and the major rail-water port at Duisburg-Ruhrort. With all these targets situated in major industrial areas any additional damage was important for the effect on factories and the working population. If weather was bad over the prime targets, secondary targets included Bremen, Frankfurt, Hamburg, Hannover, Mannheim and Stuttgart. On 8/9 July both 35 and 76 Squadrons bombed the Leuna oil installation at Merseburg. Night bombing continued on a larger scale against targets in Germany from August until October, hampered by bad weather, but results were poor and losses increased from night fighters. On 12 August, a heavy raid was made by 4 Group squadrons on Berlin in bad weather, preventing many of the aircraft from identifying the Air Ministry buildings target and two 76 Squadron Halifaxes were lost, including one which crashed on return killing the entire crew. Both Halifax squadrons continued to operate at night for the next three weeks against major German cities including Hannover and Frankfurt. With poor results and heavy losses continuing during August, Bomber Command capability was in question. In addition, the Butt Report issued in the same month, the analysis found that on night raids during June and July only one fifth of bombs dropped were landing within 5 miles of the target. As a result of this report, the development of increased accuracy bombing aids was accelerated, and despite weaknesses, in September 1941 plans were made to increase the front-line strength of Bomber Command to 4,000 aircraft.

On one particularly wild night with snow and sleet, Tait crash-landed on return to base with the bombs still on board, as he had been unable to find the target. The aircraft had to be lifted carefully off its belly, as it was located on the far side of the airfield from the hangars, and fortunately well clear of the runway. The weather was bad and the work had to be done in darkness, the damaged aircraft being slowly lifted from starboard to port wings, and as height was achieved, sandbags were pushed under as support. No lifting bags were available, but it was gradually lifted to allow heavy duty trolleys with big wheels to be pushed underneath. At this point, an armourer pressed the bomb jettison lever, and to the recovery party's surprise, they were surrounded by bombs and incendiaries, the men scattering rapidly in all directions, before returning to get the aircraft in a hangar, where the damage could be assessed.

After a pilot was injured by flack penetrating the underside of his seat, armour plating was fitted as a protection, although care had to be taken not to significantly increase the overall weight of the aircraft. Some of the crew members made their own unauthorised protection, but when a navigator was caught struggling with an overweight canvas bag, it was realised the aircraft could soon be so overweight, they would have difficulty taking-off. This practice therefore had to be stopped.

Bomber Command continued investigating the use of bombing by day to gain greater accuracy, the main criteria being the air defence capability. However, the range of fighters had been increased sufficiently in July to allow escort to provide bomber protection to nearer targets in occupied Europe. To test the theory, using up to five Spitfire squadrons fitted with long-range tanks, a surprise attack was planned on 24 July against the German battleships, *Scharnhorst* and *Gneisenau* sheltering in Brest harbour. The force was to consist of around 150 medium and heavy bombers, with three Spitfire squadrons escorting the second wave, and the other two squadrons to follow to deal with any enemy fighters which managed to rejoin the battle after refuelling.

Unfortunately, the *Scharnhorst* was moved at the last minute to La Rochelle, around 200 miles further south, with the heavy bomber part of the force tasked to attack this target without escort. The following day, with fifteen Halifaxes in the task force, nine from 35 Squadron and the other six from 76 Squadron, the task force set out from Stanton Harcourt to reduce the distance to the target and allow an increased bomb load. The formation flew out over the Lizard below 1,000 feet to avoid detection from German radar, then climbing for the bomb run, which was from 15,000 feet over the target. The weather was excellent with good visibility, which was a hazard for the bombers. A German destroyer spotted the formation and sent a warning ahead, destroying what little surprise was available. As a result, the Halifaxes were met with heavy anti-aircraft guns from the ground and the air, the latter being from around eighteen Bf 109s based locally. Flying in echelon formation, it was not long before the bombers were taking hits, with L9527 going down in a spiral, with only two parachutes seen to emerge.

The formation was scattered when taking evasive action, but were vulnerable on the bombing run. The aircraft which stayed in the protection of the formation survived better than the stragglers and on departure from the target area, the enemy fighters continued to press home their attacks. On completion of the operation, two Halifaxes from 35 Squadron had been lost, with another three from 76 Squadron. Five were extensively damaged, and the remainder suffered slight damage. As a result, the *Scharnhorst* had received five direct hits, the ship sailing back to Brest that evening with 3,000 tons of water inside the hull. The gunners from the two squadrons claimed five enemy aircraft destroyed, three probables and more damaged. Both squadrons then returned to night operations, while the advantages of day bombing were assessed. Although the results of the raid were not conclusive, it was felt in some areas improved defensive armament might have an effect.

Bad weather delayed operations at the start of October 1941 until 10 October to Essen and Nurenburg on 12 October, but the difficulties of locating targets at such long distances was difficult, in particular, Nurenburg, where the bombs were widely scattered up to 65 miles from the target. Despite the unfavourable weather forecast for 7/8 November, a long planned maximum effort to Berlin was approved. Additional targets on the same night were Cologne and Mannheim with a total of 392 bombers of all types being sent, which was the highest number so far. The weather was even worse than predicted, and many crews elected to go to the alternate targets. Those who went to Berlin suffered severe icing or had to ditch on their return due to a shortage of fuel used when attempting to climb above the cloud layers. The raid was a major disaster with thirty-seven aircraft lost, equal to 9.4 per cent, resulting in it being the last major raid to Berlin until January 1943. For the rest of November, bad weather brought bomber operations almost to a stop. The War Cabinet directed the scale of operations to be reduced, while the future operations of Bomber Command was considered.

The last production B.Mk.I, L9608, was officially named at Radlett by Lady Halifax on 12 September 1941. With the arrival in service from October of the improved Halifax B.Mk.II, there was an opportunity to further test the possibility of daytime raids.

Last production Halifax B.I L9608 naming ceremony at Radlett on 12 September 1941. This aircraft was delivered to 24 MU on 2 October 1941 and was issued to 76 Squadron on 17 October 1941. It then joined 1602 HCU on 26 February 1942 and remained with them until written off 30 November 1942. (*RAF Museum*)

Last production Halifax B.I L9608 with Merlin engines running following the naming ceremony at Radlett on 12 September 1941. (*Handley Page Association*)

4
Merlin Halifax Operations

During the introduction to operational service, a number of modest modifications had been introduced, with very little external signs. The airframe was strengthened to allow all up weight (AUW) to be increased by 5,000lb to 60,000lb. This version was designated B.Mk.I Series 2 and the aileron mass balance was repositioned above the wing. Some of the additional weight was used to increase fuel capacity by 88 gallons, with additional tankage in the wing centre section, taking total fuel load to 2,330 gallons. Increased diameter engine oil coolers were introduced to overcome engine overheating; this version being designated B.Mk.I Series 3.

There was a need for a step change in improvement modifications, and the thirty-first production Halifax, L9515, was allocated to the development programme. The goal was to further improve performance and increase range. This started with the installation of a 123-gallon fuel tank in the outboard wing section, known as the No. 6 tank, and was connected to the No. 5 tank, with a capacity of 245 gallons, and increasing overall standard fuel capacity to 1,886 gallons, and maximum capacity to 2,576 gallons. This allowed the range to be increased from 1,700 to 2,000 miles. The next major improvement was the replacement of the Merlin X engines by Merlin XXs, which had been developed by R-R to deliver 1,280hp for take-off as against 1,075hp for the earlier engine. The new engine was much more reliable, with increased performance for the Halifax. It could maintain an improved altitude, for example at 1,175hp it could cruise at 21,000 feet, as compared with 17,750 feet under Merlin X power. With an increase in dry weight of only 8.5 per cent, the new engine was fully interchangeable with the Merlin X and could be immediately introduced on the production lines.

The new Merlins were fitted to L9519 with a series of test flight made from 18 to 31 August 1941, at an AUW of 60,000lb. The aircraft was to a similar configuration to the B.Mk.1 Series III, but was not fitted with the additional fuel tanks or beam guns. Speed tests were made at up to 26,000 feet, and continuous operations were made at 23,000 feet for over an hour. The bomb doors were also functioned at 23,000 feet on 4 September.

The initial contract for Handley Page called for 200 B.Mk.Is, but this was amended from L9609 onwards to allow for upgrade to B.Mk.II Series 1 aircraft, with similar changes to the other suppliers, resulting in Handley Page being the only producer of the B.Mk.Is. The first production B.Mk.II had drag reducing modifications, including revised engine cowlings, and later had the addition of the distinctive Boulton Paul mid-upper gun turret. The first production B.Mk.II, L9485, was retained for armament trials, when it was fitted with the mid-upper turret and a Boulton Paul K.Mk.I ventral turret, the latter specifically for the Halifax. All Boulton Paul gun turrets were power operated by a combination of electro-hydraulics, and the ventral one could be retracted until almost flush with the fuselage, reducing drag on the way to the target, although it was not eventually adopted on the Halifax. With the installation of the mid-upper turret, the beam guns were removed, although many early production aircraft still featured the hatches, pending modification of the jigs.

The first delivery of a Halifax B.Mk.II was R9364 to 35 Squadron on 25 October 1941 from Radlett and V9979 from Samlesbury. The squadron had carried out nine operations during the month without any combat losses, although two were damaged when making crash-landings on return to base. During November, operations were reduced to four due to bad weather, and two Halifax were lost.

A 35 Squadron Halifax B.II Srs.1 flying low over English countryside on a daytime training flight. (*Handley Page Association*)

Above: Halifax B.II TL-P 35 Squadron in 1942. (*RAF Museum*)

Below: Engine fitters working on the Nos 1 and 2 Merlins at Linton-on-Ouse in 1942. (*RAF Museum*)

Above: Servicing the Nos 1 and 2 Merlins on a 35 Squadron Halifax B.II at Linton-on-Ouse in 1942. (*RAF Museum*)

Below: Radlett-built Halifax B.II R9441 TL-S 35 Squadron on a wintry dispersal at Linton-on-Ouse in February 1942, still fitted with the original fin/rudders. This aircraft was lost on 4 April 1943. (*Air Historical Branch*)

Above: Halifax B.II V9978 TL-A 35 Squadron releasing 1,000lb general purpose bombs from the inner wing cells. This aircraft was delivered to 35 Squadron on 9 November 1941 and was written off on 18 December 1941. (*Air Historical Branch*)

Below: Radlett-built Halifax B.II Srs. 1A HR926 TL-L 35 Squadron fitted with the new fin/rudders. It was delivered to 35 Squadron on 7 August 1943 and went missing on 23 October 1943. (*RAF Museum*)

In December 1941, 10 Squadron at Leeming became the third to equip with Halifaxes, replacing its Whitleys with B.Mk.IIs; the first operation was a trial daylight raid on 18 December with Stirlings and Manchester known as Operation Veracity 1. The targets were once again *Scharnhorst* and *Gneisenau* in Brest harbour. This time, significant fighter cover was provided during the bombing and withdrawal. In excellent visibility, all three Halifax squadrons provided six aircraft each, forming up over Linton, although one 10 Squadron aircraft had to abort due to hydraulic difficulties. At the marshalling point off Lundy, the Halifaxes arrived early, but there was no sign of the Manchesters or Stirlings, which were supposed to join the raid. The Stirlings were then seen approaching, but bypassed the orbiting Halifaxes and headed for Lands End. There was still no sign of the Manchesters. The bomber stream headed out over the Channel with the Stirlings in the lead in clear, sunny weather. The Halifax squadrons were in a close defensive 'V' formation, approaching the target at 16,000 feet. The Stirlings were heavily engaged by flak and a few fighters, with some of the bombers breaking off to the right. The formation of Halifaxes then set a course approaching the battleships in dry dock at right angles. Despite heavy flak, the Halifaxes maintained their tight formation, bombed and withdrew, to see the Manchesters arriving in tight formation heading for the targets.

Radlett-built Halifax B.II Srs. 1 L9619 ZA-E 10 Squadron on 12 December 1941 armed with beam guns as the upper turret has not been fitted. It was delivered to 10 Squadron 8 November 1941 and was SOC 21 February 1942. (*Air Historical Branch*)

Above: Leavesden-built Halifax B.II Srs. 1 (Special) BB324 ZA-X 10 Squadron with nose and mid-upper turrets removed and faired over. This aircraft appears to be flying on the power of only the No. 1 Merlin. It was delivered to 78 Squadron on 28 February 1943, then moving to 10 Squadron on 18 April, before going missing on 23 June 1943. (*Handley Page Association*)

Below: The seven aircrew with their ground crew in front of Halifax B.II Srs. 1 (Special) ZA-D 10 Squadron. (*RAF Museum*)

Merlin Halifax Operations

Above: Ground crew maintaining Leavesden-built Halifax B.II BB194 ZA-E in typical primitive conditions with 10 Squadron in December 1942. This aircraft was lost on 30 September 1943. (*Air Historical Branch*)

Below: Halifax B.IIs of 35 Squadron bombing the German Navy battleships in Brest Harbour on 18 December 1941. (*Air Historical Branch*)

Samlesbury-built Halifax B.II JB910 ZA-R 10 Squadron returning to its base at Melbourne on 21 April 1943 after bombing Stettin. The aircraft was delivered to 10 Squadron on 31 March 1943 and moved to 1658 HCU on 29 March 1944. It was SOC on 10 April 1944. (*RAF Museum*)

The lead Halifax, V9978, was hit by flak in the port wing which set fire to both engines. Wing Commander Robinson was able to extinguish the fires, but could not feather the engines, reducing the speed to around 110mph and escorted by his two wing men. He was forced to ditch about 60 miles off the English coast, the aircraft floating long enough for the crew to take to the dinghies, and be rescued later in the day. No. 35 Squadron Halifax R9367 was also damaged by flak, the port inner engine failing immediately after departing from the target, and was feathered with some difficulty. Soon after, the starboard outer engine failed and caught fire, but was extinguished. With its escort, the aircraft was landed safely at Boscombe Down. There was minor flak damage to some other aircraft, and although the damage to the battleships could not be confirmed, major bomb bursts were seen on the sterns of both ships, for the loss of one Halifax. Following the raid, reports came back that there was no major damage to the enemy war ships and, in addition to the Halifax, one Manchester and four Stirlings had been lost.

Another attempt on the enemy war ships, Operation Veracity II, was planned for 30 December, but due to bad weather in the 3 and 5 Group areas, the attack was left to just the 4 Group Halifax squadrons. Fighter cover was planned with a Polish Spitfire Wing from 5 minutes before the start to the withdrawal. Although six Halifaxes from the three squadrons were to make the attack, two of 10 Squadron aircraft had to abort. In the lead was 35 Squadron, followed by 10 Squadron and 76 Squadron in the rear. The enemy defences were on full alert and responded with a concentrated and accurate barrage.

Squadron Leader Middleton and crew went down when 35 Squadron V9979 was hit in the port wing, and while on the bombing run 76 Squadron L9615 had to dive away to starboard, gliding out to sea with the starboard engine on fire and ditched about 20 miles from the coast, protected by two Spitfires. The withdrawal was slowed by many enemy fighters, which were engaged by the Spitfire escort. One of 10 Squadron aircraft, R9374, which had the port outer engine put out of action by flak, was intercepted by a Bf 109 from astern, stopping both inboard Merlins, the crippled aircraft finally ditching 80 miles south off the Lizard, where all but one of the

Radlett-built Halifax B.II W7671 W 76 Squadron in 1942. It was originally delivered to 78 Squadron on 26 April 1942 and moved to 76 Squadron on 29 June 1942, going to the Middle East on 17 July. It was declared a write off on 7 November 1942. (*RAF Museum*)

Ringway-built Halifax B.V DK176 MP-U 76 Squadron in 1943 with nose and mid-upper turrets removed and faired over to reduce drag. This aircraft was delivered to the squadron on 23 April 1943, but was SOC on 23 July 1943. (*RAF Museum*)

crew were rescued by an Air Sea rescue launch after 5 hours in the water. Pilot Officer Hacking in R9370 was attacked by a Bf 109, but when it passed over the Halifax tail, the rear gunner, Sergeant Porritt shot it down. Despite slight wounds to his hands and face, Porritt managed to defend against another two enemy fighters. When the results were analysed, they were not encouraging with three Halifaxes and two crews lost, and the remainder extensively damaged by flak. With the Halifaxes the sole attacking force, they took all the punishment from the alerted defences, and bombing results were again disappointing.

Meanwhile, two detachments from 10 and 76 Squadrons were sent to Lossiemouth in Scotland for a highly secret attack on the *Tirpitz* sheltering in Aas Fjord in Norway. It was thought that with the ship only about 50 feet offshore, special mines could roll down the steep sloping sides of the Fjord, with hydrostatic fuses set to explode under the vulnerable lower hull. Each aircraft was carrying four special 1,000lb mines, which were a bit too large to fit in the bomb-bay, resulting in the bomb doors being left partly open, increasing drag on the operation which was at the extreme Halifax range. The approach started at 2,000 feet with a timed descent to a hazardous 200 feet. In very bad weather, the four 10 Squadron aircraft failed to locate the target, as well as four of the five from 76 Squadron. The remaining failed to positively identify the target, but assumed it was the source of the fierce anti-aircraft fire, and bombed accordingly. One of the 76 squadron aircraft, L9581, lost a port engine and ditched 3 miles off Aberdeen due to fuel starvation, but the crew were rescued. During extreme cold weather in January with heavy icing, 35 Squadron was only operational five times during the month.

Towards the end of January 1942, photo reconnaissance detected preparations in Brest Harbour with *Scharnhorst*, *Gneisenau* and *Prinz Eugen* ready for a breakout to a safer haven through the English Channel. The breakout was seen on 11 February and Bomber Command deployed 13 Halifaxes, of which four were from 35 Squadron. No attack was possible due to very bad weather. The only attempt at attack was a 10 Squadron Halifax, which detected a large ship through a brief break in the clouds, and dropped its full bomb load from 9,000 feet without confirmed results. The only positive result of the departure of the ships from Brest, was a freeing up Bomber Command from having to continue destroying the French ports where the ships had sheltered. By the spring of 1942, the antiquated and ineffective Whitleys had been replaced in 4 Group by increasing numbers of Halifaxes. In February 1942, 158 Squadron reformed as a bomber squadron at Driffield from 104 Squadron, equipped with Wellingtons, until replaced by Halifaxes in June 1942.

As a result of the heavy losses on the Berlin raid of 7/8 November the previous year, the Air Ministry had placed operational restrictions on Bomber Command. With an

The air and ground crew with 158 Squadron Halifax B.II 'Miss Otis' showing the number of combat operations and decorations awarded to the crew. (*RAF Museum*)

uncertain future, the Command, with Winston Churchill's support, was allowed to continue as a strategic force providing it had a new tactical plan with a new leader. The direction to start area bombing of the most densely built-up areas in major German cities, to reduce the productive capacity of industry, and also the workforce homes, was made on 14 February, and eight days later ACM Arthur Harris was appointed AOC Bomber Command.

With Bomber Command coming under some criticism for its lack of performance during the escape of the German battleships, 'Bomber' Harris took over as head of the Command, and immediately defended the efforts made in appalling weather conditions. The first operation under his command was on 3 March with a concentration of 235 bombers against the Renault works at Billancourt near Paris. A small force from both 10 and 76 Squadron participated. All three Halifax squadrons were in the process of equipping with the new Gee navigation aid, allowing accurate identification of a target up to 400 miles from base, depending upon altitude. As the equipment could not be retrofitted in existing aircraft, new Halifaxes had to be delivered which had been modified during production. This problem also caused a delay in 102 Squadron becoming operational, which had begun to equip with Halifaxes in December 1941 at Dalton, and by six of the earlier aircraft replaced with six fully modified Halifaxes from 35 Squadron on 9 April.

By the middle of March 1942, around 150 aircraft were equipped with Gee, including 4 Group Halifaxes, resulting in a new bombing technique called 'Shaker' being developed. This consisted of the bomber force being split into three groups. The lead group would be Gee equipped dropping illuminators as a line of flares and high explosive bombs, guiding the target markers to the target where incendiary bombs would be dropped. A concentrated area of fire on the ground would be created, for the followers to release their high explosive bomb load. To test the effectiveness of this Gee assisted raid concept in determining if the use of flares would be effective, the Renault factory near Paris was attacked on 3/4 March.1942. The raid was a complete success with damage to every building and 40 per cent of machine tools destroyed, but local French civilian casualties were high with 367 killed and 341 injured. Among the bombers were twenty 4 Group Halifaxes, with many more in the process of having Gee fitted.

The first fully operational Shaker raid was on 8 March, when 211 aircraft bombed the Krupps works in Essen, but despite the use of Gee, industrial haze prevented accurate bombing. One Halifax from 35 Squadron was lost, in addition to a 158 Squadron Wellington. An attack on Cologne followed on 13 March with improved results. The lead Gee-equipped fifty bombers successfully marked the target and almost half the following aircraft were within 65 miles of the marked area.

While Gee was being supplied, 10, 35 and 76 Squadrons sent detachments north to Lossiemouth ready for another attack on *Tirpitz* on 30 March, which was sheltering in Asen Fjord near Trondheim. A special weapon was to be carried in the shape of a football, was in fact a 1,000lb spherical mine. Four of these weapons were to be carried by the twenty Halifaxes of 10 and 35 Squadrons, with a low-level approach towards the battleship, which was moored under an overhanging cliff face. At the last moment, the aircraft had to climb steeply away after release of the weapons, which would hit the cliff face and roll down under the ship triggered to explode by a hydrostatic fuse. Meanwhile, twelve aircraft from 76 Squadron were tasked with neutralising the heavy curtain of flak and searchlights by dropping 4,000lb blast weapons and 500lb high-explosive bombs.

Weather problems had not improved since the earlier attempt, and the range was still a problem. The Halifax forces flew over the sea to Norway at 1,000 feet in good visibility to avoid detection by the enemy radar. However, on reaching the target area there was full cloud cover and fog which made it impossible to locate the target. As the fuel reserves were used up, they were forced to abort the mission, but before departing, jettisoned each of their four 1,000lb mines aimed at the source of flak and searchlights, which ceased to operate. Out of thirty-four Halifaxes taking part in the raid, six were lost with the crews, almost certainly due to lack of fuel, and most that did return landed with nearly empty fuel tanks. With further attacks planned against *Tirpitz* the Halifax squadrons remained in Scotland hoping for better weather, but with no sign of an improvement, the detachments returned to their home bases.

In addition to Gee and other new navigation aids, in early 1942, the high capacity 8,000lb bomb was introduced, with trials carried out with a single 8,000lb weapon and two 4,000lb Cookies. Despite the size of the loads, there was no reduction in take-off performance, and handling was unaffected. The bomb doors had to be left partially open, and to reduce drag a canvas strip covered the protruding bomb doors. The first of many 8,000lb bombs was dropped on the Krupp works at Essen on 10 April by Halifax R9487 of 76 Squadron, a large explosion being observed.

With the final withdrawal of the Whitleys from Bomber Command, Halifaxes were used to equip additional units. Nos 78 and 102 Squadrons began to receive Halifax B.IIs, with 78 Squadron based at Croft, and moved to Middleton St George on 10 June. No. 102 Squadron began to take delivery of B.IIs at Dalton in December 1941, with a move to Topcliffe on 7 June. Both squadrons became operational in April and participated in its first raid on 15 April, sending two aircraft with a bomber formation against Le Havre. The second operation on 27 April was not good for 102 Squadron as out of three aircraft on mixed raids to Cologne and mine laying off Dunkerque, two were lost with the crews. Meanwhile, another Shaker raid was made on the Baltic port of Rostock on 23 April, with nearly two thirds of the city destroyed.

The three other Halifax squadrons were tasked once again to attack *Tirpitz* with 10 and 35 Squadrons carrying the 1,000lb mines, and 76 Squadron armed with conventional bombs to be used against the defences, this time in darkness. The Gee sets were removed to save weight, as the target was way beyond the range of the aid. A total of thirty-two Halifaxes departed from Lossiemouth on 27 April, with one aborting soon after take-off. The route was over the Orkneys and Shetlands, then towards Trondheim for about 3 hours over the sea. Visibility was better than the previous attempts in clear moonlight, and the defences were much more challenging. Descending from 2,000 feet to mast height, the aircraft were met with a heavy concentration of flak. Several Halifaxes were able to do the 250-foot altitude drop near the target, but others were unable to identify it due to dense smoke screens. However, 76 Squadron was able to suppress some of the anti-aircraft guns with its bombs.

Above: Samlesbury-built Halifax B.II W1245 EY-B 78 Squadron. It was delivered to the squadron on 3 August 1942, but went missing 9 days later. (*Newark Air Museum*)

Below: Personnel with 78 Squadron in front of a Halifax B.II at Croft in May 1942. (*RAF Museum*)

Halifax B.II Srs IA EY-E 78 Squadron. (*RAF Museum*)

One of the attacking Halifaxes was W1048 from 35 Squadron, which was hit by flak in the starboard outer engine, but the pilot, Pilot Officer Don McIntyre, was able maintain control and cleared the cliff tops around the fjord. The instruction had been that, if damaged, the aircraft were to head for neutral Sweden, but Don believed the aircraft would be unable to achieve such a flight safely. He therefore elected to make a successful crash-landing on the ice of Lake Hoklingen, with the crew mainly uninjured. Apart from Vic Stevens, the flight engineer with a damaged foot, who was taken prisoner, the remainder of the crew avoided capture and reached Sweden, to be interned and returned to Britain. The aircraft sank through the ice and remained on the lake bottom until raised in June 1973 and is now conserved at the RAF Museum at Hendon in the condition which the aircraft was recovered.

One other Halifax was lost by 35 Squadron, and two more by 10 Squadron, including W1041 which was flown by the commanding officer, Wing Commander D. C. T. Bennett, who pressed home his attack despite damage, and maintained flight to allow his crew to abandon the aircraft. Don Bennett crash-landed in snow and made his way to Sweden with his radio operator, returning to command 10 Squadron within a month. He would later become leader of the Path Finder Force (PFF) in 8 Group, with the rank of Air Vice-Marshal.

To make the best use of the force while it was deployed in Scotland and the *Tirpitz* still afloat, as the weather was still favourable, another attack was made the next night, this time by twenty-four Halifaxes from the three squadrons. Two aircraft failed to return from 35 Squadron, but there were no losses from the other two, although 10 Squadron W1057 was badly damaged by flak which caused the flaps to come down. The hazardous flight at 110mph was just able to reach the safety of Sumburgh in Shetlands. The battleship remained undamaged despite the heroic attempts of the crews.

Bomber Command was still under criticism due to the inaccuracy of destroying targets, with some wishing it to be disbanded and become an Army and Navy support force. However, Gee had begun to improve target destruction, as demonstrated with Billancourt and other major enemy targets during April and May. To forestall further criticism, Harris decided to demonstrate the full potential of strategic bombing by assembling a larger force than ever seen before. Three more squadrons began conversion to Halifaxes in April and May, with 78 and 405 (RCAF) Squadrons becoming operational in time to participate in this major Operation Millenium, a

Halifax B.II with 405 (RCAF) Squadron being loaded with 31,000lb bombs and 30lb incendiaries. (*Air Historical Branch*)

'thousand-bomber raid'. In April 1942, 405 Squadron had exchanged its Wellingtons for Halifax B.IIs at Pocklington.

A combined force of 1,047 bombers, code named Operation Trout, was launched against Cologne on the night of 30/31 May, with the first wave consisting of Gee-equipped Wellingtons and Stirlings as the pathfinders, carrying incendiaries to mark the target aiming points. During the next hour, the second wave bombed the targets, followed by the Halifaxes and Lancasters of the third wave, who bombed during the last 15 minutes of the operation. The Halifax contribution consisted of 131 aircraft from 10, 35, 76, 78, 102 and 405 Squadrons as well as instructors and students from 1652 Heavy Conversion Unit (HCU). The raid was an outstanding success, leaving the entire city centre on fire and dense smoke up to 9,000 feet. The visibility was excellent with no cloud cover. While anti-aircraft guns were active when crossing the coast, and in the defensive zone around the city, the guns and searchlights in Cologne appeared to have been overwhelmed by the earlier attacks. As an example of the weapons carried, in 76 Squadron twenty-one Halifaxes dropped sixty-one 1,000lb bombs, 488 30lb incendiaries and 16,380 4lb incendiaries. Over 600 acres of the city were destroyed including some 250 factories, including manufacturing units, blast furnaces and chemical works, in addition to many public buildings. Over 59,000 people were made homeless, with 486 killed and 5,027 injured.

Only four Halifaxes failed to return, with the first being L9605, one of thirteen aircraft contributed by 1652 HCU which was shot down by a night fighter. Damaged and out of control, the experienced pilot, Flight Lieutenant Wright with

Radlett-built Halifax B.II Srs. 1 W7710 *The Ruhr Valley Express* LQ-R 405 (RCAF) Squadron. (*Handley Page Association*)

Nose art on Halifax B.II W7710 LQ-R 405 Squadron (RCAF) *The Ruhr Valley Express* at Pocklington. (*Air Historical Branch*)

a training crew on their first operation, all managed to bale out before the crash. A 10 Squadron Halifax, W1042, was shot down near Eindhoven by a night fighter and 405 Squadron W7707 crashed after what was believed to have been a collision with a Lancaster. The fourth loss was 78 Squadron, which emerged from cloud over England, and collided with a 14 OTU Hampden just below, which was also returning from the raid. Both aircraft crashed in flames in Plantation Farm fields in Huntingdonshire, with three of the Halifax crew surviving, but only the pilot of the Hampden. Overall losses on the raid were forty-one failing to return, with 4.8 per cent from the first wave, 4.1 per cent in the second wave, and only 1.9 per cent in the most concentrated third wave.

To maintain the momentum, Harris launched a further two thousand-bomber raids, the second was Operation Stoat against Essen on 1/2 June, with 956 aircraft, where the massive industrial conglomerate of Krupps was located in the Ruhr Valley. The area was permanently covered by industrial pollution and ground mist, making target identification difficult. A large building in the centre of the Krupps Works was allocated to 76 Squadron, supported by twenty Wellingtons illuminating the target for the pathfinders. Due to the poor visibility, the precise targets were difficult to identify with bombs dropped over eleven local towns, with relatively light damage to

The air crew of 405 Squadron (RCAF) Halifax B.II W7710 *The Ruhr Valley Express* all of whom were killed on the night of 1/2 October 1942 when the aircraft was lost following a raid on Flensburg. (*RAF Museum*)

Essen. Nine Halifaxes were among the thirty-one bombers lost that night, with one 76 Squadron Halifax shot down by an enemy night fighter.

The third attack, Operation Salmon, targeted Bremen on the night of 25/26 June with the Focke Wulf factory the main target, when 1,067 bombers were dispatched. There were eight 76 Squadron Halifaxes as part of the marker force, but care had been taken to provide good reference positions for the targets, with Bremen on the banks of the River Weser giving a clear location, as long as weather was good. The attack was to be completed within 65 minutes and only a short way inside the enemy night fighter belt was expected to reduce RAF casualties. The bomber force was raised from all sources in addition to the main Bomber Command front line and again included in training with the OCUs and HCUs, and with the addition of Coastal Command Wellingtons and Hudsons. Unfortunately, there was cloud cover over Bremen during the attack, but results were improved over Essen, as with the assistance of Gee, fires were started and acted as a guide for the following bombers. Damage was caused to the Focke-Wulf factory, as well as well as shipyards and warehousing in the dock area, but nowhere as much as the Cologne raid. Of the 124 Halifaxes dispatched, six were lost. One was with the 76 Squadron marker force downed by a night fighter, and four ditched in the sea mostly due to fuel shortage, including 158 Squadron

DG225. Overall, losses were high with forty-eight bombers lost, nearly half coming from the training force who were operating largely obsolete and war weary aircraft, making Operation Salmon the worst losses of the war to date, although it was deemed acceptable due to the conditions involved.

Despite the mixed results of these 'thousand-bomber raids', the critics had been silenced, with Bomber Command potential being confirmed. It had created a serious delay with the training programme, and although future thousand-bomber raids were not practical, it was possible to regularly build up to 700 or 800 numbers over the target over a period of less than 20 minutes, minimising RAF losses. Morale was high, even though the practice of easing new crews into operations was changed to putting new crews immediately into combat. The intensive bombing campaign against Germany began to develop with the heavy bombers carrying 4,000lb and 8,000lb bombs, both at night and occasionally during daylight, when there was cloud cover in the target area. On the first of these daylight raids on 3 August, the cloud cover stopped at the coast of the Netherlands, resulting in the raid being abandoned. Eventually these daylight raids were left to the more nimble Mosquitos, the heavies concentrating on night bombing.

Bremen was again the target for 4 Group, which by this stage was fully equipped with Halifaxes for the seven squadrons. Three raids were made on Bremen on 27 and 29 June, followed by 2 July, flying 108 sorties over the three raids with the loss of six aircraft, five of which were from 405 (RCAF) Squadron.

Regular night bombing continued with a raid on 11/12 August as the first against Mainz with 154 bombers including twenty-five Halifaxes, with much damage to the city centre. Sadly, the only losses were from 78 Squadron, with four failing to return and only five crew survivors being taken prisoner. The following night, Mainz was again the target with equal success as the first raid in inflicting damage on the ground.

With the sending of 10 and 76 squadrons to the Middle East and transfers to Coastal Command, 4 Group strength had been drastically reduced. To help improve the balance, 425 (RCAF) Squadron was formed at Dishforth on 25 June 1942 with Wellingtons and did not equip with Halifax IIIs until December 1943. During the short summer nights of 1942, less distant targets were selected, including Duisburg on 13 July, followed six nights later by the Vulkan submarine construction yards at Vegesack on the River Weser, where cloud cover resulted in bombing with the aid of Gee. Then on 26 July, seventy-three Halifaxes were part of a raid by 403 aircraft on Hamburg, where there was significant damage. However, the cost was high with twenty-nine aircraft lost. Additional Canadian squadrons were formed within 4 Group, in preparation for the all-Canadian 6 Group to be established in January 1943 with bases in Yorkshire and Durham.

By the late summer of 1942, Halifax performance had deteriorated badly, particularly at high all up weights, and high loss rates of 5.3 per cent were being experienced with Halifaxes, compared with all other types at 3.3 per cent, and Lancasters reported less than 0.2 per cent. During training, operation of fuel controls had been difficult, and could also be the reason for unexplained operational losses, but the main problem appeared to be poor performance, partly caused by drag of the many operational modifications, but mainly inadequate engine power. It was difficult to go higher than 15,000 feet and the maximum cruising speed was only 140mph, even at climbing power. An answer was to ask HP to reduce drag as much as possible, and supercharged Merlin 61 engines were considered. The aircraft were obviously overloaded and underpowered, making it very vulnerable in combat. When flown by less experienced crews, during violent manoeuvres, the aircraft tended to turn on its back, or dive steeply, with loss of control. The HP proposed drag modifications were expected to increase the speed by between 25 and 30mph.

By August 1942, there was increasing concern about the rising losses to Halifaxes, following a 4 Group conference. It was found the aircraft were flying close to stalling speed at all times, mainly due to excessive drag. The main sources of this drag were the bomb doors being partly open when carrying 4,000lb bombs, the mid-upper gun turret and the addition of equipment. This resulted in the loss of around 25mph since the aircraft had been introduced to service. Violent evasive action could not be tried due to the Halifax cruising speed being only 15mph more than its stalling speed, often resulting in the aircraft entering a spin, and flak blasts close to the Halifax could cause it to become inverted. It was recommended that until new bomb doors had been constructed by Phillips and Powis, 4,000lb bombs should not be carried. To overcome the excess drag, the engines were run at full climbing power for extended periods, which also reduced the range due to excess fuel being required. If one engine failed, the performance on three was so poor, the bomb load had to be jettisoned to maintain height.

The only way to reduce drag was to clean up the exterior of the airframe in two stages, the first being minor modifications like a smoother finish, fairing in the front turret, improved exhaust shrouds and replacing the Fraser-Nash upper gun turret with the lower drag Boulton Paul version. This was expected to increase cruising speed by 8 to 10mph and operational height by 800 feet, to 18,700 feet. A second stage would consist of designing a new powerplant with under wing nacelles and larger radiators. All the initial changes could be fitted retrospectively, as well as on production aircraft.

All the first stage improvements were in hand by October 1942, incorporated in production by November, with the second stage improvements fitted in October and flight trials to start in December. The need for these improvements was clear earlier, but Sir Frederick Handley Page had been reluctant due to increased costs and time to incorporate in production. However, the programme was threatened with drastic reduction in favour of more Lancasters if improvements in performance and reliability were not made. The Lancaster was known to be faster, fly higher with a larger bomb load and with greater reliability. Out of four Halifax Mk.IIs evaluated at Boscombe Down during 1942, the final aircraft, W7776, incorporated all the suggested improvements. It had served with 138 (Special Duties) Squadron, with both front and mid-upper turrets removed. A service ceiling of 21,750 feet was achieved with a top speed of 253mph at 12,100 feet, which was equivalent to when it first entered service. However, further aerodynamic improvements and more powerful engines would be required to carry a larger bomb load at increased speed and cruising altitude with greater reliability. A mid-upper gun turret was still required on bombing operations for better defence, but the installation of the Boulton Paul mid-upper turret in prototype Mk.II L9515 had a top speed of 275mph. A major improvement to the

Halifax was the installation of Merlin 22s, replacing Merlin XXs in Mk.II Series IA, improving both performance and reliability.

Another problem with the Halifax was rudder stalling, which could put the aircraft into an uncontrollable dive. It was found after a prolonged and demanding period of testing that under certain conditions the triangular fin stalled, and the resultant turbulent airflow through the gap between the fin and rudder caused the rudder to lock hard over. During the autumn of 1942, modifications to Halifax tail assemblies were made, reducing the overall operational capability during the period of this essential work, which continued until September.

Having had success with greater accuracy on the thousand-bomber raids using pathfinders to illuminate the target area, it was decided to form a dedicated Path Finder Force (PFF) to develop the process. Out of four squadrons allocated to this task was 35 Squadron, moving to Graveley on 15 August 1942, joining 8 Group under the command of Group Captain Donald Bennett, despite opposition from Bomber Harris who was against the formation of an elite force. The four new squadrons were not immediately available as they were being modified with special navigation equipment and given training for the new challenge.

With tail modifications completed, main force operations restarted by September—the targets being Bremen, Duisburg, Frankfurt, Wilhelmhaven and Essen. Dusseldorf was attacked on 10 September, the pathfinders marking the target with 'Pink Pansies', which were modified 4,000lb bombs converted into super incendiaries, causing widespread damage. On the night of 1 October, the U-boat base at Flensburg was bombed by 27 Halifaxes, but it was a disaster for 4 Group with a dozen aircraft lost due to very accurate and intense flak.

During October 1942, Halifaxes of 4 Group began mining operations, known as *Gardening,* which were used to introduce novice crews to combat. Most popular target areas were off occupied ports of Brest, Lorient, St Nazaire and Ostend, as well as off Texel and Frisian Islands as a means of disrupting enemy shipping.

On a raid against Kiel on 13 October, twelve PFF Halifaxes were to take part with five being tasked with marking and, if clearly identified, illuminating the target. The remaining four Halifaxes with 35 Squadron dropped five 1,000lb bombs and were part of the main force. Among the main force were also sixty-six Halifaxes, with one aircraft lost in addition to seven other types within the formation. As an enemy deception, a decoy fire was lit and the flak batteries withheld fire, causing nearly half the force to miss the target, but the remainder bombed Kiel causing widespread damage. Part of the bomber stream that night was 103 Squadron in 1 Group, which exchanged its Wellingtons for Halifaxes at Elsham Wolds in July 1942, but reequipped with Lancasters in October. It had made its first Halifax raid on 1 September, and was used against fourteen major targets in Germany and Italy before its last operation on the type on 25 October. The reason for the short use of Halifaxes was 1 Group was largely a Lancaster force, and there was a need to concentrate aircraft types within groups to facilitate logistics and maintenance.

The next unit to reequip with Halifaxes was 408 (RCAF) Squadron at Leeming in September 1942 with Mk.V Series Is, and Mk.IIs three months later. The major difference with the Mk.V was the replacement of the British Messier main undercarriage units with a set produced by Dowty. The change was caused by doubts about the continued supply of the Messier units, and with some redesign of the hydraulic system, the conversation was straightforward. The installation was tested on Mk.I L9520 in January 1942, and the Dowty units proved to be an improvement, particularly over rough ground although of increased weight. Tailwheel shimming had been a long-term problem, particularly during cross wind landings. A modified Dowty tailwheel was tested on L9520, but it was not overcome until a damping device was fitted to new production, and retrofitted to existing Halifaxes over a period of two months. By the end of October, 408 Squadron had taken delivery of thirteen Mk.Vs, which were then replaced by Mk.IIs from 30 November. A dozen Mk.Vs were delivered to 18 MU at Dumfries for modification to Mk.V Series 1 (Special) configuration, one Mk.V remaining with the squadron. From 5 October 1942, 77 Squadron at Elvington converted from Whitleys to Halifax MK.IIs.

The introduction of the Halifax B.Mk.II (Special) allowed operations to be expanded to cover not just Germany, but also Italy, with a reduction in losses. There was only the cover of darkness during the long winter nights for the longer-range targets. On 23 October 1942, 158 Squadron was part of a force of 122 bombers attacking Genoa, but with a solid cloud cover over the target, Savona received the brunt of the attack, with some bombs dropped on Turin. Two Halifaxes were lost on this raid.

It was not just enemy defences which were hazardous, an example being an attack on Turin by 35 Squadron on 18/19 November, when Wing Commander Robinson in

Personnel of 77 Squadron in front of a Halifax B.II at Elvington. (*RAF Museum*)

Samlesbury-built Halifax B.II Srs I (Special) JB911 KN-X with 77 Squadron flying low over another Halifax being serviced at Elvington in July 1943. The aircraft was delivered to the squadron on 31 March 1943 and went to 1658 HCU on 24 June 1944. It was finally SOC on 1 November 1946. (*RAF Museum*)

DT488 was returning in the vicinity of the Alps when one of four hung up flares caught fire in the bomb-bay. With the fire appearing to be spreading, Robinson ordered the crew to abandon the aircraft, but before he could follow them, the fire reduced and eventually went out. He decided to attempt to bring the aircraft back single-handed to Gravely and had the comforting news on return via Italian radio, his crew had landed safely and been taken prisoner. The crews were still experiencing Merlin failures and a starboard engine in 158 Squadron W1091 failed on the way to bombing Turin, and leaving forty incendiaries hung up. The reduced power meant they were unable to climb over the Alps and Wing Commander Fletcher flew south-west to the Rhone Valley, then west to Le Havre, before crossing the channel and landing at Rufforth in a visibility of 500 yards.

Before starting a sustained offensive against Germany in early 1943, Bomber Command was tasked with attempting to destroy the heavily defended and practically bomb-proof U-boat pens and supporting facilities along the Bay of Biscay, on the coast of France. The U-boat threat in the Atlantic was taking its toll on Allied shipping and supplies with over 200 merchant ships lost during the months of November and December 1942, threatening Britain's sustainment. The ports where the U-boats were based were Lorient, St Nazaire and La Pallice. With some reluctance, Harris launched 3,170 sorties between 14 January and 6 April, regrettably using area bombing on these French ports. The first of the two largest attacks was a daylight attack on 13 February when 466 bombers attacked La Pallice. Then, on 28 February, 437 bombers attacked St Nazaire. No. 35 Squadron sent eight Halifaxes on the St Nazaire raid. On the approach to the target from 13,400 feet, W7877 lost the port outer engine, forced to descend to 9,000 feet and was able to complete the bombing run. Just after starting the flight home the starboard inner engine failed with flames shooting out, the Halifax slowly descending to 3,000 feet. With preparations made for a ditching under heavy cloud, the English coast was seen, and an emergency landing made at Harrowbeer near Plymouth. The aircraft overshot and the undercarriage collapsed, but the crew were all safe.

The anti U-boat campaign consisted of fourteen raids with thirty-eight aircraft lost in combat and nine more destroyed in accidents over England. Harris's reluctance to use his valuable bombers against these impregnable targets had been justified. Despite major damage to the French ports and towns, the U-boat pens and their supporting facilities were virtually undamaged, and no U-boat was put out of action. It was going to be a major task of Coastal Command with special weapons and equipment which would defeat enemy submarines.

During 1943, a range of new navigation and bombing aids were introduced to Bomber Command to significantly increase accuracy of target destruction at night. One was code named 'Oboe' and was controlled by a pair of ground stations by sending signals from locations in Britain and receiving a signal back, to precisely locate the position of the aircraft. The message could then be sent when the aircraft was over its target, releasing the bombs. Range of the aid was limited by the aircraft altitude, as it was only by line of sight, and the limited number of aircraft which could be controlled resulted in the use of Oboe being best used by target marking aircraft with the PFF.

Meanwhile during 1942, the enemy had been improving its night fighter defences to counter the bombing offensive, with sophisticated airborne interception radars. By early 1943, over 360 German night fighters could be deployed against the RAF bombers, with the latest Bf 110s not only carrying radar, but armed with highly destructive 20mm cannons, which were lethal against the lightly armoured RAF heavy bomber force. The night fighters were directed from the ground by the Himmelbett fighter control sector, which monitored the Kammhuber Line stretching from Troyes, 80 miles south-east of Paris to the northern tip of Denmark, from the coast to 100–150 miles inland. This formidable defence protected the low-countries, the Ruhr industrial valley, Westphalia and Hanover–Hamburg areas. The only way for RAF bombers to avoid these night fighter defences was to fly several hundred extra miles to the north or south of this area. In an effort to overwhelm the night fighter defences, bomber streams were made more compact, taking between 30 and 40 minutes to fly through the Kammhuber Line, rather than a number of hours, as in the past.

It was during this campaign that the RCAF squadrons were collected into No 6 (Canadian) Group which included both Halifax and Wellington bombers, remaining operational until 1 January 1943. The Path Finder Force (PFF) was also allocated group status as 8 Group on 8 January.

Even during the diversion of resource against the French ports, the remainder of Bomber Command was busy in the build-up of a major offensive from March. This started with an attack on Berlin on 16 January 1943, which had been left alone since last bombing in 1941. It was way beyond the range of British ground-based navigation aids, and target marking had to be done by the PFF using basic dead reckoning navigation, which in a cloud covered sky relied on unknown wind speed and direction. Fortunately Berlin was a large widespread target. The initial approach was three Lancasters, which released flares 2 minutes before zero hour, followed by five each Lancasters and Halifaxes whose task was to visually identify the aiming point and drop target markers. Not only did the cloud cover on the way to the target make navigation demanding, but although clear over Berlin, the target was covered by a thick haze.

The main force bombed on the target indicators resulting in some devastating damage with high explosive (HE) and incendiaries. The target was left burning over the entire area, which was still visible from Hanover on the way home. The main target was in the area of Templehof Airport, but some of the force also bombed a scattered area of southern Berlin suburbs. The following night, another force returned to Berlin consisting of 170 Lancasters and seventeen Halifaxes by unfortunately the same route, but results were very similar. The mistake of using the same route was confirmed with only one Lancaster lost on the first raid, but rose sharply to twenty-two aircraft, three of which were Halifaxes, with an overall total of thirty damaged. The majority of the 11.8 per cent losses were due to pre-warned enemy night fighters. As a result of these losses, target marking against the heavily defended Berlin was suspended pending the development of a new independent navigation aid.

On 24 January, Dusseldorf was bombed by Halifaxes from 51, 76, 78 and 102 Squadrons as part of the main force. This was the first time the target was marked by Oboe-equipped Mosquitos using 250lb markers, which burst just above the ground scattering bunches of coloured flares around the targets. Widespread damage resulted with the loss of one 51 Squadron Halifax. No. 51 Squadron had changed its Whitleys for Halifax B.Mk.IIs at Snaith in November 1942.

Also during January, Bomber Command targeted Essen six times, but an attack on Hamburg at the end of the month introduced a whole new bombing aid known as H2S, which was carried in the aircraft, and independent of any ground signals from Britain. With the gradual development of radar since the late 1930s resulting in centimetric wavelength, initial airborne trials were carried out on 1 November 1941 with a Blenheim. It was fitted with an AI (Airborne Interception) radar developed for RAF night fighters to detect a hostile target. In these tests, the radar beam was directed downwards to determine if it detected ground features. This was progressively developed into H2S which allowed accurate navigation by distinctive ground features, and accurate target identification in all weathers. This blind bombing technique gave the RAF a much greater capability from 1943 onwards.

The scanner system was rather large causing difficulties finding an aircraft capable of carrying the new aid. With its high-volume fuselage, the Halifax was the ideal

Above: Damage to Radlett-built Halifax B.II Srs IA HR868 MH-B 51 Squadron at Snaith on 20 December 1943 after a raid to Frankfurt. The aircraft was delivered to the squadron on 31 May 1943 and moved to 1656 HCU on 10 May 1944. It was damaged beyond repair on 25 January 1945. (*RAF Museum*)

Below: Radlett-built Halifax B.II Srs. 1A HR952 MH-X 51 Squadron being refuelled and loaded with 500lb bombs and incendiaries at Snaith in August 1943, ready for the next raid. The aircraft was delivered to the squadron on 31 July 1943. It went to 10 Squadron on 4 January 1944 and was lost on a raid to Berlin on 29 January 1944. (*RAF Museum*)

candidate for the trials and V9977 was chosen and flown to Hurn on 27 March 1942. It had been fitted with a large Perspex electronically transparent radome where the ventral turret was normally located, and boffins from the Telecommunications Research Establishment (TRE) installed the first 10cm H2S radar. As covered in Chapter 1, this aircraft crashed while flying to Defford, killing the entire crew of experts, destroying the prototype H2S radar. The aircraft was replaced by Halifax V7711, and by the end of September, the first production H2S had been fitted in W7808 for service trials with the Bombing Development Unit. The major problem was poor serviceability of this early equipment.

A group of navigators were being trained in the use of H2S at the Telecommunications Research Establishment (TRE), which produced an image of ground features on a cathode ray tube covering a limited circle around the aircraft. Its definition was limited, but a well-trained operator could interpret the picture with some accuracy, particularly where water and land masses were clearly shown.

The first operational trial was an attack against Hamburg on the night of 30/31 January 1943 with the target completely covered by cloud, making visual identification impossible. The target was marked for the main force by six 35 Squadron Halifaxes and seven Stirlings from 7 Squadron. Three Halifaxes aborted due to H2S failures, with another having to return due to mechanical problems. Three Stirlings also aborted due to unservicability with H2S. Two Halifaxes navigated using H2S and successfully marked the target. Some damage was caused to the target area, but many bombs fell outside the city, and five Lancasters were lost.

Harris's main offensive from the spring of 1943, over a twelve-month period, committed Bomber Command to the systematic destruction of one city at a time. Berlin was too far to attack except during the longer winter nights and required more effective navigation aids to achieve accuracy. The first four-month campaign was against targets in the industrial might in the Ruhr Valley, with forty-three raids, of which some two thirds were against Ruhr targets.

After the first raid using H2S, three further raids quickly followed with the first at Cologne on 2/3 February, then Hamburg again on 3/4 and Turin on 4/5 where the success was clearly demonstrated despite relatively poor results, except Turin where there was widespread damage for no losses to Bomber Command. By the end of May, the maximum number of bombers equipped with the new system was eighteen, due to initial production delays. However, early problems were quickly solved and by August, 840 sets had been completed, followed by fitting to 155 Halifaxes, 225 Lancasters and seventy Stirlings by mid-October.

With the directive delivered to Bomber Command on 4 February for '... primarily the progressive destruction and dislocation of the German military, industrial and economic system and undermining of the morale of the German people to a point where their capacity for armed resistance is fatally weakened', the early introduction of H2S was welcome. The directive defined a series of targets which were to be attacked, taking account of weather and tactical considerations. The main targets were U-boat construction facilities, aircraft manufacturing, transports, oil production and storage and anything which contributed to war production. Berlin was also to be targeted, when possible, to reduce German morale, while also showing support for

Russia. Harris interpreted the directive as the destruction of the industrial capability of Germany with the force he had available. Before the first great attack of the offensive, the tempo of attacks had to build up allowing experience to be gained with H2S and target marking.

The Ruhr Valley was an essential part of Germany's munitions production with over 75 per cent of coal production and the centre of heavy industry. It had excellent surface access by road, rail and water. Because its location was within easy range of RAF bombers, it had formidable defences, providing it with the Bomber Command aircrew name 'Happy Valley'. Approaching RAF bombers could be detected in advance by a widespread surveillance radar network, complemented by tracking radars as guidance for airborne interception by enemy night fighters. Bomber Command had coming into service increasingly more effective heavy bombers fitted with various counter measures. From 1942, the aircraft IFF (Identification Friend or Foe) was used to jam the ground based German radars and the early warning *Freya* radar could be interfered with by *Mandrel* carried by RAF bombers, with 158 and 408 Squadrons being among the first to have it fitted.

Berlin was the target for a heavy attack on 1/2 March, where widespread bombing by around 300 aircraft appeared to saturate the defences. Although it was achieved using H2S, features were difficult to identify in the overall ground clutter without any distinctive outlines. It was found that the Telefunken factory was hit, fortunately destroying a rebuilt H2S set salvaged from a crashed Stirling in Holland. This success was countered by a 35 Squadron Halifax crash-landing with little damage, providing an instant H2S example.

In addition to H2S, the highly industrialised region of the Ruhr Valley was well within the range of Oboe. This vast area contained steel and iron production, as well as chemical plants, oil refineries and coal mines, with Essen at the centre where the Krupps giant works complex was located. The Krupps Works were the largest armament manufacturer in Germany, producing tanks, heavy guns, bombs, armoured vehicles and railway rolling stock. The entire Ruhr Valley had extensive means of surface communications, with a major rail network and navigable waterways leading to the River Rhine, and the extensive inland port of Duisburg. Identifying any specific target was difficult due to a blanket of industrial haze, and the defences were formidable with major flak batteries assisted by searchlights protecting the approaches to the industrial areas and surrounding night fighter airfields, making bombing a hazardous operation.

The main Battle of the Ruhr began on 5/6 March with the Halifax force assisted by Oboe leading three waves to Essen, using the latest navigation and defensive aids. The battle lasted for five months, consisting of forty-five Main Force attacks, of which twenty-five were over the Ruhr. This was by no means the first Bomber Command raid on this city, which had accounted for some 10 per cent of the bomber effort during 1942. Target marking was highly effective with the pathfinder yellow markers attracting the Halifaxes. The red target indicators flared up as the bomber stream passed over the final turning point. The searchlights lit up above the whole target area directing heavy flak at the bombers. As the attack progressed, the searchlights became less effective and anti-aircraft guns were suppressed. The target of Krupps was blazing with incendiaries and HE bombs causing widespread destruction. Following the raid, photo reconnaissance confirmed major damage over around 300 acres in Essen. Out of 442 bombers dispatched, 362 crews claimed hitting the target while in the area for 40 minutes. This was the start of similar raids over the coming months. Losses were very low with fourteen aircraft lost, including one each from 76, 78 and 466 Squadrons.

While the intention was to follow up the raid rapidly, bad weather caused a delay for a week, but then the devastation was repeated. On the second raid, the German defences shot down twenty-three of the 457 bombers dispatched, although the returning crews were enthusiastic about the raid's success. Later bomb damage assessments estimated 27 per cent of the Krupps Works had suffered damage. In addition to the Ruhr Valley, other targets selected included Nurenberg, Stuttgart and Munich, creating a dispersal of German anti-aircraft defences, causing reduced defence in the Ruhr Valley. No. 77 Squadron took part in these raids, suffering the loss of JB795 and DT734 over Munich on 9/10 March, the only Halifax losses on the raid, in addition to five Lancasters and a Stirling. The next night, Stuttgart was bombed, and on 26/27 March Duisburg was attacked. Bombing was from 19,000 feet aiming at red target markers, following a timed run from yellow markers. Visibility was good enough to identify fires in the target area, and moderate flak was experienced, but the bombs were scattered because the Oboe-equipped PFF Mosquitos failed to arrive due to technical difficulties.

During an attack on Berlin on 27/28 March, two 300 plus main force raids were dispatched, but for a second raid two nights later, the weather was so bad with heavy icing, it caused poor bombing results and the loss of twenty-one bombers out of the force of 329 aircraft. As a result, further attacks on the 'Big City' were delayed until the protective darkness of longer autumn nights. The first major operation of April was to Essen on the night of the 4 April, when there were 113 Halifaxes as part of the total force of 348 aircraft. With clear weather conditions, bombing was accurate on this continuing important target, which was marked by the PFF. Unfortunately, the clear visibility also favoured enemy night fighters, which accounted for twenty-one bombers, including at least seven Halifaxes, while others were damaged, but returned to base. Attacks continued during the first week in April, with Kiel, Duisburg and Frankfurt. But the attack on Frankfurt failed due to thick cloud over the target.

Raids on less well defended more distant targets continued with a mixed force of 327 Halifaxes and Lancasters sent to bomb the Skoda armament factories at Pilsen in Czechoslovakia on 16 April, with a diversionary raid to Mannheim by 271 bombers, which gave good results with 6.6 per cent loss rate. The Skoda works however was considered a failure as the target markers were dropped around 7 miles from the Skoda works and eighteen Halifaxes and eighteen Lancasters were lost, equivalent to 11 per cent, when between 4 and 6 per cent were considered normal. The Halifax losses included five from 51 Squadron and three each from 76 and 78 Squadrons.

On 20 April, there was another attack on a long-distance target, this time Stettin, situated on the Baltic coast at a range of around 600 miles. A new technique was flown to avoid alerting the defences by flying across Denmark at under 700 feet and climbing over the Baltic to 14,000 feet for bomb release. The return was back down to low-level over Denmark, but a number of bombers were lost to flak, both from the ground and flak ships on the approach to target. Marking was accurate and of 304 crews who claimed to have hit the primary target, 256 were within 3 miles of the aiming point.

The Battle of the Ruhr continued at the end of April with major raids on Duisburg on the 26th and Essen on the last day of the month. The first bombing raid of the war was made on Dortmund on 4 May when a force of 600 bombers caused major damage on the town centre, industrial area and docks were destroyed.

The Dowty-equipped main undercarriage Halifaxe B.V Series 1 (Special) began to equip the squadrons from April 1943 which were otherwise identical to the Mk.IIs. These aircraft were issued to the 6 (RCAF) Group squadrons and 76 Squadron. Also, the improved Halifax B.II Series IA, began to reach the squadrons during the spring of 1943 with all the drag reducing modifications improving performance by some 10 per cent over earlier marks.

Enemy defences continued to become more effective with anti-aircraft guns capable of reaching targets up to 21,000 feet complimented by increasingly aggressive night fighter attacks, often using one as a decoy, while another closed in on the kill, when the bomber gunners opened up on the decoy. On the raid to Dusseldorf on 11/12 June, German night fighters were able to destroy thirty-eight out of the force of 783 bombers, although a number of crews claimed successes against night fighters. In return, damage to the city was extensive. On the same night, seventy-two aircraft equipped with H2S from the PFF bombed Munster effectively over 10 minutes, with the loss of five of their number.

The Ruhr Valley campaign continued with an attack on Bochum on 17/18 by 503 bombers and despite cloud cover, was very successful. The target was marked accurately using sky markers positioned by Oboe. Defences were again heavy, but losses were light. Another hazard in the crowded night sky was bombs dropped from above could hit the aircraft at lower altitudes. During an attack on Stettin, a 35 Squadron crew had just marked the target when their Halifax was hit by falling incendiary bombs, one of which broke through the pilot's escape hatch, setting his seat on fire, then exploding in the flight engineer's position. With loss of control, the pilot ordered the aircraft abandoned, but immediately regained control and cancelled the order. With often only seconds to get clear from a doomed aircraft, when this aircraft returned safely to base, two of the crew were found to have abandoned the aircraft over the target. Following release of bombs over Cologne on 28 May, 158 Squadron Halifax HR837 was attacked with cannon shells from a Ju 88, and at the same time a 1,000lb bomb hit the aircraft from above. The bomb went through the fuselage and port wing, leaving a large hole in the fuselage, although the aircraft was able to return to base.

Following five heavy raids on Duisburg, where the Thyssen steel works were badly damaged on 12 May, the nearby towns of Oberhausen and Mulheim were attacked in June. Mulheim was bombed on 22/23 June by a force of 557 bombers, including 77 Squadron Halifaxes. Bombing was from 19,000 feet on an accurately marked target by the PFF, with major damage to about half the town, although losses were thirty-four bombers, including four crews from 51 Squadron, up to 6.3 per cent.

Bomber Command crews were expected to complete thirty operations on their first tour, and after a 'rest' period of training new aircrew, followed a second tour of another twenty operations. The chance of surviving the full fifty operations was not good. At a total loss rate of only 1 per cent, a crew had a 60.5 per cent chance of survival, but with an average loss rate of 4 per cent, the chances of crew survival dropped to just 3 per cent. Although the average at this time was around 4 per cent, some raids had suffered losses of up to 15 per cent, which was totally unsustainable.

On 29/30 May 719 bombers were sent to the Barmen area of Wuppertal, which was highly successful, with the majority of the bombs falling within 3 miles of the accurately placed target markers. Over 90 per cent of the target was destroyed in major fires, destroying some of the town's factories and nearly 4,000 houses, making 118,000 people homeless. Bomber Command losses were thirty-three aircraft, twenty-two of which had been shot down by night fighters. By this stage in the Battle of the Ruhr, Bomber Command were losing between thirty and forty aircraft on every operation, mostly to night fighters, the bombers being extremely vulnerable. As another example of the heavy bomber losses, 783 bombers made a main force attack to Dusseldorf on 12/13 June causing severe damage, but despite the success, thirty-eight bombers failed to return. However, it was not always one sided. On a raid to Bochum the next night a 51 Squadron rear gunner spotted a single engine night fighter in the moonlight, and while the captain took evasive action, the rear gunner was able to hit the fighter, causing it to explode and crash. On return to base, a 158 Squadron was attacked by two Bf 110s, but despite guns jamming and damage to the Halifax, they were able to shake off the attacker by skilful corkscrewing. Yet a third escape was with a 76 Squadron Halifax which as it was flying home over the Dutch coast, the rear gunner shouted to the pilot to corkscrew, avoiding the night fighter cannon fire. As the enemy fighter broke off the gunner fired into his vulnerable underside from 200 yards, the aircraft falling in flames into the sea.

On 19 June, instead of the regular 'Happy Valley' operations, 290 aircraft were sent to bomb the Schneider armaments factory at Le Crousot, which was reasonably successful. Two nights later, a return was made to the Ruhr where Krefeld on the Rhine was bombed accurately destroying the town centre.

As the Battle of the Ruhr was coming to an end, Cologne was targeted in June and July, with a devastating attack on 28/29 June by a mixed force of 608 Halifaxes and Lancasters. Despite difficulties providing accurate marking, there were comparatively light losses of twenty-five bombers. Damage was extensive with heavy casualties on the ground. On 3/4 July, a force of 653 bombers returned to Cologne, but were met with single-seat fighters without AI radar, which meant the defending force could not be detected by the RAF electronic devices. As a result, twelve of the bombers lost that night out of thirty, were destroyed over the target. As an additional defence against radar-equipped German night fighters, *Monica* was fitted as a tail warning beacon. If another aircraft approached from the rear, the pilot was warned by a signal in his headphones, and could take evasive action. The final attack of the series on Cologne was 8/9 July.

The Halifax was also vulnerable from below, where the enemy night fighters could make an approach undetected. As a result, one of 419 Squadron Halifaxes was modified with hand operated machine guns in the lower fuselage. No. 419 Squadron had replaced its Wellingtons for Halifax B.Mk.II at Croft in November 1942. The crowded bomber streams approaching targets in the dark often resulted in mid-air collisions, only the known ones being those which despite heavy damage managed to return to base. The final bomber operation of the battle was to Gelsenkirchen and Aachen in early July, and before moving into the next bomber campaign, 4 Group Halifaxes attacked the Peugeot factory at Sochaux, led by thirty-one PFF Halifaxes, which unfortunately were marked inaccurately, causing many deaths and injuries to the French population in the town, while only minor damage was caused to the factory. During the attacks on the Ruhr Valley, while nearly all the town centres had been destroyed, Bomber Command had lost 872 aircraft, which was equivalent to 4.7 per cent of aircraft despatched. This was mainly due to the German night fighters, and threatened the whole effect of the night bomber offensive. Despite this, ACM Harris was confident the bomber offensive would succeed in the end, with the raids becoming a war of attrition over the next eight months.

During 1943, the Halifax force began to expand with the re-equipment of a number of squadrons with 6 Group forming on 1 January, with the RCAF squadrons operating

Ringway-built Halifax B.V LK735 ZL-Z 427 Squadron at Coltishall in February 1944. It was originally delivered to 431 Squadron on 18 December 1943, before going to 427 Squadron on 26 December 1943. It entered the training programme at 1659 HCU on 14 May 1944, and moved to 1669 HCU on 22 October the same year. It was SOC on 1 November 1945. (*RAF Museum*)

Halifax Mk.Vs. No. 4 Group 76 Squadron began to replace its Mk.IIs with Mk.Vs at Linton-on-Ouse in February 1943, but for the sake of logistics commonality, transferred to 6 Group. On 3 May 1943, 427 (RCAF) Squadron moved to Leeming and replaced its Wellington bombers with Halifax B.Vs.

Meanwhile the Handley Page design organisation was continuing to investigate improvements in performance, maintainability, armament and navigation aids as they became available. What had been known as the Tollerton nose fairing had only been an interim solution, and L9515 was modified to test a revised shape. Other efforts were made to smooth airflow and reduce drag. Halifax HR679 incorporated these modifications, and was further modified to become the prototype B.Mk.II Series IA with the nose slightly extended and covered in Perspex. Power was increased by replacing the existing Merlin XXs with 1,480bhp Merlin 22s fitted with new radiators and oil coolers. The tailwheel could also be retracted. The comprehensive flight test programme with HR679 was made from December 1942 to May 1943, with modifications and equipment being added as it became available. The aircraft was flown to the A&AEE on 28 February where tests were carried with a single nose mounted Vickers machine gun. Overall results of the trials were good with most of the modifications introduced to the production lines, although the tailwheel remained non-retractable.

Rudder overbalance was still the contributory cause of a number of accidents, and while a larger fin could be a cure, it would take time to incorporate on the production lines. In an effort to find an interim solution, HR679 was joined by HR727, but despite a number of local modifications, an effective cure was not identified. A much-modified fin with straight leading edges was fitted to R9534 giving an increased area of 40 per cent.

A 4,000lb 'Cookie' being loaded on Halifax B.II of 419 Squadron at Middleton St George. (*Air Historical Branch*)

The new fin was tested in June 1943, with sideslip and asymmetric flying compared with the same tests before the modification. The new fin and rudder assembly was considered satisfactory overall, although the controls were heavier at higher speeds. To confirm the results, B.Mk.V Series 1 (Special) DK145 was fitted with the same new fins and rudders and passed the test satisfactorily. The new modification was introduced onto the production lines as soon as practical. Modification of existing serving aircraft was more demanding, but was achieved by a working party from 13 MU at Henlow consisting of a warrant officer, five NCOs and thirty-six other ranks. A total of 225 Merlin-powered Halifaxes were converted over a period of three and a half months, followed by 277 more over the next two months, finishing at St Davids where a further sixty Coastal Command Halifaxes were modified.

With the Cologne raids completing the Battle of the Ruhr, Harris directed Bomber Command to make raids deeper into Germany, taking advantage of H2S to navigate to, and identify targets. The first of these targets was Hamburg, where the topographical features were easy to recognise with H2S. Four major raids were made between late July and early August, when, within ten days, around 8,000 tons of bombs were dropped. Although Hamburg had been bombed by the RAF on ninety-eight previous occasions, it had only suffered minor damage, and its armament factories and shipyards building U-boats were a high priority, resulting in the city being earmarked for destruction.

The first operation of what was known as Operation Gomorrah was by 791 bombers on 24/25 July 1943, when 'Window' was dropped for the first time. This was bundles of aluminium foil, which consisted of strips 27 cm long and 1.5 cm wide, which made the force appear much larger to the enemy radars, both on the ground and in the air, hiding the bombers in interference. The large clouds of fluttering aluminium strips disrupted all German fire-control and air reporting systems, making it impossible to either direct the night fighters, or fire radar predicted flak barrages. As a result, losses were very light with only four of 246 Halifaxes lost from the first raid and only a 1.5 per cent loss rate of twelve Halifaxes overall. This compared with an average loss rate of 5.4 per cent over Hamburg during the previous year and a half.

The second raid on Hamburg on 27/28 July resulted in around three quarters of the closely packed residential area badly damaged, and out of 787 bombers sent, only eleven were lost. Despite a two-mile marking error using H2S, damage was extensive and intense fires were started, resulting in a fire storm which killed around 40,000 residents. The fire storm exceeded 1,000 degrees centigrade and caused wind updraughts of 150mph destroying nearly 16,000 apartment blocks. This was followed two nights later, and although no fire storm resulted, there was still extensive damage. On the raid, out of 777 bombers twenty-eight aircraft failed to return. In addition to the high number of deaths in the population, another two thirds had evacuated the city. The final raid to Hamburg on 2/3 August was not a success, as although the defences had been suppressed, extreme weather conditions resulting in bombs being jettisoned, or dropped on alternate targets, due to heavy icing and violent electrical storms in the target area. Out of a mixed force of 235 Halifaxes, 329 Lancasters, 105 Stirlings, sixty-six Wellingtons and five Mosquitos, thirty aircraft were lost mainly to weather conditions. RAF losses over the four nights were eighty-seven aircraft with over two thirds relatively inexperienced crews with five or less combat operations. During the raids on Hamburg, nearly 600 industrial premises and 2,632 commercial buildings had been destroyed or badly damaged.

Following the destruction of Hamburg, the next target selected was Mannheim-Ludwigshaven on 9/10 August, followed on 17/18 August by Operation Hydra, a force of 596 bombers to the secret German scientific research centre at Peenemunde on the Baltic coast. The site was known to be undertaking rocket research into what turned out to be V1 flying bombs and V2 rockets, capable of the indiscriminate bombing of Britain. The PFF included 35 and 405 Squadrons and the operation was led by Group Captain John Searby of 83 Squadron in clear moonlight, even though there was a high risk of enemy night fighters. It was the first raid to use the master bomber technique, where the bombs were directed on the target by radio running commentary identifying the precise position of the target according to the target markers, correcting any errors. Visibility over the target was excellent, with ground features clearly seen, and hits were seen on three separate aiming points, with fires still visible some 150 miles away, on the way home. Out of a force of 324 Lancasters, 218 Halifaxes and fifty-four Stirlings, a total of forty bombers were shot down, including fifteen Halifaxes, mainly in the third wave. The night fighters employed, for the first time, the very effective upward firing 20mm cannons, which fired into the unsuspecting bomber without any warning, accounting for at least six of the bombers lost.

In an effort to persuade Italy to exit the war, a number of Italian targets were attacked during August, when Milan was bombed on 12/13 August by 504 bombers, including 138 Halifaxes, when the Alfa-Romeo works and main railway station were badly damaged.

This was followed by a return to German targets, with the Battle of Berlin at the start of the longer nights, when on 23/24 August the first of three raids was made, although the main Battle of Berlin did not start until the much longer nights in mid-November. Although the pathfinders were unable to identify the centre of the city, considerable damage was caused to the southern areas, resulting in high casualties. A return was made to Berlin on the night of 31 August, where among the 622 bombers despatched, were 100 Halifaxes from 4 Group. There were a number of aborted flights due to technical problems, including lack of power to climb to the designated altitudes. There were unforecasted winds over the target, and erratic marking resulting in reduced damage on the ground. Also for the first time, German highflyers used parachute flares to illuminate the bomber streams for the night fighters below. With daunting German defences, forty-seven bombers were lost, of which around two thirds were from night fighters. Despite claims of widespread damage, it was found that overall damage was minor, with many bombs falling to the south of the city and the sustainability of Bomber Command again being questioned.

The third preliminary raid was with just Lancasters on 3/4 September, due to the high losses of Halifaxes and Stirlings on the earlier attacks. Although overall damage was modest, the German population began a panic evacuation of the city, following the experience of the Hamburg raids.

With a continued increase in the number of bombers available, it had become practical to start a winter campaign against the German capital, which required a minimum seven-hour flight of 500 miles over hostile territory, and the initial raids were used to determine the effect of enemy defences before starting the main attacks. Meanwhile, after the destruction of Hamburg, Berlin's defences had been considerably strengthened, in particular the improvement of night fighter performance.

While waiting for the longer dark nights, operations switched back to other German targets. On 5/6 September Mannheim and Ludwigshaven armament and chemical works were subject to a double attack by a force of 605 bombers causing widespread damage. The very active Mannheim defences were responsible for the loss of thirty-four aircraft, including at least nine Halifaxes, with four lost from the twenty-one bombers sent by 78 Squadron. The next night, Munich was the target for the first time in over six months by a force of 147 Halifaxes and 257 Lancasters, where high level fighter flares were again in use at the long-range target.

By September 1943, all 4 Group squadrons were equipped with Halifax Mk.IIs apart from 466 (RCAF) Squadron which was converting to the Mk.III. During this month, forces of mainly Halifaxes and Stirlings from 3, 4 and 6 Groups were flown against French targets, with the Dunlop rubber factory at Montlucon badly damaged on 15/16 September. The next night, the railway communications between France and Italy were bombed by 340 aircraft, including 100 4 Group Halifaxes, attacking marshalling yards at Mordane close to the Mont Cenis tunnel mouth. The following week, a return was made to Germany when Hanover was bombed in the first of four major attacks on 22/23 September. Although the weather was clear, winds over the target resulted in the bombing to be concentrated to the southeast of the city. With active night fighter defences carrying vertical firing cannons, twenty-six bombers were lost, including eight 4 Group Halifaxes. Five nights later, Hanover was visited again, followed by Kassel, Frankfurt and Hanover during the first week of October. No. 4 Group was in action again over Germany on 22/23 October when 130 4 Group Halifaxes were part of a force which bombed Kassel, resulting in major destruction and a fire storm, and many armament factories destroyed, particularly V-1 flying bomb production. Thirteen Halifaxes were lost on this raid, and bad weather stopped further raids until 3 November, when the target was Dusseldorf.

The hazards of the long dangerous flights to distant targets took its toll on the crews, as even if they survived the attack itself, the fatigue and nervous tension could result in accidents where maintaining control of a badly damaged aircraft could cause loss of control, particularly if bad weather was encountered at base.

Efforts continued to improve Halifax performance, with a major drag reduction by lowering the engines, with the rear end of the nacelles extended, and modified undercarriage doors to completely enclose the wheels. The Merlin engines fitted with Morris block radiators with thermostatically controlled radiator flaps and six-way exhaust ejector stubs were all fitted to HR756, which became the prototype Halifax B.Mk.II Series 2, with flight testing between April and May 1943. Although cruising speed was only 9mph faster than the Series 1A, the operational ceiling was increased to 16,000 feet, although 20,000 feet could be reached with full power, using less fuel than the fully loaded earlier version. Apart from putting the Series II into production, there were only two other possible improvements towards increasing the operational ceiling of the Series IA Halifax. One solution was drag reduction by removing the mid-upper turret, or more power would have to be obtained from the engines without an increase in fuel consumption. Removal of the mid-upper turret was not an option with the increasing threat of enemy night fighters. Installation of supercharged Merlins was a possibility, but by the time testing was complete, the B.Mk.III had entered service, resulting in it being impracticable to introduce the more powerful Merlins.

The expanding Bomber Command heavy bomber fleet had grown sufficiently by November 1943 to begin the long-awaited full Berlin Campaign. By this time, over 90 per cent of heavy bombers were equipped with H2S, and the purpose was to break the morale of the Germans and reduce their capability of continuing the War. Using the long winter nights, the Battle of Berlin commenced in mid-November, but although the PFF was using the latest version of H2S, the sprawling area of the city with few defining features still made precise target marking a challenge. All but one of the targets was beyond the range of Oboe, with an initial thirty-two targets identified. A major hazard was freely roving German twin-engine night fighters, which headed towards the bomber stream, identified by the cloud of Window, when high flying reconnaissance aircraft would drop flares over the bombers, illuminating them for the fighter defences. In an effort to reduce the night fighter threat, intruder operations were made against night fighter airfields, with additional protection from RAF night fighter squadrons complimented by radio counter measured from 100 (Bomber Support) Group.

Berlin was an important target, not just because it was the centre of Nazi government, but housed important armament manufacturing facilities, which were essential to the enemy war effort. On the west side of the city was the massive Siemens electrical factories, with nearby the L Lowe plant producing naval fire control equipment. Another major plant in the western side was the enormous BMW aero engine factories. Elsewhere, were three sites used by AEG manufacturing accumulators and operating zinc smelting plants, as well as the Henschel aircraft production and many other major engineering and chemical works, all serviced by a significant power station. To the north of the city Dornier and Heinkel produced aircraft parts, the Argus aero engine factory and many armament producers. Near Tempelhof Daimler Benz produced aero and diesel engines, with many machine tool and engineering factories nearby. ACM Harris believed Berlin could be reduced to rubble, but the destruction of the entire city was estimated to cost between 400 and 500 Bomber Command aircraft.

The Battle of Berlin started with an all-Lancaster attack to Berlin on 18/19 November, complemented by a mixed force of Halifaxes and Stirlings to Mannheim, splitting the night fighter defences. Although considered a success, twenty-five bombers out of the force of 395 were lost. With the opening of the emergency runway at Woodbridge in August 1943, the other two being Manston in Kent and Carnaby in Yorkshire, the first emergency bomber landing was 431 Squadron Halifax LK918 after the 19 November raid, when short of fuel. Berlin was again the target on 22/23 November with the force of 764 bombers, including 234 Halifaxes, the largest attack to date, and bad weather kept the enemy night fighters on the ground. This was also the last Stirling mission over Germany, as this rather more vulnerable bomber had seen high losses in the past. PFF marking was accurate using H2S, resulting in major destruction of the target area with a number of major firestorms created. Important government buildings were also damaged, including the British and French embassies. In addition to destruction of major factories, the railway system was disrupted with stations and tracks damaged. The results of the raid were estimated to be over five times the Luftwaffe had been able to achieve over London. With the night fighters unable to get airborne, losses were relatively light with twenty-six bombers shot down, of which ten Halifaxes failed to return.

The following night, conditions were more favourable for the very aggressive night fighter defences. The night fighters were over the target area when the bombers started to arrive, and Mosquitos released flares north of the bomber stream as a diversion. Sky markers were dropped accurately resulting in high levels of destruction on the ground. Frankfurt was the target on 25/26 November including 419 and 102 Squadron as part of a force of 236 Halifaxes, accompanied by twenty-six Lancasters. Once again, defences were aggressive with eleven Halifaxes and one Lancaster destroyed, the planned target having been clearly identified by German controllers. The following night, Berlin was again the target, but by using the same route as before made the German controllers think it was a repeat run to Frankfurt. The bomber force split with 443 Lancasters and seven Mosquitos turning towards Berlin, and 157 Halifaxes plus twenty-one Lancasters on a diversionary raid to Stuttgart. The German fighters headed mistakenly for Frankfurt, and by the time it was realised it was not the target, they were only able to intercept the last wave of RAF bombers. Berlin Lancaster losses were high at 6.2 per cent, while Halifax losses over Stuttgart were 3.4 per cent.

Forecast winds for the night of 2/3 December resulted in a complete failure of the Berlin attack with losses of 8.7 per cent from the force of 458 bombers, but only fifteen Halifaxes were involved with the loss of two aircraft. Leipzig was the target the following night when a force of 527 bombers appeared to be heading for Berlin, before heading for the real target, while Mosquitos made a diversionary attack on the Big City. Although the raid on Leipzig was very successful, fifteen Halifaxes and nine Lancasters were shot down.

Bad weather prevented operations over Germany for two weeks until on 20/21 December. A total of 257 Halifaxes, 390 Lancasters and three Mosquitos bombed Frankfurt, but they were met by accurately positioned German night fighters. Bombing results were effective, but Halifax losses increased alarmingly to twenty-seven and fourteen Lancasters were also shot down, a loss rate of 6.3 per cent. Damage to the centre of the city was high and 466 (RCAF) Squadron sent sixteen Halifax B.IIIs for the first time having just converted to the improved version. By the end of 1943, Halifax Mk.IIIs were beginning to replace all the earlier Mk.IIs in service.

The last Berlin operation for the year was on 29/30 December when 252 Halifaxes and 457 Lancasters were accompanied by three PFF Mosquitos, having reached around halfway through the battle. Bombs and incendiaries were dropped on south and eastern districts of Berlin, causing widespread devastation. More Mosquitos made diversionary attacks on Dusseldorf, Leipzig and Magdeburg, diverting the night defences, and bad weather helped to protect the bombers, with losses low at nine Halifaxes and eleven Lancasters lost. Radar-assisted flak defences were diverted by dropping window, and despite 10/10^{ths} cloud cover over the target the PFF sky markers were accurate. This made a total of eight raids on Berlin up to the end of the year; numbers being restricted by bad weather and the need to avoid clear moonlit nights over Germany.

Bad weather prevented operations in early January, but with marked improvements in German airborne radars at the start of 1944, Halifax losses began to increase during January, with 76 Squadron going from practically no losses in 1943 to six aircraft lost in the first two operations in January, while 102 Squadron lost eleven Halifaxes in the first two months. Operations restarted to Berlin on 20/21 January with 769 bombers, the largest force to the city to date, with a diversionary raid by Mosquitos to Dusseldorf, Hanover and Kiel. No. 4 Group provided a maximum effort with 154 Halifaxes. Post-raid reconnaissance was prevented by cloud cover over Berlin, but damage was scattered and thirty-five bombers were lost, fourteen of which were Halifaxes. No. 102 Squadron was still operating the underpowered Halifax Mk.II Series 1As, losing five out of the sixteen aircraft despatched.

On 21/22 January while bombing Magdeburg Halifax losses reached an unsustainable 15.6 per cent, represented by thirty-five aircraft destroyed out of a force of 224 Halifaxes. As the force of 648 bombers crossed the enemy coast, they were immediately met by many fully fuelled and armed night fighters. Additional night fighters were attracted by PFF route marker flares dropped south of Hamburg, resulting in the total Bomber Command losses being fifty-seven aircraft.

In January 1944, 4 Group Halifax losses reached 11.4 per cent from 544 sorties against targets in Germany, with an overall loss of 10.1 per cent from 613 sorties against all targets. With a 24.2 per cent loss rate, 434 Squadron was the highest, with three other squadrons at 15 per cent, or more. On 19/20 January, Leipzig was the target for 255 Halifaxes in a force of 823 bombers, but it was not successful with aggressive defence by night fighters, from crossing the coast of Holland. The main force arrived early due to incorrectly forecast winds and had to orbit while waiting for the target to be marked. It is believed flak was responsible for the loss of twenty aircraft, with a total thirty-four Halifaxes and forty-four Lancasters shot down. On the night of 21 January, 136 4 Group Halifaxes were despatched to Magdeburg, with twenty-one aircraft lost, the highest number lost by the Group in one night during the entire war. Four each were lost by 76, 77 and 102 Squadrons, with most losses to the underperforming Mk.II and Mk.V, while B.IIIs were reequipping units as quickly as they could be produced. A week after the Magdeburg raid, a force was sent back to Berlin including 241 Halifaxes with 432 Lancasters and four PFF Mosquitos for the 13th raid in the battle, which was followed by another very effective raid on 28/29 January with many fires seen to be burning from long distances, but forty-six aircraft failed to return.

Bad weather delayed further Berlin bombing in early February, but the virtual end to the Berlin Campaign was 15/16 February when the highest number of 891 bombers despatched to any target, apart from the 'thousand-bomber raids', were sent to the Big City. A major effort by 4 Group was 175 Halifaxes from ten squadrons, the majority by this time equipped with the improved Mk.III, and 226 Lancasters were sent by 5 Group.

With an overall loss rate of Halifaxes at 10.8 per cent overall during February, all Merlin-powered Halifax operations over Germany were stopped, apart from a few Mk.IIs with the PFF. This, in practice, only affected 10, 77, 102 and 419 Squadrons, as the remaining squadrons had already converted to the more effective B.Mk.III. By March, 10 Squadron had converted to Halifax Mk.IIIs, followed by 102 and 77 Squadrons in May and June, while 419 Squadron converted to Lancaster Xs in April.

The Merlin-powered Halifax squadrons, despite being withdrawn from German targets, were still kept busy mine laying and bombing manufacturing installations in occupied France, which were being used by Germany for the benefit of the war effort. While Coastal Command had been responsible for mining operations up until 1942, some Bomber Command aircraft were adapted to carry mines. These gardening operations within the early stages the mines had to be dropped at low-level on a timed run, but for obvious reasons they became very hazardous. From 1943, it was found that it was possible to drop mines from as high as 15,000 feet with the assistance of an improved H2S. On 4 January, mines were laid in Brest Harbour by six Halifaxes from 15,000 feet. The techniques were developed by 10 Squadron on the night of 25/26 February with thirteen Halifaxes, three illuminated the dropping zone with flares, before laying their own mines.

Mine laying operations were highly successful with 13,776 mines laid during 1943 in the waters around north-west Europe, with a further 11,415 in the first half of 1944. During this period, German shipping losses reached 175,000 tons, mainly carrying supplies from Scandinavia, against an RAF loss rate of only 2.1 per cent. As the Merlin-powered Halifaxes were withdrawn from Bomber Command, they were usefully employed by other branches of the RAF.

5
Support Operations by Merlin-Powered Halifaxes

With a significant fleet of potentially unemployed crews and operational aircraft becoming available, new roles could be filled. One of these major new roles was glider towing in airborne operations. The success of such operations had been used by the German army during the rapid advances across Europe in 1940, delivering an effective fighting force in advance of the ground troops. The potential was quickly appreciated by the British Government with the formation of the Airborne Forces Development Unit (AFDU) at Ringway in October 1940, starting from basics with no previous experience and a wide collection of aircraft, including Tiger Moths, Hector gliders and a Vickers Wellington. Progress was slow until the Germans used glider borne forces in the conquest of Crete in May 1941, and Churchill urged the Chiefs of Staff to rapidly expand the airborne forces capability. The response was to form a plan to create two parachute brigades and a glider force capable of lifting 10,000 men and their equipment. The gliders would be wooden construction to be produced by the woodworking industries to avoid interference with existing bomber and fighter production. Being a non-strategic material, it could be abandoned after landing following its often one-way trip.

At the same time, specifications were issued for four troop carrying gliders, starting with the eight-seat General Aircraft Hotspur, with the first flight on 21 January 1941. With the need for larger gliders capable of carrying more troops and equipment, in January 1941 mock-ups of the Slingsby Hengist and Airspeed Horsa were inspected, followed on in May by the very much larger General Aircraft Hamilcar, which was capable of carrying vehicles or tanks. The Horsa could carry twenty-five men and equipment, with the two army pilots being part of the squad, or a Jeep towing a gun. With the significant increase in size of the gliders, it was clear that large and powerful tugs would be required. As a result, a visit was made to Boscombe Down in June to consider the Halifax, Manchester, Lancaster and Liberator as potential glider tugs.

Although not initially involved with glider towing, the AFDU took delivery of its first Halifax Mk.II, R9435, on 12 October 1941, which was configured for paratroop dropping trials, with a hatch in the lower part of the fuselage. The early drops using dummies were made on 23 October, but there were difficulties retrieving the static lines and a special winch was fitted to overcome the problem. A wind break was fitted to protect the troops when they jumped to keep them clear from the initial slipstream, allowing the first successful live drop on 10 December. During November, three more Halifaxes were added to the test fleet at Ringway and in December R9443 was delivered configured for glider towing, with the previous aircraft also brought up to the same standard. With the towing rig installed under the rear fuselage aft of the tailwheel, flight trials were moved to Snaith to join the Hamilcar trials, which started on 29 January 1942. The Halifax-Horsa trials started from Snaith in January 1942 and were practically completed by the end of May, with two more, W7719 and W7720, added to the trials on 7 June to be used on Hamilcar towing development. By the end of May, there were seven Halifaxes used on glider towing trials, mainly with the Hamilcar.

The Halifax-Horsa combination was soon to be tested operationally. Norway was the base of the Norsk Hydro establishment at Vermok where duterium oxide, better known as heavy water, was being produced. A month after their occupation, the Germans were demanding a substantial increase in production, the requirement being increased by more than three times in 1942 as part of their atomic research programme. It was therefore essential to stop the production of heavy water. The plant was well protected by surrounding terrain, resulting in great difficulty with

Halifax Mk.II towing an Airspeed Horsa troop carrying glider from Tarrant Rushton. (*Philip Birtles* collection)

Above: Horsa II glider RN334 at Christchurch where many were test flown after assembly. (*Philip Birtles*)

Below: General Aircraft Hamilcar LA634 LA634 after assembly at 33 MU Lyneham. This glider was capable of carrying a light tank to the battlefield. (*RAF Museum*)

destruction by bombing. It was therefore proposed to attempt a glider assault force with Norwegian guides. Sixteen volunteer parachutists from the 9th Field Company RE (Airborne) with sixteen more from the 261st Field Park Company (Airborne) made up the ground force. Airborne support was from a specially formed detachment from 38 Wing with three Halifaxes and two crews. The glider pilots consisted of two from the Glider Pilot Regiment and the other two from the RAAF, each crew training independently from each other, with either capable of completing the mission.

Support Operations by Merlin-Powered Halifaxes

Above: A Halifax Mk.II (Special) ready to tow into the air Hamilcar glider at RAF Lyneham. (*RAF Museum*)

Below: Halifax Mk.II (Special) aerial tow of Hamilcar glider. (*Handley Page Association*)

Training for the attack involved long-distance towing of fully laden gliders around Britain and Norwegian resistance members with Eureka beacons were located along the route to the target for precise guidance. With the code name Operation Washington Party, three Halifaxes and three Horsas were deployed to Skitten on 17 November 1942. The operation was planned for the night of 19/20 November commanded by Group Captain T. B. Cooper, providing the weather was suitable. With a prediction of weather deteriorating during the moon period, a departure was made as planned with the first combination leaving at 17.50hrs, followed by the second 20 minutes later, each combination flying individually 340 miles across the North Sea. Following the crossing of the coast by the first combination, difficulties were experienced with failure of the beacon, and map reading was made difficult by patchy cloud. The target was not identified on the first approach, and while flying in thick cloud, the aircraft was gradually descending due to heavy icing. Just north of Stavanger the tow rope broke, and with marginal reserves, the Halifax only just managed to return to base. Meanwhile the Horsa crashed into snow covered mountains at Fylesdalen, resulting in the death of eight occupants, including the two army pilots, with four others seriously injured. The injured personnel were executed by a German doctor, and after a period in prison, the remainder were executed by the Gestapo on 18 January 1943.

The second combination was lost soon after crossing the coast, with the Horsa crash-landing in the mountains, killing three of the occupants. The survivors were captured and shot within hours of the crash. The Halifax was able to clear the mountain range, but crashed into another line of hills, with the loss of the entire crew. The operation had always been considered hazardous with the long sea crossing and arriving over unknown terrain at night. Bad weather made navigation and identification of the target difficult, with the whole operation a total failure. Eventually a successful destruction of the plant was achieved by an SOE (Special Operations Executive) force supported by Norwegian resistance.

Despite the disaster of the high-risk operation in Norway, the formation of glider towing units started with 295 Squadron, which formed at Netheravon on 3 August 1942, initially with Whitleys, but adding Halifax Mk.Vs from February 1943, which it continued to operate until November 1943. The squadron was part of 38 Wing in Army Co-operation Command, and had a mixture of Horsa and Hotspur gliders. Halifax operations started on 19/20 February when two aircraft bombed a transformer unit at Distre in France which despite the attack being successful on this well defended target, one of the Halifaxes was lost. Delivery of additional aircraft was delayed, but six more were eventually delivered on 21 April. On 1 May, the squadron moved to Holmsley South in the New Forest, and was fully operational by 3 May, when glider towing training continued.

As early as the spring of 1943, there were concerns regarding very severe vibration in Merlin-powered Halifaxes, which had caused a high level of operational failures and crashes. A number of fatal accidents were caused by indiscriminate failure of the magnesium propeller blades, which was cured by fitting wooden propeller blades. However, this caused an increase in vibration, which was breaking up radiators, oil coolers, header tanks, thermostats, nose cowling rings, air intakes, and reduction gear casings. For example, there were 429 radiator failures in a period of three months.

To improve reliability many of the services were mounted on rubber blocks, but the source of the vibration still persisted, resulting in cracking of reduction gear casings, the superchargers and wheel cases were shaking loose from the crankcase, and engine mountings were breaking. Because Handley Page rather than Rolls-Royce were responsible for the Merlin installation, the excessive vibration was attributed to poor design of the outer engine mountings. The result of low stiffness in pitch and yaw caused by wing flexing was resulting in engine installation failures, with urgent action required to stop the vibration becoming out of control, giving the Halifax a poor reputation.

The Halifax Mk.II Series 2 was fitted with Merlin 22 powerplants designed by Rolls-Royce, with much stiffer side bearers, which were satisfactory with the Lancasters, but the vibration in existing Halifaxes required the vibration to be cured urgently. The only practical answer was to fit four blade propellers and isolate the engine installation components by rubber mountings. Many of the earlier Merlin-powered Halifaxes were relegated to training as Merlin 22 examples became available. The final Merlin-powered Halifax was delivered in the summer of 1944, with all subsequent aircraft Hercules-powered, while a total of 2,967 Merlin-powered Halifaxes were built. A total of twenty-three RAF Bomber Command squadrons had been equipped with Merlin-powered Halifaxes, but by June 1944, only one squadron in Italy was not Hercules-powered. The Special Duties squadrons began to reequip during 1944, although three units continued with Merlin power until 1945, as well as Coastal Command and the two meteorological squadrons. Merlin-powered aircraft equipped the sixteen Heavy Conversion Units.

With the Merlin Halifax difficulties apparently solved, there was suddenly a new problem identified. On 16 September 1944, Air Commander Roach of Bomber Command wrote a letter highlighting the continuing unreliability with Merlin XX engines fitted to Halifax Mk.IIs and Mk.Vs operated by the Heavy Conversion Units. During the month of August, it was necessary to change 251 engines, of which only forty-eight had run their full service life of 300 hours. Of the remaining 203, 173 were primary engine failures unconnected with engine installation faults. This level of unreliability was considerably in excess of any other engine type in use with Bomber Command. It was obviously damaging Rolls-Royce reputation, and although these engines were no longer in production, the standard of repair was inadequate. Reducing the service life of the engines would have been of little help, as many of the failures were occurring between only 100 and 150 hours. Bomber Command was therefore considering retiring the Merlin Halifaxes due to the unreliability, which not only affected airworthiness, but also the safety of the crews. The engines were a challenge for the ground crew both for maintenance and repair. Fortunately, Merlin 22-powered Halifaxes served much better, with 75 per cent reaching their full overhaul life. The underlying problem was caused by Handley Page insisting on designing the Merlin installation, instead of using the Rolls-Royce design, which worked well on the Lancaster with the same engines.

Training for basic glider towing involved the tug aircraft moving gradually forward on the runway until the row rope was taught, and then starting the take-off run with the glider becoming airborne first at around 70mph. The tug then climbed away with the glider out of the slipstream, usually below the tug, but could be above. Communications between the two elements was by intercom via a wire in the tow rope, and while together, the tug captain was in command.

The first two Horsa troop carrying gliders were designed and built at Salisbury Hall near St Albans, where the prototype Mosquito had been created in 1940. In late 1940, the Airspeed design team moved from Hatfield to Salisbury Hall after their premises had been destroyed by a German bomb at Hatfield Aerodrome in October 1940. Work started on design and construction with the first Horsa taken to Fairey's Great West Aerodrome, now part of Heathrow, where it was first flown on 12 September 1941. Main flight trials were conducted at Portsmouth where two versions were built, the Horsa I with a side ramp in the forward port side of the fuselage, and the Horsa II with a swing nose allowing direct access for jeeps and mobile guns. Horsa gliders were built entirely of wood in widely dispersed factories, and major assemblies delivered to RAF maintenance units (MUs) for assembly and flight test in preparation for their often one-way trip. The two pilots were in the Glider Pilots Regiment as part of the fighting unit, until collected together and flown back to base to ferry out more troops and equipment.

With deliveries beginning to the RAF, preparations were made for the first major operation, the planned invasion of Sicily from North Africa. With 295 Squadron still the only unit equipped with glider towing Halifaxes, the requirement was sending enough Horsa gliders to Tunisia, from where the invasion was to be launched. Known as Operation Beggar, the Horsas were towed without payload across the often-hazardous Bay of Biscay, over a distance of 1,200 miles initially to Sale in Morocco, and then another 1,000 miles to Sousse. With favourable weather and no enemy interruptions, the Halifax and Horsa combinations should just be able to reach their destination in North Africa. The training programme included 10 hour cross country flights around Britain to prepare for the long ferry flight to Tunisia.

On 8 May 1943, a working party from 13 MU was sent to Hurn with the task of modifying twenty-three Halifaxes to the glider tug configuration, which was completed on time by 1 June, despite the loss of two Halifaxes due to accidents. The Halifaxes had their nose and mid-upper turrets removed and the rear fuselage was strengthened. The Horsas were also prepared at Hurn by the Heavy Glider MU, and once ready, the Halifaxes towed the Horsas to the departure point at Portreath in Cornwall. With the runway at Portreath ending above a sheer cliff, many of the departures were interesting, as the Halifaxes were fully loaded with fuel, and would sink towards the waves before struggling to climb away. Departures started on 3 June with four combinations, but one had to return with an unserviceable glider, and another tow rope broke, resulting in the Horsa and crew ditching, with the crew rescued successfully after 10 hours in the sea. The remaining two combinations reached the destination safely. The following fourteen combinations arrived at Sale by 14 June, after flying in daylight within 100 miles of enemy airfields in south-west France. Unfortunately, on 14 June, a combination was intercepted by a pair of FW Condors, and despite the Halifax rear gunners attempting to defend the combination, the Horsa had to cast off and was forced to ditch, with the tug shot down into the sea. Rather unexpectedly, the crew were the same who had ditched on the first day of the operation, but this time spent eleven days in their life raft before being rescued by a Portuguese fishing boat.

While some Halifaxes stayed in North Africa to assist with training, others returned to Britain to bring more Horsas for the landings. With one more combination lost, the last was delivered on 28 June, about a week before the planned start of the invasion, leaving little time for additional training and preparations. The American contributions were combinations of C-47s towing Waco gliders with limited navigation capability. The combined force was launched from six airfields in Kairouan on the night of 9/10 July with seven Halifax combinations of 295 Squadron and 28 Albemarles of 296 Squadron, complemented by 109 US Troop Carrier Command combinations in hardly ideal weather conditions of 30mph cross winds. With the inexperienced crews and difficult approaches, sixty-nine of the 137 gliders came down in the sea, and a further fifty-six were scattered widely along the coast. Part of the 38 Wing tug force, consisting of a dozen Horsas arrived at the landing zone, with one close to the vital Syracuse canal bridge. By dawn, this bridge had been taken together with many prisoners captured.

The last airborne assault of the Sicilian Campaign was Operation Fustian with the target being the Simento Bridge, which controlled the routes from high ground on to the Catania Plain. A force of 107 C-47s and Albemarles were used to drop paratroops, while eleven Horsas and six Wacos were towed by five Halifaxes and Albemarles, departed in the evening of 13 July. Not all went to plan due to a break down in communications with the glider force routed through a balloon barrage protecting the troop ships waiting off the coast. At least two of the Albemarle combinations were shot down by Allied guns under attack from German Ju 88s just as the gliders were passing overhead. As the drop zone was being approached, anti-aircraft fire from the shore damaging one Halifax and completely destroying another, the only one to be lost that night.

The operation was considered a success with thirteen gliders arriving in the correct places, although one crashed, with four failing to arrive. In addition to the one Halifax, ten C-47s and three Albemarles were lost, and the objective was taken allowing the US Seventh and British Eighth Armies to advance across Sicily. Despite the airborne operations not being totally successful, many lessons were learned for the benefit of future operations.

There was concern about the loss of some glider towing Mk.Vs in September 1943 caused by numerous defects, which was attributed to poor workmanship by Fairey Aviation, who built the Halifax Mk.Vs. Most failures were a result of pipes fouling each other and chafing through, resulting in loss of oil or coolant. Handley Page arranged for Fairey to send working parties to remedy the defects on the spot. Tests at Boscombe Down found a loss of speed in the lower range of 125mph, which was exactly where the aircraft were operating. In addition, take-off distance was 1,120 yards in the existing configuration, with a further 50 yards, allowing insufficient margin for a 2,000-yard runway, especially as the aircraft were very heavily loaded. Engine reliability was also a problem, as if one engine failed, the glider had to be released, as three engines provided insufficient power to continue the tow. On two recent operations of 9.5 hours, en route losses were as high as 40 per cent, with only two being credited to enemy action.

No 295 Squadron returned to Britain for Operation Elaborate, ferrying gliders to North Africa over the following two months. Although losses were light, on 17 September, Halifax DG396 was towing a Horsa over the Bay of Biscay in clear weather. With the Beaufighter escort returned to base, the combination was attacked by Ju 88s. As the enemy prepared for attack, the Horsa pilot bravely requested permission to cast off to give the Halifax a better chance of survival. The Halifax captain was determined to attempt to save the glider and headed for a distant cloud bank, just as the enemy aircraft started their attack. At this point, the glider crew released the tow, and ended up in the sea from which they were eventually rescued by ASR. Meanwhile the Halifax was badly damaged by rockets fired by the Ju 88s, many of them missing due to the violent evasive manoeuvres, until two were fired from head on, resulting in serious damage to the aircraft, after which it flew into the cloud. The aircraft was obviously too badly damaged to land on the short, crowded runway at Gibraltar, but was able to reach Sale safely, the pilot, Flying Officer Norman being awarded a DFC, and the rear gunner a DFM. The last ferry combination departed for North Africa on 23 September, with Albemarles replacing the last Halifax on 10 October.

No. 38 Wing was expanded into becoming 38 Group in November, consisting of nine squadrons of which 298 Squadron was the only Halifax unit, which formed

Halifax Mk.II (Special)s lined upon either side of the Tarrant Rushton runway with Horsa and Hamilcar gliders ready for launch from the runway to head for Normandy. (*RAF Museum*)

Samlesbury-built Halifax A.III LW385 L9 190 Squadron which replaced its Stirlings with Halifax A.IIIs at Great Dunmow in May 1945. The A.Mk.IIIs were interim conversions from 30 B.IIIs, pending availability of the A.Mk.VII, and were equipped to tow both Horsa and Hamilcar gliders. LW385 was delivered to 424 Squadron on 25 December 1943 and also was operated by 431 and 190 Squadrons. It went to RAE Farnborough on 28 February 1946 and was scrapped on 12 March 1948. (*Handley Page Association*)

at Tarrant Rushton on 4 November. Initial equipment included seventeen Mk.V Halifaxes and seven Horsa gliders, with ten crews posted from 295 Squadron to form A Flight and twelve crews from 297 Squadron forming B Flight. Training started with Horsa gliders in preparation for the much larger General Aircraft Hamilcar, which could carry a light tank to the battlefield.

The first of 344 wooden-structure Hamilcars, DP206, made its maiden flight on 27 March 1942 and it was the largest glider used operationally. It had a wingspan of 110 feet and was over 20 feet high. At an empty weight of 18,500lb, it was nearly 3,000lb heavier than the AUW of the Horsa. The 1,920-cubic-foot hold could carry a load of 17,500lb. Development testing started at the Airborne Forces Experimental Establishment at Newmarket in August 1942, including both tug and glider at maximum AUW, but DP206 was damaged when its undercarriage collapsed, with replacement by the first of a pre-production batch of ten gliders. Testing continued into 1943 with a Halifax carrying out dive tests from 10,000 feet on 30 January with a fully loaded Hamilcar. Contractor's Trials were flown with a Halifax/Hamilcar combination on 26 February. Training began with the new gliders at Tarrant Rushton in November 1943.

In addition to glider towing, Halifaxes were used to develop other methods of supporting ground forces, including recovery of Hamilcars from landing spots. A Halifax was used to recover a Hamilcar without its undercarriage, and performance trials with one of the pre-production gliders. A Halifax was fitted with a Jeep and 75mm gun slung in the bomb-bay, with a parachute drop test on 11 June. On 17 June, mixed loads of containers and dummy parachutists in quick succession, culminating in a group of thirty parachutists from a Halifax/Horsa combination at Sherburn-in-Elmet during the month of August. With Hamilcar trials almost complete by October, Halifaxes were used to continue Jeep and 75mm gun dropping over Sherburn-in-Elmet, with container numbers increasing to fifteen dropped in November. By January 1944, Halifaxes were dropping a pannier with dummy parachutists and in March a collapsible motorcycle was dropped by parachute followed by a 4,000lb container. In May, the Jeep and 75mm gun combination was tested with a gun crew of six parachutists, with other combinations to follow in July, just when 38 Group were busy supporting the advances in France.

Meanwhile, training by 298 Squadron had been delayed by bad weather, with only a small number of flights achieved by the end of January. Despite limited training in Exercise Co-operation in February, eleven paratroops carrying Halifaxes were airborne in 4.5 minutes, followed by three Stirlings and ten Halifaxes each towing a Horsa in just under 10 minutes. On 5 February 1944, a third flight was added to 298 Squadron with crew numbers of forty by the end of the month. These additional crews were trained to gain experience in preparation to form 644 Squadron on 23 February also at Tarrant Rushton, with half the crews transferred to the new unit. The first Halifax Mk.Vs were delivered in March, totalling twenty aircraft each, of which two were reserves.

There was a requirement to land gliders close to key battlefield targets to maintain an element of surprise. A number of Horsa and Halifax crews received specialist training at Tarrant Rushton, with the Halifax navigator providing a course to fly after release, the only additional equipment being a gyro compass. To be effective, constant practice was required, and its success was more than proven with the three Horsas landing within a few meters of 'Pegasus Bridge' in the early hours of 6 June 1944.

With 38 Group preparing for the planned invasion of occupied Europe, the Halifaxes were fitted with Gee and Rebecca to improve navigation accuracy. With Merlin XX serviceability still poor, the decision was made to re-engine the Halifaxes with the much more reliable Merlin 22s, although as production was delayed, only just over half had been replaced by the end of March.

With the glider towing squadrons ready for Operation Overlord, the D-Day landings in Normandy, the airborne part was known as Operation Neptune, headed by six 298 Squadron Halifaxes, each towing a Horsa glider with the intention of capturing two vital bridges, one over the River Orne, and the other over the Caen

Canal. It was essential these bridges were captured intact to maintain land routes for the 6th Airborne Division advances. Three Horsas were allocated to each bridge, and because of the silent approach, were able to achieve complete surprise, the bridge over the Orne being named Pegasus Bridge after the crest of the Glider Pilot Regiment. The gliders landed soon after midnight and were tasked with holding the bridges until relieved by the main forces.

The second stage was the first main assault of the day consisting of 350 gliders known as Operation Tonga. Each of the two Halifax squadrons towed fifteen Horsas and two Hamilcars. The Horsas were loaded with Jeeps and 75mm guns, while the Hamilcars carried 17 pounder guns and Morris tractors for the Royal Artillery anti-tank unit. Weather was bad over England, but improved as they approached France, although some of the cloud was below the ideal release height of 1,500 feet. Three of the gliders towed by 298 Squadron had to abort, with two landing in England, and the third ditching in the Channel. One 298 Squadron Halifax was shot down by enemy coastal flak, but the crew survived. Only two gliders had to abort with 644 Squadron, both landing in England. All the other gliders achieved their objectives successfully.

Halifax A.V towing Horsa glider on 12 October for Operation Market Garden at Arnhem. (*RAF Museum*)

Above: Halifax Mk.II (Specials) with 298 and 644 Squadrons lined up on either side of the runway at Tarrant Rushton on 12 October 1944, waiting for aerial tow of Hamilcars which still have control locks in place. (*RAF Museum*)

Below: Halifax Mk.V 9U-L 644 Squadron towing a Hamilcar glider for Operation Market Garden. (*RAF Museum*)

Above: Halifax Mk.V LL338 9U-J 644 Squadron at Tarrant Rushton on 12 October 1944. This Halifax was delivered to 297 Squadron on 9 November 1944 and finally SOC on 1 November 1945. (*RAF Museum*)

Below: Halifax Mk.Vs, including LL275 KK and LL350 9U-Z 644 Squadron at Tarrant Rushton 12 October 1944. LL275 also was operated by 297 Squadron from 16 November 1944 and SOC on 31 May 1945. LL350 was delivered to 644 Squadron on 23 April 1944 and also served with 297 Squadron from 23 November 1944. It was SOC on 4 March 1945. (*RAF Museum*)

Above: Halifax Mk.II towing a Horsa glider off from Tarrant Rushton. (*RAF Museum*)

Below: Halifax Mk.V with the crew of 644 Squadron at Tarrant Rushton on 12 October 1944. (*RAF Museum*)

Halifax B.V 9U-U 644 Squadron loading with canisters at Tarrant Rushton on 12 October 1944. (*RAF Museum*)

The final stage in the airborne assault was Operation Mallard, the largest daylight operation attempted to date. The main requirement was to provide reinforcements for the airborne troops already in France using 256 gliders, the whole formations being escorted by fighter squadrons. Each of the Halifax squadrons towed fifteen Hamilcars and one Horsa; the Halifaxes towing Horsas were each loaded with containers for release in the DZ (dropping zone). All of these gliders reached the DZ safely, but a 298 Squadron Halifax was hit by enemy fire and forced to ditch in the Channel. The crew were all picked up by a ship, with neither squadron losing a single crew member during the invasion support operations. On 10 June, both squadrons were active in a resupply of the airborne troops with six Halifaxes. Each Halifax successfully dropped a Jeep and 6 pounder gun from 1,000 feet, as well as six containers, with both squadrons continuing the resupply until 27 June. Special operations included a drop by 298 Squadron when four Halifaxes dropped additional paratroops, Jeeps and containers to SAS personnel on the ground in France. A 644 Squadron Halifax towed a Hamilcar loaded with a replacement set of Spitfire wings to a beach head airstrip.

Halifax parachute supply drop. (*Handley Page Association*)

Demonstration parachute supply drop from a Halifax. (*RAF Museum*)

With the completion of airborne resupply missions, both Halifax squadrons reverted to continuing training in preparation for future operations, while also supporting the SOE and SAS, as well as some tactical bombing sorties. To give some idea of the intensity of operations, in August 1944, 298 Squadron supported 156 SOE and SAS missions and delivered 999 containers with the loss of three Halifaxes. Both Halifax squadrons led the first Hadrian operation on 5 August, when five tugs from each unit achieved a successful SAS incursion to Brittany. Each Hadrian carried three equipped men and a Jeep.

With Allied advances progressively over occupied Europe from the D-Day landings, natural barriers were the Maas, Waal and lower River Rhine, Field Marshal Montgomery devised a plan to capture strategic bridge crossings to ensure a crossing across the River Rhine. The 1st Allied Airborne Army was allocated the task of securing the Grave, Nijmegan, Arnhem areas to allow capture of the main river and canal crossings. The aerial support, including glider towing, paratroop drops and resupply was the responsibility of 38 and 46 Groups in the Arnhem area. The main parachute drops in the Nijmegan-Grave area were the responsibility of the US IX Troop Carrier Command (TCC), except glider towing the British Airborne Corps HQ which was left to 38 Group. The US TCC was also responsible for the Eindhoven area. The glider force was positioned on the runway at Tarrant Rushton with the Halifax tugs on either side and preparations were completed by 18.00hrs on 16 September 1944, ready for the departure of the first combination at 10.20hrs the next day. The remainder of the force followed at 45 second intervals, with the airborne formations split into three parallel lines, one and a half miles apart. Seven Hamilcars and thirteen Horsas were towed by 298 Squadron, with seven Hamilcars and fourteen Horsas behind 644 Squadron. Each squadron had one abort, with 298 Squadron Halifax having engine trouble and returning to base, while the Hamilcar tow rope broke behind a 644 Squadron Halifax, and the glider managed to return to the coast. Weather was fair over the target with some haze near the ground, but the gliders were seen to arrive on the Rhine north bank. Two Hamilcars overturned when landing on soft ground with the loss of their 17 pounder guns. There was minimal anti-aircraft fire from the ground and all the Halifaxes returned to base safely.

On the second day, there was a delay to the start of 3 hours due to unsuitable weather, with 298 Squadron towing eight Hamilcars and eight Horsas, and 644 Squadron taking seven Hamilcars and eight Horsas. With time to prepare the flak was more aggressive, damaging one of 298 Squadron Halifaxes and injuring the navigator. Two gliders were lost over the Channel by 644 Squadron, but they did not suffer any flak damage. The weather had deteriorated further by the third and final day, resulting in

Halifax A.VII NA366 April 1945. The A.Mk.VII was an interim conversion of the B.Mk.VII and could carry twelve paratroops, as well as tow gliders. On 24 March 1945, 298 Squadron operated seven A.VIIs on Operation Varsity. This version was operated by RAF squadrons in Britain, the Middle East and Asia from 1944 until after the war. NA366 was delivered to 45 MU on 23 March 1945, and was sold for scrap to J. Dale on 5 January 1949. (*RAF Museum*)

Radlett-built Halifax A.VII PP350 with Universal 8,000lb Freight Container loaded in the bomb-bay. This combination was shown at a demonstration at Watchfield on 6 March 1951. This aircraft was delivered to RAE Farnborough on 11 April 1947 and SOC on 29 May 1952. (*Air Historical Branch*)

Contemporary Giles cartoon from the *Daily Express* as Halifaxes tow gliders over the Normandy coastline. (*Handley Page Association*)

Above: Hamilcar gliders lined up at Tarrant Rushton on 12 October 1944, framed under a Halifax wing. (*RAF Museum*)

Below: A 298 Squadron Halifax Mk.II landing at Tarrant Rushton ready for a dusk take-off, with a mobile 'Chance' light by the runway to assist with night time landings. (*RAF Museum*)

a delay of nearly 5 hours, the first combination not becoming airborne until 12.10hrs. Only ten Horsas were towed by 298 Squadron with 644 towing another ten, plus the Hamilcar which had to abort the previous day. Visibility in the DZ was reduced due to low-level haze.

By this time enemy defences had increased significantly, both fighters and on the ground. There was no RAF fighter escort for the gliders due to a misunderstanding. Although some gliders were seen to be shot down, 298 Squadron were able to release their gliders over the DZ, and two Halifaxes were damaged. Due to determined resistance by flak, 644 Squadron experienced damage to some Halifaxes and three gliders failed to reach the DZ, two because of broken tow ropes.

Although the Arnhem operation was overall a disastrous failure, partly due to inadequate resupply and poor communications, two river crossings were established by the Allies and the airborne operation was considered an overall success. The glider force carried some 4,500 troops, ninety-five guns and 544 Jeeps to around 60 miles behind enemy lines with a high success rate.

During the Arnhem operation, 296 Squadron began to convert from Albemarles to Halifax Mk.Vs at Brize Norton, moving to Earls Colne on 29 September 1944, the crew being trained by 1665 HCU at Tilstock. Glider towing training started in October, with Halifaxes from 298 and 644 Squadrons, which were being replaced by the more powerful Halifax Mk.IIIs and 297 began converting to surplus Mk.Vs at Earls Colne in October. Both of these squadrons flew SAS, SOE and bombing operations, while training for glider towing until February 1945, when they were reequipped with Halifax Mk.IIIs. The special operations were flown by a single Halifax, which, to disguise its intentions, would drop bombs on a target near the DZ.

The last major glider operation was Operation Varsity, the long-awaited Rhine crossing, leading into the heart of Germany in March 1945. All four squadrons were tasked with towing gliders with sixty Halifaxes from 296 and 297 operating from Earls Colne, and 298 and 644 Squadrons flying sixty Halifaxes from the emergency runway at Woodbridge. Operation Varsity started on 24 March 1945 involving 16,000 paratroops and several thousand aircraft, and was the largest ever airborne operation to be conducted in one day to one location. The British 6th Airborne Division was tasked with the capture of the villages of Schnappenberg and Diersfordt Wald to clear the area of German forces and secure three bridges over the River Issel near the town of Wesel. In an attempt to ensure accurate drops on the DZs, beacons were located at various turning points to guide in the air assault.

At Woodbridge, 298 and 644 Squadrons were each split into two flights for the operation, with 298 Squadron towing twelve Horsa combinations and 644 Squadron leading forty-eight Hamilcar combinations. From Earls Colne, 296 and 297 Squadrons shared the towing of sixty Horsa combinations. In preparation at Earls Colne, half the tugs and gliders were set up with tow lines attached and lined up along about one third of the runway ready for departure. The remaining Halifaxes and Horsas were parked around the perimeter, ready to be positioned on the vacated runway. Weather conditions were good allowing on time departures for the overall 1,500 aircraft and 1,300 gliders, with Allied air

Above: The vast Woodbridge runway on 24 March 1945 with Hamilcars on the runway and 298 and 644 Squadrons Halifaxes ready to tow them off for Operation Varsity, the Allied crossing of the Rhine. (*Handley Page Association*)

Left: Halifax Mk.Vs towing Horsa II gliders over the French coast on 24 March 1945 for Operation Varsity. (*RAF Museum*)

supremacy ensuring an absence of German fighters. As was to be expected in such a large operation, there were some premature losses with some six gliders failing to reach their DZ. There were some losses to flak with five Halifaxes shot down, but the major hazards were failing tow ropes and collisions in the crowded sky. To overcome the resupply problems experienced at Arnhem, six DZs were allocated and three Halifaxes were tasked as master supply aircraft to direct operations. When asked now about Operation Varsity, people often have no knowledge of its existence. Probably because it was a complete success and had benefitted from earlier experiences.

With the Allied advances into Germany, the outcome of the War was only a matter of time. While there was no further requirement for airborne assaults, there was still a need for the Halifaxes to undertake SOE operations in Norway and Denmark. There were two final non-combat airborne operations, the first being on 8 May 1945, the day the war finished, when troops and equipment of the 1st Airborne Division were dropped at Copenhagen. RAF Halifaxes and Stirlings were joined by C-46s of the US IX TCC, with 38 Group responsible for resupply sorties for the remainder of May. The final airborne operation of the war was the delivery to Norway of 7,000 troops and 2,000 tons of equipment known as Operation Domesday by 38 Group. The requirement was to occupy Oslo, Stavenger and Kristiansund following the German surrender, in four stages from 9 to 13 May. Bad weather delayed the start by 36 hours, but the operation was completed successfully with a warm welcome from the Norwegian population.

Although a much smaller scale of operations to those in Europe, two Halifax Vs were deployed to the Far East, starting with the formation of 1577 Flight in August 1943, also with two Lancaster Mk.IIIs. The aircraft were delivered to Llandow in early September for the necessary preparations, particularly to the engines, to ensure a high level of reliability when operating so far from home. The aircraft departed for India on 26 September, the Halifaxes arriving at Karachi on 6 and 7 October. The operational trials started on 1 November with exercise Bulls Eye to Calcutta to assess operational performance under tropical conditions. These tests were normally combined with meteorological duties, and started on 3 November when DK254 took off at the hottest point in the afternoon, with an all-up weight of 62,000lb, reaching 19,000 feet. This flight was repeated on 17 December with the all-up weight increased to 62,000lb, achieving 17,200 feet in just less than an hour. A week later, the other Halifax, DK263, with an all-up weight of 62,000lb, took off after a run of 1,200 feet and reached 20,000 feet.

The supply ship carrying the aircraft spares was lost, which resulted in high unserviceability and delays in completing the trials. With the eventual successful completion, on 5 December, the flight was allocated to non-combat transport duties. However, these were not without hazard under primitive operating conditions. Both Merlin-powered Halifax Vs were lost due to accidents, DK254 on 3 January from a flight from Bombay, when it swung on landing and collapsed the port undercarriage. DK263 was destroyed on 26 January when landing on the short 600-yard strip with the loss of power in two engines. The aircraft overshot down the bank of a river, landing on its back killing nine of the crew and passengers.

Above: Halifax B.III with 1577 Special Duties (SD) Flight landing at Maripur in September 1945. (*Handley Page Association*)

Below: Halifax B.III of 1577 (SD) Flight with air and ground crew at Dhamial in September 1945. (*Handley Page Association*)

Support Operations by Merlin-Powered Halifaxes

Above: Close-up of Halifax B.III nose of 1577 (SD) Flight at Dhamial in September 1945. (*Handley Page Association*)

Below: Servicing Halifax B.III of 1577 (SD) Flight at Dhamial in September 1945. (*Handley Page Association*)

Following the loss of both Halifaxes, the Lancasters moved to Mauripur on 7 May and were allocated to glider towing trials, with four Horsa and two Hamilcars, and additional Dakota and Commando towing aircraft. Replacement Halifax Mk.IIIs (see Chapter 7) were allocated in October for glider towing, paratroop and supply dropping; the new aircraft arriving on 10 November, after the Lancasters had been withdrawn. The more robust air-cooled Hercules radial engines were better suited for the trials which started on 15 November and continued until April, including some long-distance tows, the results being positive.

Five more Halifax Mk.IIIs arrived in May 1945 to equip 1341 Flight at Digri, with the role of Japanese radio and radar counter measures, shared with Liberators. Although there were only a few sorties, the ones flown were often in bad weather over long-ranges. No significant new information was obtained on Japanese radars, but the Halifaxes were also used by 159 Squadron on transport duties, with the last mission on 1 August. When the Japanese surrendered, the Halifaxes were used to fly medical supplies, cargo and fuel over the 'Hump' to China, and were able to bring back a number of ex-prisoners of war. The flight finally disbanded on 30 October 1945.

Meanwhile 1577 Flight continued to tow gliders with one Halifax and a Dakota ferrying forty-three gliders over a distance of 320 miles in a period of eight weeks.

Halifax B.III with 1341 Flight at Raipur in December 1945. (*RAF Museum*)

Gliders towed included both Horsas and the larger Hamilcar. Halifax NA644 was fitted with an 8,000lb bomb beam fitted with electro-magnetic releases and in June began dropping tests of a jeep and gun. On the first test from 1,000 feet, there was a fault with the gun parachute, which caused it to drop without assistance, writing it off, but the jeep landed safely.

As the war came to an end in Europe, plans had been made to transfer some of the 38 Group squadrons to Asia to undertake glider operations against the Japanese, following the proving of the concept by 1577 Flight. On 6 July 1945, nine tropicalised 298 Squadron Halifax A.Mk.VIIs departed Tarrant Rushton for India. A second batch of eight left on 13 July with seven more following on 18 July and were based initially at Raipur moving to Digri on 9 December. The Halifax VIIs were fitted with 3,000lb capacity freight panniers, but these were soon replaced by 8,000lb capacity panniers. All armament, armour plating and glider towing gear were removed. From August, the aircraft were used to carry passengers and freight to destinations around India and Ceylon mainly in monsoon weather conditions, and also flew over the 'Hump' to China, again bringing back released POWs. The squadron was soon flying a number of regular scheduled services, with some aircraft configured for the carriage of twenty-four passengers, while 100 hospital patients had to be taken from Bilaspur to Mauripur in January 1946 in two Halifaxes at the rate of sixteen per flight.

With a change of command into 228 Group, the squadron went back to the airborne training role, but it was still available for famine relief in India, when each aircraft carried 50 × 80lb bags of rice in the pannier, with the same amount in the fuselage. The rice in the fuselage could be air dropped to specific remote locations, while the load in the pannier was delivered to main bases. With a reduction in fuel load it was possible to increase the rice load to a total of 12,000lb, equally distributed between the pannier and fuselage interior. With the initial phase completed by the end of March, it was realised that the famine was continuing, and further airborne support was provided in April. The squadron then returned to airborne training, but in July it was tasked as the Bomber Airborne Support and Heavy Equipment Dropping Squadron until it was finally disbanded on 21 December 1946. Meanwhile 1577 Flight disbanded on 1 June 1946.

With its roomy fuselage interior, the Halifax was easily adapted to airborne forces duties with comparatively easy modifications. The first A.Mk.V Series 1 (Special) was first used operationally by the RAF from February 1943, and by D-Day in June 1944, both 38 (Airborne Forces) Group Halifax Squadrons, 298 and 644 had been reequipped with the much-improved A.V Series 1s. The major changes were a paratroop dropping hatch and glider towing hook, with the mid-upper turret removed. The A.Mk.III was an interim conversion of thirty B.IIIs for glider towing and troop transport, pending the delivery of the A.Mk.VII in August 1945. The A.IIIs could tow both Horsa and Hamilcar gliders. The A.Mk.VII was an interim conversion of the B.VII which could carry twelve paratroops and a glider towing hook was fitted. This was the first transport Halifax version to be fitted with an 8,000lb capacity Universal Freight Container in the bomb-bay, from which the doors had been removed. This version was used by 298 Squadron on Operation Varsity, and used by British, Middle East and Asia based squadrons from 1944 until after the end of the war. The final version of the Halifax to be built was the A.Mk.IX which was converted from the B.VIs. As well as being used by airborne forces, this version could also be used as a bomber or transport, but the first examples were not delivered to the RAF until November 1945. There was accommodation for twelve paratroops aft of the wing centre section. The port side door and paratroop cone were replaced by a rectangular hatch in the floor. A glider hook was fitted, and defence was by a Boulton Paul Type D rear turret armed with two 0.5-inch Browning machine guns. The A.IXs briefly replaced A.VIIs with 620 and 644 Squadrons from August 1946 in the Middle East, before both squadrons were disbanded in the next month. Only two A.IXs were used in the Berlin Air Lift with Bond Air Services and thirty more were operated by Aviation Traders as civil aircraft from Southend. With the ending of the Berlin Air Lift, nine Mk.IXs were sold to the Egyptian Air Force in 1950 and the remainder scrapped the following year.

Meanwhile the Special Operations Executive (SOE) was formed to organise support for the resistance in occupied Europe, by sending volunteer agents at great personal risk, and sabotage supplies. To undertake this hazardous, but vital task the RAF formed 419 (Special Duties) Flight at North Weald on 21 August 1940, equipped with Lysanders to undertake clandestine flights with agents, known as 'Joeys'. A month after forming it moved to Stapleford Tawney with operations commencing from Tangmere. On 9 October, a move was made to Stradishall by which time Whitleys had been added to increase the load carrying capability and range. On 1 March 1941, it was redesignated 1419 (Special Duties) Flight and on 25 August 1941, became

Radlett-built Halifax A.Mk.IX RT760 November 1945. This was the last Halifax type built and a comprehensive modified B.Mk.VI. (*RAF Museum*)

Radlett-built Halifax A.IX RT938. Although it was for use by airborne forces, it could also be used as a bomber or transport. (*RAF Museum*)

138 (Special Duties) Squadron at Newmarket. The Lysanders equipped A Flight and Whitleys B Flight.

With a requirement to assist the Polish Home Army with supplies and equipment, there was a need for an aircraft with greater range, resulting in Halifaxes being supplied in August 1941, followed by move to its long-term base at Tempsford on 11 March 1942. Five Halifax B.IIs, starting with L9612, were allocated from service aircraft already fitted with additional wing fuel tanks. The major modification programme was for drag reduction, which included nose and top turret removal if time allowed, and replacement with fairings. All unnecessary external items were removed and any apertures sealed to ensure the highest standard of finish. Additional long-range tanks were installed in the bomb-bay and provision was made for dropping paratroopers with a circular hatch on the fuselage underside. All these modifications were made by Tollerton Aircraft Services, with 138 Squadron responsible for fitting a retractable tail wheel, and the later B.Mk.VI having enclosed main wheels when retracted.

Special duties operations were operated by single aircraft and the need for secrecy was essential. Crews were briefed individually with the pilot and navigator, the only crew members to know the DZ location in case captured crew members were forced to give away essential information. Each crew operated alone with no knowledge of what other aircraft might be doing and navigation over enemy territory to locate an isolated field was challenging without aids, resulting in the need for accurate map reading and stellar navigation. Flying was often at low-level in all weathers to keep in the ground view, often at the limits of the aircraft endurance. In addition to the

Above: Speke-built Halifax B.V(SD) DG245 NF-W 138 Squadron was one of two with the SOE at Tempsford. This aircraft failed to return from an operation on 14/15 March 1943. (*Air Historical Branch*)

Below: The personnel of 138 Squadron at Tempsford in front of one of the two Halifax B.V(SD)s. (*RAF Museum*)

risks associated with flying low and slow over occupied territory, there was also the unknown threat of hoping the ground-based reception party was friendly. If an agent's cover was blown and the equipment and documents captured, after interrogation, the enemy would try and attract Allied support, and because of security and bureaucracy it may be a long time before it was realised an agent had been compromised. An example was when the first two agents were dropped in The Netherlands in November 1942 and immediately captured by the Germans. This allowed them to set up a spoof organisation which continued for a year with losses to new agents and aircraft during operations. Losses to 138 Squadron increased steadily, with twenty-two lost between March and September 1943 all while operating over The Netherlands. This finally alerted the SOE to what was happening, and further operations over the country were abandoned. This was the worst failure by the SOE during the Second World War.

The first volunteer Polish crews were allocated from 300 and 301 Squadrons in October 1941, having been converted from Wellingtons at Linton-on-Ouse. They were ready for the first clandestine operation to Poland on 7/8 November 1941 with L9612, which flew from Linton-on-Ouse where there was full Halifax support, unlike Newmarket. Aboard the Halifax were three instructors and equipment, which were to be dropped west of Warsaw. Despite bad weather on route to the target, the three men were dropped as planned, but with hydraulic failure causing the undercarriage to drop and a higher-than-expected head wind on the return flight, it was clear there was insufficient endurance to reach base. Over Denmark, a decision was made to divert to neutral Sweden, where a crash-landing was made without injury to the crew, but writing off the aircraft. The crew returned to their squadron early in the new year.

The squadron duties were not just to Poland, but also in support of the resistance in other occupied territories. On 28/29 December, L9613 flew to Czechoslovakia carrying two training and communications squads and the proposed Heydrich assassination team. Despite bad weather, all three teams were dropped, although the third group were some 12 miles from their target, all without the benefit of reception committees. A safe return was made by the aircraft to Tangmere.

The targets in Poland were mostly at the extreme Halifax range, even with additional fuel tanks. To avoid the worst of the defences, the route to Poland was over the North Sea to Denmark, and along the Baltic coast to a point between Danzig and Kolobrzeg when a turn was made inland on a southerly heading. The shortest distance flown was around 800 miles to DZ in Pomerania, with Warsaw a distance of 1,000 miles. Even with long-range fuel tanks, the round trip to Warsaw of 2,000 miles, was even in good weather on the Halifax endurance limits. To maximise on fuel load, it was necessary to reduce payload to 2,400lb. An example was on the third supply trip on 6 January 1942, bad weather resulted in the flight lasting 14 hours, with tanks close to empty when landing.

On 25 January 1942, the Halifaxes with 138 Squadron were increased to the full five conversions, with more crews posted in, including a Czech one. Weather during February was responsible for the failure of a number of sorties, but conditions improved in March. Operations were not able to restart until May, when the protection of darkness was lost.

With the move to Tempsford in March, it joined 161 Squadron, the second special duties unit which had moved there from Graveley, receiving its Halifax Mk.IIs in September and Mk.Vs in October, replacing the Mk.IIs by December. Tempsford therefore became the centre for special operations, under the control of Assistant Chief of Air Staff (Intelligence) instead of Bomber Command. The Polish crews also made supply drops in Norway, Austria and Czechoslovakia. The first loss of a crew was 20 April in V9976 when the aircraft hit high ground in Austria.

With the return of the longer nights in September, supply flights to Poland restarted including additional SOE operations, with the release of more Halifaxes from Bomber Command. W1046 being the first to arrive with 161 Squadron on 6 October, followed by two more on 18 October. With the longer nights, additional destinations were Norway and Czechoslovakia. On the night of 29/30 October both squadrons flew sorties over Poland, The Netherlands and Denmark, one of the flights to Poland being the longest yet at 14.25 hours. One of the Polish sorties in W7774 was damaged by night fighters and was forced to ditch off the English coast, but the crew were rescued.

With the planned Allied offensive in Libya in October 1942, every available aircraft capable of carrying supplies was pressed into service, including both 138 and 161 Squadrons sending detachments to 511 Squadron at Lyneham, with seven aircraft from 138 Squadron and two from 161 Squadron. The first departure was from Hurn on 4 October, but two aircraft were lost with experienced crews during the operations. To cope with the extreme long flights, 138 Squadron aircraft were fitted with additional fuel tanks, taking overall capacity to 2,752 gallons, 180 gallons more than with other Mk.IIs and Mk.Vs.

SOE operations continued with B Flight, 161 Squadron Halifaxes on 14/15 January 1943 taking two agents with packages of coffee and pigeons to a DZ in Belgium, near the border with the Netherlands. However, due to thick cloud on approach to the target, the flight had to be aborted. Overall, during January, out of sixteen SOE and SIS sorties, three were achieved successfully, five partly completed, five not completed due to no reception committee at the DZ, and two were abandoned. Failures were often due to conditions out of the crew's control, but every effort was made to achieve some positive results. A successful operation was achieved on 25/26 January when Halifax DG245 dropped six containers from 1,000 feet near Loire, followed by two agents dropped from 800 feet. The aircraft returned safely to Tempsford after 7.5 hours flying at low-level over enemy occupied territory and navigating by map reading at night. The first loss was on 13/14 January with a load of containers and other items, but no agents, which failed to return. A report from the French resistance reported the crash of a four-engine bomber near Rennes, for an unknown reason, with the loss of seven crew.

Operations to Poland were always a challenge, but on 13/14 March six 138 Squadron crews were all successful, despite the extreme distances involved. The following night, two Halifaxes were lost, one crashing in Denmark and the other shot down near Munich. Losses were also experienced by 161 Squadron, as out of five aircraft two were lost. Following the high losses experienced in early 1943, the original route to Warsaw was changed to a more northerly one over Sweden, which increased the distance to targets by 160 miles. This resulted in the supply flights only being practical in very good weather conditions.

An additional SOE unit was formed at Tempsford on 28 May 1943 in the form of 1575 (Special Duties) Flight equipped with four Halifax and two Venturas, plus crews detached from 138 Squadron. The task was to undertake SOE and SIS operations in the Mediterranean area from Maison Blanche in Northwest Africa, where the first two Halifaxes arrived on 11 June. The flight moved to Blida on 25 June, and operations were flown over Italy, Corsica and Sardinia with occasional flights to southern France. During its short existence, three Halifaxes were in use, and on 22 September 1943, the flight was redesignated 624 Squadron. It was still based at Blida operating Halifax IIs and Vs, with Venturas, until the Halifaxes were replaced by Stirlings in July 1944. No. 148 Squadron was already based in the Middle East on SOE duties and was reformed for Special Duties at Gambut on 14 March 1943 equipped with Liberators and Halifax Mk.IIs.

With Bomber Command in constant need of additional aircraft and crews, the decision was made in October 1943 to gradually replace 138 and 161 Squadrons' Halifaxes with Stirlings. The Stirling had a poor high-altitude performance, which was not required by the special duties' units, and was an ideal aircraft for the SOE role. This allowed the Halifaxes to be returned to the main force, but there was no let-up in operations, pending the change-over. Hudsons were also used by 616 Squadron, when only one or two agents were being dropped, rather than the larger Halifax. This resulted in 138 Squadron becoming an overall operator of Halifaxes from January 1944.

With the start of the new year in 1944, plans began to evolve in support of the expected invasion. For the first time, agents were to be dropped in Germany, with

Above: Leavesden-built Halifax B.II BB335 FS-M 148 Squadron loading supplies in the Middle East. It went to 148 Squadron in the Middle East on 1 March 1944 and was SOC on 24 April 1945. (*RAF Museum*)

Left: Leavesden-built Halifax B.II JP246 FS-B 148 Squadron fitted with improved fin/rudders. It was delivered to 10 APU on 12 March 1944 and SOC on 18 November 1944. (*RAF Museum*)

Above: Halifax B.IIs 148 Squadron. (*RAF Museum*)

Below: Halifax B.II JP245 being refuelled and prepared, ready for the next operation. It was delivered to 10 APU on 12 February 1944 and SOC on 1 April 1945. (*RAF Museum*)

two dropped by 161 Squadron at Schwarzwald near Stuttgart on 6/7 January. With some crews becoming tour expired at the end of January, personnel were transferred from 138 Squadron to balance the operations of both units during February. With the increased numbers of agents and supplies needing to be delivered, the intensity of operations became demanding for all special duties' squadrons. An example of the increased pressure was on the night of 9/10 April. No. 138 Squadron fielded sixteen Halifaxes and 161 Squadron sent up another seven, compared with the solo flights a year previously, but naturally losses increased.

On 5 April, 148 Squadron moved to Derna to make supply drops over Greece and the Balkans, where they achieved high accuracy. Despite primitive maintenance conditions and provision of supplies, the squadron continued a steady stream of operations, dropping seventy agents, plus containers and packages during August. So intensive were the operations, that it was estimated some 50,000 German troops were deployed away from the front lines to Greece, Albania and Yugoslavia. A move to Tocra on 1 September started with leaflet dropping over Greece, and although night fighters and flak were very much reduced compared with northern Europe, additional hazards were faced with weather and high ground. Many drops to partisans involved flying up valleys between high mountains in poor weather and unknown turbulence, which could easily cause loss of control, creating a challenge for recovery.

Further SOE support was provided in the Middle East by the formation of 1586 (SD) Flight at Derna on 3 November 1943, with crews from 138 Squadron Polish Flight to drop supplies to partisans in Poland, Yugoslavia and north Italy. There were ten crews with three Halifaxes and three Liberators. A move was made to Brindisi in January 1944, and it became 301 Squadron on 7 November 1944.

With the formation of 624 (SD) Squadron from 1575 Flight at Blida on 22 September 1943, the unit was equipped with Halifax Mk.IIs, Mk.Vs and Venturas, with Stirlings added briefly in July 1944. A detachment of 624 Squadron moved to Sidi Amor on 16 October, from where it operated until the whole squadron moved to Brindisi in late December, where, with 1586 Flight, it became part of 334 Wing. Operations restarted on 4 January 1944, consisting mainly of leaflet drops over Yugoslavia, Albania and Italy, but also supply and agent drops. A total of ninety-three missions were flown during January with a very high success rate. Unfortunately, the squadron suffered its first loss on 1 February when BB444 crashed at the DZ, from which only the rear gunner survived. The squadron was recalled to Blida on 8 February, with operations over France of between 12 and 14 sorties a night until it was disbanded on 4 September 1944, the Halifax crews transferring to 148 Squadron.

With the departure of 624 Squadron from Brindisi, its place was taken by 148 Squadron on 22 January. Working with 1586 Flight, operations were concentrated over the Balkans and central Europe with additional weapons drops in distant Poland. An early operation by 148 Squadron was a supply drop to Yugoslav partisans, with six out of eleven Halifaxes making successful deliveries.

In early 1944, most of the early Halifax Series Is (Special) with SOE units were replaced by Halifax Mk.IIs or Mk.Vs, with crew numbers reduced to give priority to larger payloads. The crews with 1586 Flight were reduced to two pilots, a navigator and dispatcher. A typical gross load was between 7,000 and 7,400lb, with agents usually between two or three, but sometimes up to five.

The Warsaw uprising commenced on 1 August 1944, supported by the Polish Home Army, taking control of large sections of the city. Having been taken by surprise, the SOE supply effort did not start until 4 August, with flights by both 148 Squadron and 1586 Flight that night. The conditions were chaotic with dense smoke masking flares required to mark the DZ with precision due to opposing forces being very close to each other. With the aircraft having to fly as low as 300 to 400 feet, four 148 Squadron Halifaxes were lost on the first night. Another Halifax crash-landed with the crew surviving the burning wreck and the sixth aircraft returned to base with its load due to being unable to identify the DZ. The Polish crews with 1586 Flight were more successful with three drops on target.

The high loss rate of experienced crews prompted Air Marshal Slessor to withdraw permission for further operations, but political pressure forced him to allow Polish crews to continue in the defence of their homeland, while British crews were to abstain until longer nights. Polish operations restarted on 8/9 August, soon supported by SAAF Liberator squadrons with equally disastrous results. As the battle continued, enemy flak defences were increased along the supply route, with a very heavy concentration around Warsaw itself. To get below the line of fire of the flak batteries, crews were having to fly as low as 100 feet with losses still high. An example was the loss of five aircraft over the city on one mission. The surviving aircraft were usually so badly damaged on return, they needed extensive repairs. The ultimate price paid by Allied aircrews was recognised by the general in command in Warsaw, General Bor-Komorowski.

The Polish 1586 Flight was already short of aircraft and crews due to losses during operations over Yugoslavia and Italy, and some Halifaxes were loaned by 148 Squadron, but in the event they were only able to make a token effort, with Halifax reserves eroded throughout the Mediterranean. In an effort to make up the numbers of aircraft, ten Halifaxes were passed to 334 Wing from Bomber Command, but delays were caused by having to strip out bomber systems and configure them for SOE operations, all of which took too much time. Despite this, the first nine modified aircraft were delivered to Brindisi from 30 August and 1 September, while 1586 Flight flew eighty supply missions and 148 Squadron 116 supply missions during August. Further aircraft deliveries were delayed to 334 Wing when a number of Mk.Vs were delivered to 144 MU and found to require major inspection and overhaul. The Merlin XXs fitted had to be replaced by Merlin 22s before going on operations. Unfortunately, due to the raging fire and activities of the enemy, less than half the supplies reached the Warsaw defenders. With bad weather starting in September, the Polish forces surrendered.

With 138 Squadron re-equipping with Stirlings from June 1944 at Tempsford, the last Halifax sortie was on 31 August in a mixed force of Halifaxes and Stirlings, as part of large drop on a French DZ. One Halifax was shot down by an enemy night fighter, as well as two Stirlings. In October, 148 Squadron were also allocated to daylight operations, but weather conditions were demanding with high turbulence over the mountains, together with frequent thunderstorms, reducing accuracy of the drops. With the flares difficult to detect in daylight, they were replaced by smoke markers, allowing a precision accuracy of supplies delivery from the bomb-bay and out of the supplies hatch.

The Polish crews with 1586 Flight continued night operations over Czechoslovakia, Yugoslavia, Bulgaria, Austria and Crete, with twenty additional drops to Polish troops behind enemy lines. With its increased strength, the flight was brought up to a full squadron and became 301 (SD) Squadron on 7 November 1944 at Brindisi, equipped with Halifax IIs and Vs, plus Liberators until March 1945. The squadron made the last supply drop to Poland on 28 December due to advancing Soviet forces. A couple of Stirlings were delivered to 148 Squadron in November, but in the next month the decision was made to convert to Liberators. The delivery was delayed, resulting in a successful Halifax supply drop to Soviet forces in January. Agents, a Jeep and supplies were dropped to partisans in northern Italy during January.

With the reduced need for the SOE operations, 301 Squadron was transferred to transport duties on 28 February and 624 Squadron was disbanded on 5 September 1944 at Blida, leaving only 148 Squadron, which was allocated to the support of final ground operations in Italy, continuing until VE Day. With the coming of peace, the squadron flew five Halifaxes to evacuate POWs from Yugoslavia, and made its conversion to Liberators on 23 May 1945, the surviving Halifaxes going to 144 MU at Maison Blanche in North Africa.

6

Mediterranean Operations with Merlin Halifaxes

In June 1942, Rommel's Afrika Korps had advanced along North Africa and was facing a British force from Tobruk, which, if defeated, would threaten Britain's oil fields in the Middle East, as well as denying Allied use of the vital Suez Canal. The British 8th Army had been driven back by Rommel's Africa Corps, but left a powerful garrison in Tobruk, which was the only major port between Benghazi and Alexandria. To sustain his thrust forward, Rommel needed to capture the port for essential supplies of fuel and ammunition, without which his army would become stagnated. British army troops in Tobruk provided a garrison to the German forces rear, which would allow a counterattack to be mounted. With Tobruk in Rommel's control, his supply lines would be greatly improved, ready for his armour, supported by bombers, to sweep forward across Egypt to Cairo and the Suez Canal.

Tobruk fell on 21 June 1942, with the surrender of 25,000 men to enemy forces less than half their number. As a result, the Royal Navy Eastern Fleet had to withdraw from its role in hampering Rommel's supplies across the Mediterranean and preventing a seaborne invasion of Egypt. To avoid enemy air attack, it withdrew south through the Suez Canal from Alexandria, with the role of the fleet taken over by the air forces.

There was an urgent need for more aircraft, with Air Chief Marshal Tedder looking for additional resources in the Mediterranean Theatre. The Minister of State for the Middle East also requested Winston Churchill for more heavy bombers. As a result, two Halifax squadrons were rapidly deployed. Both 10 and 76 Squadrons each sent sixteen aircraft to Aqir in Palestine, with the Italian fleet at Taranto as targets, becoming 249 Wing in 205 Group. The 10 Squadron detachment with the first two Halifax Mk.IIs arrived at Aqir on 5 July as 10/227 Squadron, becoming 462 Squadron on 7 September 1942. Halifax IIs with 76 Squadron arrived on detachment at Aqir in October as 76/462 Squadron, joining 462 Squadron also on 7 September 1942. The combining of the two Halifax units from Britain was for maintenance efficiencies. Two 10 Squadron Halifaxes were lost on the delivery flight, and three were delayed in Gibraltar due to unserviceability.

Above: Radlett-built Halifax B.II W7755 MP-A 76 Squadron at Fayid before becoming 462 Squadron. This aircraft was delivered to 76 Squadron on 22 June 1942 and flew to the Middle East on 18 July. It was SOC on 1 March 1944. (*RAF Museum*)

Below: Armourers rolling 500lb bombs under a 462 Squadron Halifax B.II at Fayid in December 1942. (*Air Historical Branch*)

Above: Radlett-built Halifax B.II W7671 W 76 Squadron flying over the desert on another sortie in 1942. (*RAF Museum*)

Below: A 76 Squadron Halifax B.II being bombed up at Fayid, including a 4,000lb 'Cookie' with extended tail fin fairing. (*RAF Museum*)

Halifax B.II of 462 Squadron at Fayid in 1942. (*RAF Museum*)

On arrival at Aqir, the crews were expecting a short detachment of sixteen days, but were told to prepare for a long stay, which would have impacted on domestic arrangements at home. The first operation was flown on 11/12 July by 10 Squadron against Tobruk with a single Halifax. On the night of 13/14 July, one of the four Halifaxes was lost when W1171 was brought down by flak and crash-landed. The port of Tubruk remained the main target for RAF Halifaxes and Wellingtons, complemented by USAAF Liberators bombing Benghazi, depriving German forces of essential supplies. The extended time of the detachment resulted in many equipment failures, particularly hydraulic systems and engine overheating, with inadequate spares support.

With less hostile skies than mainland Europe, despite continuous raids on Tobruk, loss rates were low with a 76 Squadron Halifax forced to crash-land after being hit by flak, but without injuries to the crew. Bombing of Tubruk was reasonably successful despite reduced visibility caused by haze which made damage assessment difficult. A 10 Squadron Halifax was lost on the night of 5/6 August when an engine was hit by flak and another engine overheated with the pilot having to ditch, although the crew were all rescued.

The failure of Rommel's offensive in September was mainly caused by lack of supplies, in particular fuel stocks being critical. A convenient staging point for German supplies was the island of Crete, Heraklion airfield presenting an excellent target for 249 Wing on 5 September, each squadron to provide six aircraft.

Crash-landing after flack damage of Samlesbury-built Halifax B.II W1176 462 Squadron at Fayid on 29 September 1942. It was delivered to 10 Squadron on 25 June 1942 and flown to the Middle East on 6 July. As a result of the crash-landing, it was SOC on 6 October 1942. (*RAF Museum*)

However, unserviceability reduced this number, with two 76 Squadron Halifaxes aborting, plus one from 10 Squadron. On the way to the target, the force was further reduced when a 10 Squadron Halifax had to abort due to engine failure. The first wave hit many of the aircraft dispersed on the airfield and damaged the runways for no RAF losses. One Halifax from the second wave was shot down in flames and a second was badly damaged by defending Bf 109s, but was able to return to Fayid. In the third wave, the lead Halifax was shot down soon after dropping its bombs and the remaining two aircraft suffered minor flak and fighter damage, but returned to base.

On 7 September, when the two squadron detachments were amalgamated to become 462 Squadron RAAF, Tobruk was still the primary target. In support of a combined army and naval offensive on 13 September, fourteen Halifaxes bombed the target without loss, some coming down to 8,000 feet, while the surface forces suffered heavy casualties. Crete was bombed again on 10 October as part of a sustained programme between 6 September and 24 October to reduce the supplies to the Afrika Korps, in addition to 183 sorties to Tobruk, leading up to the decisive Battle of El Alamein on 23 October 1942. In support of the British ground forces, 462 Squadron bombed targets in the battle zone, the first of four night attacks being made on 5 November with enemy transport as the targets. In addition to bombing, Halifaxes reduced altitude progressively from 9,000 feet to 5,000 feet using their guns against ground target. Following the first series of attacks, the crews flew as low as 1,200 feet to increase effectiveness of ground strafing.

The squadron then made a number of moves around some of the specially prepared, but spartan landing grounds, to be closer to potential targets in Crete and Tripolitania. A move was made back to LG237 on 17 December, from where about 90 per cent of the crews were returned home due to becoming tour expired. With new crews becoming trained, a move was made to Solluch in January 1943, bringing targets in Sicily within range due to Allied advances. The new campaign was started on 29 January when six Halifaxes dropped 29,000lb of bombs on a rail ferry terminal at Messina, with a repeat two nights later by seven aircraft.

With a short lull in the land battle, General Montgomery was able to consolidate his forces ready for the next offensive. In support, the bomber force made a series of attacks on German airfields by 462 Squadron bombing Gabes-West airfield each night from 23 to 26 February. Major enemy troop reinforcements were identified by reconnaissance to the south of Garbes, where there were concentrations of motor transport and armour, resulting in bombing by 462 Squadron, moving on to other targets in El Hamma, Oudref and Wadi Akrit. A high number of engine failures were experienced in April, reducing capability, the unavailability of replacements requiring often cannibalising unserviceable aircraft to keep as many as possibly operational. Eventually, with some 60 per cent of the Halifaxes affected, they were transferred to 61 RSU to wait for replacement Merlins. With supplies improving by the end of the month, the squadron was returned to strength, but even the locally overhauled replacements caused problems with failures within 40 flying hours from being fitted. To help reduce some strain on the Merlins, permission was given to remove the drag and weight of the front and mid-upper gun turrets.

The North African Campaign finally ended with the defeat and surrender of the Afrika Korps on 13 May 1943. During early May, attacks were mainly against troop and transport concentrations in Tunisia and 462 Squadron was joined by 178 Squadron based at Hose Raui which began to replace its Liberators with Halifaxes during the month. With North Africa in Allied control, the next major step was the invasion of Sicily, to be followed by the Italian mainland. This increased the 205 Group target areas to include the industrial north of Italy, Austria and the Balkans.

The first operation to Italy was on the night of 31 May 1943, by 462 Squadron from Hose Raui. As with all the short-term airfields in North Africa, conditions were primitive, and often a muddy mess due to heavy rain. Merlin engine failures continued to plague operations, with some aircraft coming off an overhaul and experiencing engine failure on the delivery flight to the squadron. For night raids. the flare path party remained on standby for at least an hour after departure, in case of any premature returns. In the high temperatures and with a heavy full load, if one engine failed. the crew had to unload the bombs and return to base, as height could not be maintained on three engines. With the extra strain on the remaining three engines it was not unheard of for at least one more to lose power, some Halifaxes managing to just get back to base on just two engines.

With an almost total lack of navigation aids in the Mediterranean theatre, crews were forced to resort to the basic principles of astro-navigation and dead reckoning, which made operations less accurate. In an attempt to overcome these restrictions, four most able crews were selected, with two on each night operation to act as pathfinders, to locate and mark the target with flares over the 5 to 10 minutes of each raid. To confirm accurate target marking, as well as assessing damage, crews took photographs during the attack, with both air and ground crew morale improving significantly. The hardworking ground crews particularly benefitted, many having served in the desert for over eighteen months without any break in the most demanding conditions.

Major improvements were made with overhaul standards of Merlin engines following visits by Rolls-Royce representatives, and further benefits to reliability with the arrival of Merlin 22-powered Halifaxes. Some of these improved aircraft came from 178 Squadron, which converted back to Liberators in September 1943, making its last Halifax flight on 7/8 September, having only operated them from May 1943. The replacement aircraft made a significant improvement to operational efficiency with a marked reduction in engine failures. With a great of effort by the ground crew, Halifax Mk.II W1169, which was an original 76 Squadron aircraft, achieved fifty operations by September, and continued in service until March 1944, when it was finally struck off charge due to age.

For the remainder of the year, 462 Squadron continued bombing Italian and Greek airfields during October and November, followed diversionary raids to cover mining operations around mainland Greece and Crete, and anti-shipping raids in Suda bay and Piraeus. On 1 January 1944, the squadron moved from Terria to El Adem, the road transport for the move being a collection of captured German and Italian vehicles. Due to bad weather in January, only seven raids were made, with news received on 19 January of a planned move to Italy when the unit would become the pathfinding squadron for night bombing forces. In preparation for these new duties, a number of crews were returned to Britain for training in the navigation skills, returning by the end of the month with Halifaxes fitted with H2S and the Mk. XIV bombsight. Due to an intense training period for the ground crews on the new equipment, only twenty-one sorties were flown and the squadron began its move to Celone in Italy on 15 February, where it was renumbered 614 Squadron, with the demanding duties of pathfinding and target marking for the 205 Group night bomber force using basic dead reckoning and astro navigation. Weather conditions from northern Europe improved and, quite often, targets were close to the coast which made target location more successful.

The new squadron was soon operational with eight Halifaxes marking railway a marshalling yard on 10 April near Sofia in Bulgaria, successfully illuminated the target and returned to base without loss. This was followed by a marshalling yard in Genoa, bombing successfully from 16,000 feet in poor weather conditions. The next operation was a disaster for the squadron, with four out of nine Halifaxes lost, mainly due to very bad weather, and one crew successfully abandoning their aircraft. Following more operations, the squadron stood down for more specialised training, in preparation for full target marking duties for 205 Group. There were two operational flights of eight H2S-equipped Halifaxes each and a training flight consisting of four

Above: Leavesden-built Halifax B.II Series 1A JN976 of 614 Squadron at Celone, Italy after heavy rain in March 1944. It was originally delivered to the RAF on 6 November 1943 and SOC in April 1945. (*Air Historical Branch*)

Below: Leavesden-built Halifax B.II JP321 V 614 Squadron damaged by anti-aircraft rockets while on a pathfinding raid on marshalling yards at Szombatheley, Hungary 22/23 November 1944. As a result of this damage, the aircraft was struck off charge in February 1945. (*Air Historical Branch*)

Leavesden-built Halifax B.II JP259 614 Squadron being reassembled, having had major repairs at 144 MU Maison Blanch in November 1944. In the background is a 301 (Polish) Squadron aircraft. JP259 went missing on 23 August 1944. (*Air Historical Branch*)

H2S aircraft, and two dual non-H2S Halifaxes. The specialist crews were experienced in night operations, many converting to Halifaxes from other types and training on marking techniques with the squadron. During training, the first operational target marking was carried out on 10 April, when eight Halifaxes successfully illuminated marshalling yards at Plovdiv. The following raids achieved many successes at a very low loss rate.

On 10 May, the squadron moved to Stornara with oil installations becoming prime targets during June and July. For a mine laying operation in the Danube on 1/2 July, three of the squadron Halifaxes provided route markers, the purpose being to delay shipments of oil by barges. Five nights later, 614 Squadron marked Fuersbrunn airfield for a bomber attack which destroyed nineteen enemy aircraft and the damage to the site was so complete, the remaining fifty or so aircraft were unable to operate. One Halifax was shot down by night fighters, in addition to ten Wellingtons and two Liberators. As well as performing its pathfinding operations, 614 Squadron also was allocated to bombing duties. Targets were allocated further north and spreading out across France including on 3 August, identifying marshalling yards at Valence for an attack by Wellingtons and Liberators. This was followed by the well-defended Ploesti oil refineries in Rumania, when two Halifaxes were shot down.

On 15 August 1944, the invasion of southern France commenced as Operation Dragoon with the Mediterranean Allied Strategic Air Force in full support. In preparation for the operation, 614 Squadron successfully marked the docks at Genoa and Marseilles on 13 and 14 August, but due to thick haze over the target, the attack on Valence airfield was unsuccessful. With Allied advances progressing well, 614 Squadron supported the British 8th Army by bombing troop concentrations at Pesaro in Italy, as well as marshalling yards at Bologna and Bovenna.

As part of the overall reequipping of all 205 Group squadrons, in August 1944, 614 Squadron began to convert to Liberators at Amendola, although Halifaxes were still used for bombing marshalling yards in Zagreb on 16 October, together with Liberators. With selected crews awarded the PFF badge in October, their skills were formally recognised. Two Halifaxes were detached to the Balkan Air Force to mark DZs in Yugoslavia for SOE operations, as a start of a number of marking or supply drops. These were followed by bombing troop concentrations and airfields, including mixed operations of Halifaxes and Liberators against bridges, including Matesevo on

Radlett-built Halifax B.III LW125 on a visit to North Africa. This aircraft was delivered to the A&AEE at Boscombe Down on 2 May 1944, flying to the Middle East on 31 August and North Africa on 30 November. It was finally SOC at A&AEE on 26 July 1945. (*Alan Dowsett*)

Above: Halifax B.III LW125 with the name 'Sarie Marais' on the nose. (*Alan Dowsett*)

Below: A top side view of Halifax B.III LW125 showing the camouflage pattern. (*Alan Dowsett*)

Radlett-built Halifax A.VII PP375 620 Squadron at Aqir. It was delivered to the RAF on 25 September 1945 and went to Pershore on 11 March 1946. It was flown to the Middle East on 10 April and was sold for scrap to J. Dale on 5 January 1949. (*Alan Dowsett*)

19 December. The bridge was destroyed and a motor convoy shot up by the aircraft guns.

With so many active operations, pathfinding by 614 Squadron was limited to marking three northern Italian bridges in late December, while still becoming highly skilled in supply dropping. In late January 1945, after being grounded due to bad weather, marshalling yards at Udine were bombed, with attacks on Italian targets and dropping supplies to the Yugoslav partisans continuing. On 3 March 1945, 614 Squadron made its final Halifax operation against an oil installation at Port Marhamo.

In July 1945, 620 Squadron replaced its Stirlings with Halifax A.VII at Great Dunmow with a move to Aqir on 15 January 1946. A move was made to Cairo West on 6 March 1946, when Dakotas were added in June at Aqir, with Halifax A.IXs in August. The squadron was disbanded on 1 September 1946 when it was renumbered 113 Squadron.

7

The Hercules-Powered Halifax Bomber Development and Operations

During the Second World War, many combat aircraft retained their basic airframe, but relied on improvements by using engines of ever-increasing power, reliability and economy. The Halifax was no exception. With original examples powered by early versions of the Merlin, there was a definite need for improvement in reliability and performance. The answer came in the form of the air-cooled Bristol Hercules radial engines, the initial example being the Hercules VI developing 1,615bhp with two speed superchargers, four of which were fitted to Mk.II HP development aircraft R9534. This prototype was delivered to Boscombe Down in February 1943, ready for full scale testing, not only of engines, but overall handling. On 4 June 1943, this aircraft was designated the prototype Halifax B.Mk.III. A retractable tail wheel was fitted in time for intensive flight trials starting on 17 July, by which time the aircraft had flown some 85 hours, to which the trials added a further 67 hours. The initial climb performance tests from Boscombe Down were disappointing due to drag from engine cooling gills, which had to be open to maintain satisfactory temperature limits. Control with the new large 'D' fins was completely satisfactory.

Prototype Halifax B.Mk.III R9534, converted from a Radlett-built B.II, at Boscombe Down in November 1942. It is fitted with a mid-upper and rear gun turrets. (*RAF Museum*)

Classic side view of Halifax B.III prototype at A&AEE Boscombe Down in November 1942. It still features the original fins and rudders shape. (*RAF Museum*)

Flight trials in R9534 were carried out by two crews seconded from active squadrons in addition to service test pilots from 4 Group, with engineering support from operational squadron ground crews. From 27 August to 7 September, the prototype was operated away from base and flown by regular RAF Bomber Command crews, with a routine 150-hour check carried out in the field during the deployment. After forty-four flights, it was returned to Handley Page to have any resulting modifications incorporated, particularly to control services and wing structure.

The first production B.Mk.III, HX226, made its first flight on 29 August 1943 and following HP flight testing, was delivered to Boscombe Down on 12 September as a fully operational capable aircraft, powered by Hercules XVIs fitted with automatic carburettors. Service flight trials were undertaken from 14 September to 22 October with forty-five flights totalling 150 flying hours, the results being good with the trials completed quicker than any other four engine aircraft. Engine tests were found to achieve an increase in altitude of 1,000 feet. The AUW was cleared to 63,000lb, which included a total fuel load of 2,688 gallons. The Halifax had now become the aircraft it should have been, with improved all round performance and reliability.

As production became established, three of the early Mk.IIIs, HX227, HX229 and HX238, were allocated to further flight trials. HX227 and HX229 were delivered to the A&AEE to investigate air intake, carburetion and heating improvements, with cooling problems still persisting until June 1944, when fully flared propellers were fitted. HX226 was then allocated to fuel consumption measurement. At a take-off weight of 63,000lb and a bomb load of 8,500lb, range was estimated to be 1,800 miles, increasing by 50 miles with a 5-foot increase in wingspan.

Three B.Mk.IIIs were allocated to armament trials at Boscombe Down, including the Type D tail turret with two 0.5-inch guns assisted by radar in HX226 in early

Above: Early Radlett-built Halifax B.III HX283 fitted with new fins and rudders and H2S ground mapping radar under the fuselage. It is carrying guns in the nose, mid-upper position and tail. (*RAF Museum*)

Below: Radlett-built Halifax B.III HX833 fitted with new fins and rudders, plus H2S, but no gun in the nose. (*Alan Dowsett*)

Above: Radlett-built Halifax B.III LV838 fitted with a pannier under the bomb-bay. (*Handley Page Association*)

Below: Showing the camouflage pattern of Halifax B.III armed with mid-upper and tail turrets and H2S radar under the fuselage. (*Alan Dowsett*)

Above: Halifax B.III with Hercules engines apparently stopped, in formation with a Halifax engine development aircraft. (*Alan Dowsett*)

Below: Production Halifax B.III at Boscombe Down in January 1944 with full defensive gun armament, H2S and improved fins and rudders. (*RAF Museum*)

1944. This resulted in a slight yaw when rotated at cruising speed. Later in the year, HX238 was fitted with deflectors to assist rotation, but reduced top speed by 3mph. In August 1944, LV999/G covered further tests on the Boulton Paul Type D turret with radar assistance.

The first batch of B.Mk.IIIs were allocated to 35 Squadron at Graveley in October 1943, plus another three squadrons. On 3 November, 466 Squadron took delivery of its first example, HX244 at Leconfield, but it crash-landed four days later. Number 433 Squadron began reequipping at Skipton-on-Swale in November, but had an early loss when control was lost in HX345 on 19 December. It crashed inverted on a parked HX277 at Skipton-on-Swale, killing five flight crew and one on the ground. During December, 424 Squadron began to exchange its Wellingtons in return for Halifax B.IIIs also at Skipton-on-Swale, which it kept until January 1945 when Lancasters replaced the Halifaxes.

Crews became familiar with the Halifaxes, which were fitted with H2S by working parties, after converting from Wellingtons, and 466 Squadron started operations on 1 December with twelve Halifaxes mine laying off Terschelling. On 21/22 December, 35 Squadron sent four Mk.IIIs to Frankfurt, with one shot down and another made an emergency landing when a target indicator exploded on the final approach. The pilot climbed to 2,000 feet to allow five members of the crew to bale out, but as the mid-upper gunner's parachute had been destroyed by the fire, Squadron Leader Sale landed the burning aircraft and taxied off the runway. Both remaining crew members were able to evacuate the aircraft and were clear when it exploded. On 29/30 December, 466 Squadron sent fifteen Mk.IIIs as part of the Berlin offensive, returning to Leconfield without loss.

By the middle of January 1944, nine Bomber Command squadrons had become operational on Mk.IIIs with 35 Squadron sending nine Mk.IIIs and four Mk.IIs to Berlin on 21/22 January. The experienced crews of the Mk.II-equipped C Flight of

Poor quality image of 424 Squadron Halifax B.III taxiing with two crew members on the fuselage top. (*RAF Museum*)

Above: Samlesbury-built Halifax B.III MZ896 QB-O 424 Squadron at Skipton-on-Swale on 13 November 1944 with 57 mission score on the nose. (*Handley Page Association*)

Below: Take-off of Halifax B.III with mid-upper and tail gun turrets, H2S radar and the improved fins and rudders shape (*Handley Page Association*)

158 Squadron became the nucleus of 640 (RCAF) Squadron at Leconfield, when it formed on 7 January and similarly, the C Flight of 51 Squadron became the nucleus of 578 Squadron, which formed at Snaith on 14 January 1944. Diversionary raids to Kiel and Hanover failed to conceal the target destination with large numbers of night fighters meeting the bomber stream as it crossed the German coast. No. 640 Squadron managed to send eight Halifaxes, but one had to return to Coltishall with major damage from a night fighter. Of the remaining seven, five were able to drop their bomb load on, or close to the aiming point. The other two returned early, one with

640 Squadron personnel in front of Halifax B.III at Leconfield on 6 May 1945, celebrating the end of the Second World War. (*RAF Museum*)

engine unserviceability, and the other with an ill navigator. Six Halifaxes were sent by 578 Squadron with five bombing the target through cloud.

From December 1943, the new aircraft were also fitted with an improved tail warning system known as Visual Monica or Fishpond, which featured a cathode ray display in place of the earlier aural signal. This overcame almost continuous warnings in a busy bomber stream. The new system detected high-speed hostile fighters on the H2S screen and was in full production by July.

To achieve a greater AUW to 65,000lb, it was necessary to increase the wingspan to 103 feet 8 inches by extending the wing tips on B.Mk.II HR845, which was flight tested at Boscombe Down in January 1944. The rate of climb was increased by to

Above: Samlesbury-built Halifax B.III MZ543 LK-X 578 Squadron at Burn named 'Intuition?' with the seven aircrew. (*RAF Museum*)

Left: Samlesbury-built Halifax B.III MZ559 LK-F 578 Squadron damaged by a bomb falling from above while in formation over the target on 4 September 1944. (*Handley Page Association*)

Halifax B.III MZ559 during repairs, including replacing the entire rear fuselage, demonstrating the modular construction of the Halifax. (*Handley Page Association*)

up to 120 feet per minute, cruising ceiling by 1,700 feet and cruising speed by up to 10mph. The new wing tips were rapidly introduced on production lines with the modified Halifaxes in service by February. Meanwhile an early production B.Mk. III, HX339, was flown at Boscombe Down in January and passed the acceptance programme successfully, although the extended wing tips had not been fitted.

By the end of the year, Mk.IIIs were becoming operational with the 4 and 6 Group squadrons, reequipping continuing until July when 347 Squadron began replacing its Mk.Vs with Mk.IIIs at Elvington. Another early unit to receive Mk.IIIs was 432 Squadron which received its first Mk.III at East Moor in February 1944, replacing Lancasters. The first operational losses of Mk.IIIs were HX236 and HX273, which failed to return after a raid on Frankfurt on 21/22 December. No. 433 Squadron used four Mk.IIIs as part of a mining operation off the French coast on 2 January 1944, but the squadron lost HX283 during a raid on Magdeburg with nine Mk.IIIs on 21/22 January. No. 158 Squadron, began to reequip with Mk.IIIs at Lisset in December 1943.

Despite early losses, the overall rate was reducing over the previous operations with the Merlin-powered aircraft, an example being no losses by 433 Squadron during nearly 400 sorties in the early part of 1944. At least four Mk.IIIs were to achieve 100 or more combat operations, with many others not far short. One example was LV907 with 158 Squadron, followed by 158 Squadron aircraft LW587 (104) and MZ527 (105), which both reached 100 on the same raid to Kamen on 3/4 March 1945. Another 578 Squadron Mk.III, LV937 achieved its hundredth operation when with 51 Squadron. It is a great shame not one was preserved for posterity.

Above: Ringway-built Halifax B.III PN167 L8-D 347 (Tunisie) Squadron, Free French Air Force at Elvington. (*Handley Page Association*)

Below: Crew with Halifax B.III of 347 Free French Squadron at Elvington. Amongst the nose art are forty-seven bombing sorties recorded. (*Philip Birtles*)

Above: Radlett-built Halifax B.III LV907 *Friday the 13th* of 158 Squadron at Lisset with over 100 bombing operations recorded. (*Alan Dowsett*)

Below: The crew with Halifax B.III LV907 at Lisset with forty-five bombing operations recorded by the aircraft. (*RAF Museum*)

Halifax B.III LV907 NP-F 158 Squadron on display in London's Oxford Street in June 1945, celebrating the end of the war. Although this aircraft was not saved for preservation, it has been reproduced at the Yorkshire Air Museum at Elvington. (*RAF Museum*)

A memorial to 158 Squadron has been erected at Lisset, and shows in boiler plate an image of a typical crew walking to their Halifax, looking serious. When viewed from the other side, they have returned and are looking relaxed having survived. (*Philip Birtles*)

Radlett-built Halifax B.III LV937 MH-E 51 Squadron *Expensive Babe* with 100 bombing operations marked on the nose. (*RAF Museum*)

Berlin was always a difficult target to define precise aiming points, as there were few clear landmarks to be identified by H2S. As part of the ending of the Battle of Berlin, an all Halifax Mk.III force of fifty-nine aircraft from 51, 158, 466 and 640 Squadrons were part of a force of eighty-two Halifaxes, 446 Lancasters and twelve Mosquitos which bombed central and south west areas of the city, with no losses in 4 Group to enemy action, but one Mk.II Halifax was lost, together with thirty-two Lancasters. By February 1944, seven of the 4 Group ten squadrons had replaced their earlier Halifaxes with the Mk.IIIs. On 19/20 February, 255 Halifaxes, 561 Lancasters and seven Mosquitos headed for Leipzig including 78 Squadron, which had just reequipped with Mk.IIIs. This latest version performed better than the Lancaster, although increased fuel consumption reduced the bomb load. The main target was a major rail junction, marked by the PFF, the main force approaching in five waves with 23 minutes over the target. However, it was a bad night for Bomber Command. A diversionary raid with Stirlings mining in Kiel Bay and Mosquitos to Berlin failed to attract attention from night fighters, with interceptions starting soon after crossing the coast. The attacks became more ferocious all the way to the target. A change in winds caused some bombers to arrive early, resulting in them having to orbit while waiting for the target to be marked by the PFF, making them also vulnerable to flak. A total of seventy-eight bombers were shot down of which sixteen were Halifaxes in 4 Group. This was the highest Bomber Command losses of the war so far.

A typical bomb load being raised by armourers into a Halifax B.III, mainly consisting of 500lb bombs. (*RAF Museum*)

During the week of 19 to 25 February, Allied bombers concentrated on German towns which contained fighter production lines, or support industries. Over 8,000 sorties were flown with around 19,000 tons of bombs dropped. Throughout the remainder of February and March, the intensive campaign by Bomber Command continued, included Schweinfurt, Stuttgart and Augsburg, attacked between 20 and 25 February. A new tactic was introduced for the Schweinfurt raid, where the 734 bomber force was split into two waves, the second following 2 hours later. While German night fighters and other defences accounted for twenty-two losses, they were reduced by half in the second wave, with only four believed to have been destroyed by night fighters. Seven of the total losses were Halifaxes. The Augsburg raid on 21 February was a success with over 60 per cent of the target destroyed for the loss of five Halifaxes and sixteen Lancasters. Two further attacks were made on each of Stuttgart and Frankfurt, and on the night of 24/25 March, Berlin was the target for the last time in the year due to the shorter nights, and high losses. Bomber Command despatched 811 aircraft on this major target, but very high winds caused many aircraft to be blown off course or overshoot the target. On the return flight, the bomber stream became very scattered, making the aircraft vulnerable to flak and searchlight defences. Seventy-two bombers were lost, with at least fifty destroyed by radar directed flak guns. At least fifteen Halifaxes were destroyed by night fighters, with

78 Squadron losing six of their sixteen crews. Total bomber losses during the Battle of Berlin were worse than the 500 predicted by Harris. The actual losses during the battle were 625 bombers and the destruction of the capital city certainly did not force an early German surrender. Despite immense damage, the city continued to function as a centre of government with major armament production capability.

During this period, losses of Halifax Mk.IIs and Mk.Vs became unsustainable and they were permanently withdrawn from bombing operation over Germany. By this time, only three units in 4 Group were still flying these earlier marks, being 10, 77 and 102 Squadrons. These squadrons were then used on mining and against French targets.

The final heavy bomber raid of the winter was made on 30/31 March when 795 bombers went to Nuremberg. Due to bad weather over the North Sea, diversionary raids were not possible, resulting in massed enemy night fighters intercepting the bombers. Due to unpredicted high winds at operating altitudes, the bomber stream was widely scattered, with the protection of high cloud cover lost while crossing Belgium. The enemy night fighters were deployed over Bonn and Frankfurt where they were ideally placed to intercept the approaching bombers. It is believed at least fifty bombers were shot down before the target was reached, with thirty-one Halifaxes

Halifax B.III MZ359 KN-G 77 Squadron with H2S radar under the fuselage. (*Handley Page Association*)

Above: Leavesden-built Halifax B.III MZ359 KN-G 77 Squadron turning over Full Sutton, ready for landing. (*RAF Museum*)

Below: The aircrew of B Flight 102 Squadron in front of Halifax B.III at Pocklington on 3 April 1945. (*RAF Museum*)

destroyed out of 214 in the raid. Seven Halifaxes were lost by 51 Squadron, which included one which crashed on landing, killing the crew.

On this raid, the only Victoria Cross was awarded to a Halifax crew member. Pilot Officer Cyril Barton was flying LK979 with 578 Squadron on his nineteenth mission. Seventy miles from the target night fighters put out of action his intercom, damaged an engine and put all the guns out of action. With no intercom, a signal to the crew was misunderstood, resulting in the navigator, wireless operator and bomb aimer all bailing out. Despite these setbacks, Barton continued to the target and released the bombs on Nuremberg himself. With great difficulties, Barton successfully navigated the return, crossing the English coast, 90 miles north of his base at Burn, but with fuel running low and insufficient height to bale out, he crash-landed at Ryehope in Northumberland, killing Barton, but saving the flight engineer and two gunners, resulting in the posthumous award.

The raid cost Bomber Command ninety-five aircraft with eleven others damaged beyond repair, amounting to 11.9 per cent loss rate, the highest of the war for Bomber Command. The bombing was so scattered, that little damage was done to any significant targets. In what was known as the Battle of Berlin during the winter of 1943/44, Bomber Command suffered the highest rate of losses in the war. On the fourteen attacks on the city, a total of 384 aircraft were lost.

A reduction in bombing of Ruhr industries allowed Bomber Command to start making long-term preparations for the Allied invasion of occupied Europe. This started with some attacks against French and Belgian significant railway installations, including junctions and marshalling yards. The Transport Plan identified seventy-two transportation targets in France, Belgium and Germany, continuing until the beginning in June. The targets included railways, rolling stock, marshalling yards and major rail junctions, also including repair and maintenance facilities, roads and bridges.

The destruction of communications was intended to prevent German employment of reserves to attack the invasion forces at the start of the landings. Allied bombing started in northern France and Paris area in the hope that the German high command might believe the invasion would be along the Pas-de-Calais. Later, when the focus was on Normandy, it was still essential to destroy communications on a wide front, not only to divert enemy attention, but also to stop supplies from further afield.

This programme commenced with a 261 Halifax force bombing Trappes marshalling yards on 6/7 March 1944 marked by the PFF. Visibility for this raid was excellent with the attack led by 119 bombers from 6 Group, followed by the second wave 136 Halifaxes from 4 Group with six Oboe PFF Mosquito responsible for marking. Bombing was from 12,000 and 15,000 feet, with hits grouped closely round the aiming point and the target heavily damaged overall. In total, 1,258 tons of bombs were dropped with no aircraft losses, the installation being taken out of use for about five weeks. The next night, the railway installations at Le Mans were bombed by over 300 aircraft, including 121 4 Group Halifaxes and despite heavy cloud cover over the target, the attack was very successful, and for the second night running all crews returned safely.

Every effort was made to avoid civilian casualties when attacking Belgian and French targets and numbers were kept to a minimum by the Master Bomber ensuring bombing was accurate. Unfortunately, on 13/14 March, when Le Mans was again the target, despite the attack being accurate, some 100 French civilians were killed and one 78 Squadron aircraft was lost. Two nights later, the main force returned to Germany, with a long-range attack on Stuttgart, but bombing was inaccurate due to poor marking. Five Halifaxes were lost during the raid and two more from 578 Squadron crashed on return.

On the nights of 18 and 22 March, heavy Bomber Command raids were made on Frankfurt with over 1,600 sorties and more than 3,000 tons of bombs dropped. Out of 114 4 Group Halifaxes on the first attack, eighty-nine claimed to have bombed the target, with eight Halifaxes lost. On the second attack accurate ground marking resulted in highly concentrated bombing, with fires reaching up to 4,000 feet above the ground, but night fighters were active towards the end of the raid.

During March, 4 Group Halifaxes bombed marshalling yards at Aulnoye and Paris-Vaires, followed by a very successful attack on the Krupps works at Essen, where it was possible to outwit the German night fighter controller. On 9 April, 3, 4, 6 and 8 Groups bombed rail targets at Lille and Villeneuve-St-George causing widespread damage, but over 500 deaths were caused in the local French railway worker population. The following night, rail installations at Tergnier were bombed accurately causing severe damage, but ten Halifaxes were shot down by night fighters.

By 11 April, 2,513 bomber sorties during the pre-invasion campaign had been mounted by mostly Halifaxes to thirteen targets, with maximum damage caused by a mixture of 500lb and 1,000lb bombs, a Mk.III Halifax carrying typically nine 1,000lb

Speke-built Halifax B.III NA195 R 10 Squadron. (*Handley Page Association*)

and six 500lb bombs. Generally, loss rates were down to a welcome 0.5 per cent, but some targets were heavily defended, resulting in more serious losses of aircraft.

Tergnier was again bombed on 18 April by a force mainly of 171 Halifaxes with significant destruction to railway tracks, but six aircraft from 4 Group were lost. As April continued, crippling attacks were made on a number of targets in the French rail system, marked by the PFF. In addition, there were heavy main force attacks to Dusseldorf on 22 April, followed by Karlsruhe two nights later, but as a result of night fighters, bomber losses were heavy.

On 27/28 April, Aulnoye and Montzen marshalling yards were attacked by a mixed bomber force with inconclusive results. Bombing was concentrated at the former, with the loss of one Halifax. However, Montzen was unsuccessful with the loss of fourteen Halifaxes and one Lancaster to German night fighters and only part of the target damaged. Major damage was inflicted on 8/9 May at Haine-St-Pierre by a mixed force including sixty-two Halifaxes, six of which were shot down. On 12 May, the important rail junction and marshalling yard at Hasselt in Belgium was attacked by a force of 111 bombers, which was met by intense fighter activity. On 19 and 22 May, the marshalling yards at Boulogne and Orleans were bombed by 4 Group Halifaxes, before an attack on 24/25 May to Aachen in Germany in a mixed force of 442 aircraft, where, as expected, the defences were greater. There were eighteen Halifaxes were amongst RAF losses, but the target was heavily damaged, causing major disruption.

There was no doubt these attacks were overall successful and by early April, eighty of the most vital rail centres had been identified for Allied destruction. The main objective was to paralyse the French railway operation, denying German tactical logistics support of troop and supplies mobility to defend against the planned Allied landings. Bomber Command was allocated thirty-seven of the targets, with the US 9th Air Force and other RAF commands attacking the remainder. By the time the invasion commenced, fifty-one of the targets were heavily damaged, twenty-five with severe damage, leaving four slightly damaged.

As part of the plan to disrupt communications, an important radio listening station near Cherbourg was bombed on 2 June by ninety-nine 4 Group Halifaxes, with marking by PFF Mosquitos. The station was located close to the English Channel coast and needed to be put out of action prior to the invasion. Allocated to the task was the newly formed 346 (Free French) Squadron which was established at Elvington on 16 May, with twelve Halifax Mk.Vs, which was the first of two squadrons manned by French crews, 347 Squadron forming on 20 June, also at Elvington. Due to cloud over the target, bombing was disappointing with all twelve crews retuning safely. The Merlin-powered Halifax Mk.Vs were soon replaced by Mk.IIIs

The final raid in the programme was on Trappes railways installations on 2/3 June, just before D-Day on 6 June. Unfortunately for the RAF, German night fighters were ready, causing the greatest losses of the campaign with sixteen out of 128, mainly Halifaxes, destroyed by night fighters in clear moonlight, with others damaged beyond repair. As part of the D-Day deception plan, sixty-three aircraft bombed coastal gun batteries in the Pas de Calais.

The remainder of Bomber Command was employed on other strategic targets, including French aircraft and aero engine factories as part of the effort to reduce

German retaliation in the path of the invasion. Enemy troop concentrations were also targeted with a mixed Halifax and Lancaster force on 27/28 May, causing major destruction. With the planned date of the landings approaching, Bomber Command targeted German communications, although many were compact sites and bad weather made the task more challenging. As a result of these preparations, the German early warning systems were made inoperable, maintaining the element of surprise, vital for the Allied armada approaching the Normandy coastline.

Unfortunately, destruction of the heavy coastal gun batteries was less successful, but diversionary attacks were also made on coastal guns outside the planned landing areas. The campaign against coastal guns started on 10 April until the evening of 5 June, but the available 1,000lb bombs were insufficient to penetrate the heavily armour and concrete protected gun installation, which required precision placement of specialist weapons. However, there was considerable destruction to associated communications and other equipment, which handicapped effectiveness of the guns when facing a determined invasion force. The final attempt was made to subdue the coastal gun batteries on the night of 5/6 June, with ten targets identified. Starting at 23.35hrs some 100 bombers were allocated to each target, but heavy cloud cover made target identification impossible. By the time a second phase was launched, cloud had partly cleared making bombing more accurate. Halifaxes were used to attack one of the four remaining gun emplacements, but at one, the guns were not silenced until captured by ground forces. To achieve some deception, a number of bomber formations were used to drop Window to represent a fleet of surface shipping approaching France in the English Channel. Halifaxes and Stirlings dropped dummy paratroopers over northern France, the dummies discharging simulated gun fire.

Having established landings in Normandy, Bomber Command were tasked with slowing the supply of German reserves by bombing targets between the Rivers Seine and Loire, making attacks on road and rail centres from 6/7 June, using forces of approximately 100 aircraft on each. Targets were shared between Halifaxes and Lancasters, the former dropping bombs on Chateaudun , Saint-Lô and a bridge at Coutances. To further disrupt the railway system, four major rail centres around Paris were bombed on 7/8 June, but twenty-eight of the 337 bombers were shot down by strong enemy defences.

Bombing continued to disrupt communications in support of the advancing armies throughout the month of June, still against rail targets, with overall light losses, but the loss rate increased to 3.6 per cent for deeper penetration targets. Examples were Metz and Blainville on 28 June, where there were strong defences and the raid included aircraft from 433 Squadron. A total of twenty aircraft were shot down by night fighters and flak, with 102 Squadron losing five and 76 Squadron losing three. Bomber Command started a series of attacks on 14/15 June on the battlefield immediately behind the enemy lines, which were made mostly at night. A 4 Group force of 100 Halifaxes were used and two aircraft were lost to the initial light flak. The next night, Halifaxes from 77, 102, 158, 466 and 640 Squadrons joined Lancasters to bomb the Fischer-Tropsch synthetic oil plant at Sterkrade in the Ruhr, but on arrival at the target area, the ground was covered by thick cloud, and there was also heavy flak. With cloud up to 16,000 feet, bombing was from 20,000 feet directed by high-level target markers. Another hazard was the night fighters, which could see the vulnerable bombers silhouetted above the searchlight-lit cloud base. Losses were significant with thirty-one bombers shot down, including six Halifaxes from 77 Squadron and five from 102 Squadron.

To take full advantage of the more powerful Hercules XVI engines, interim improvements were made to the airframe resulting in the Mk.VII, which was externally similar to the earlier Mk.II-based airframe. The fuel system was completely redesigned with increased capacity, leading to the more capable Mk.VI which was powered by 1,680bhp Hercules 100 engines. The prototype B.VI was converted from Mk.III LV838 by HP ready for trials at Boscombe Down starting on 5 February 1944, with the wingspan increased to 104 feet. The more powerful engines were fitted with de Havilland or Rotol propellers with tests made to check performance improvements. Initial trials were concentrated on solving overheating problems which took until November 1944. The AUW was increased to 65,000lb and a service ceiling of 20,000 feet achieved. Handling trial with Mk.VI TW783 started in early 1945 with a new gross weight of 68,000lb, but had a very high safety speed on take-off of 170mph. In late 1945, C.Mk.VI LV838, fitted with a pannier, had rudder trim changes tested and found to improve asymmetric handling.

With an initial shortage of Hercules 100 engines, Hercules XVIs were substituted gaining the designation Mk.VII which continued in production until Mk.VI aircraft were available in June 1944. With interim B.Mk.VIIs in production, deliveries were made to units in 6 Group starting with 426 Squadron from 15 June at Linton-on-Ouse.

Halifax B.VII with guns in upper and rear turrets, and H2S radar under the fuselage, June 1944. (*Alan Dowsett*)

Above: Speke-built Halifax B.VII NA366 with no guns or H2S radar. (*Alan Dowsett*)

Below: An H2S-equipped, but unarmed Halifax B.VI in October 1944. (*Alan Dowsett*)

Halifax B.VI RG820 used by de Havilland Propellers and fitted with four-blade propellers on the inboard Hercules engines. (*Alan Dowsett*)

This was followed by 432 Squadron which began to reequip on 20 June at East Moor. The last fifteen B.Mk.IIIs were completed by HP as B.Mk.VIIs for 426 Squadron, ready for operations to start with the new version to St Harten on 20 June in daylight. In July 1944, Linton-on-Ouse-based 408 Squadron became the third unit to reequip with B.Mk.VIIs, as well as a few B.Mk.IIIs, replacing Lancasters. The only other unit to have a few B.Mk.VIIs was 415 Squadron at East Moor, which added a few of the interim version to its B.Mk.IIIs in March 1945, until disbanding on 15 May.

With enemy resistance in the Cherbourg Peninsular cleared by 1 July, the next stage was to break through congestion at the bridges over the rivers, with the German forces well established in defensive locations around Caen and the difficult bocage countryside consisting of banked hedge lined fields, which were natural barriers to armour. Therefore, Bomber Command was required to blast a route for the Allies' frontal attack on Caen. A mixed force of Halifaxes and Lancasters consisting of 467 aircraft bombed the approaches to Caen in a 2½-mile-wide corridor and 1-mile-deep approach, just 6,000 yards ahead of the advancing ground forces. Resistance was light and a large escort of fighters protected the bombers. The attack was so successful that by the evening of 8 July, British troops had entered the northern suburbs, but were slowed by the large bomb craters and rubble on their route to the bridges across the

River Orne. The delay allowed the Germans to destroy the bridges and set up defences in Vaucelles. With the success of the initial bombing, General Eisenhower approved the use of Bomber Command and the US 8th Air Force to break ways through for both British and American forces to advance.

Bomber Command were allocated the task of hitting areas directly in front of Allied positions, supporting some 2,000 American heavy and medium bombers of the Allied Expeditionary Force, starting at 05.45hrs on 18 July. A low-level precision attack was made on Colombelles by tactical bombers, followed by a mixed force of over 200 Halifaxes and Lancasters coming in at low-level under the control of a Master Bomber to ensure destruction of the target area. Losses were low, although Halifax LW127 went down when the starboard tailplane was removed by a bomb descending from above.

A force of 105 Halifaxes from 4 Group, accompanied by 1 Group Lancasters also were bombing road and rail targets at Sommerville, making a concentrated low-level attack. A mixed force of 242 bombers bombed Mannerville with a further force of 106 bombers targeting the German 21st Panzer Division concentration at Cagny. In the short period of 35 minutes, around 5,000lb of bombs were dropped with a loss of nine aircraft, which included a Halifax from both 76 and 578 Squadrons.

After initial successful rapid advances, ground forces were slowed down by heavy rains on 20 July, but despite difficulties, American forces were able to gain positions in Brittany. To stop a German reinforcement counterattack against American ground advances, the 2nd British Army made a determined attack in the area of Caumont, supported by a mixed heavy bomber force of 692 aircraft, as well as medium and light bomber ground attacks. Due to cloud cover, fewer than half the aircraft were able to bomb, resulting in only two out of the six designated targets being hit, with four Lancasters lost. On a follow up attack on 30 July, out of six targets, three were hit, again due to poor weather conditions. However, within a few days enemy forces were driven back out of the bocage, avoiding the threat to the American flank.

The unfamiliar Bomber Command tactical campaign in support of the advancing Allied ground forces continued on 7/8 August with a night attack against five precise targets along the flank of the planned advance route. It was vital not to endanger the 1st Canadian Army, which was preparing for the break-through of the Falaise Gap out of the restricted bocage country. Only some 660 out of the planned 1,019 bombers were able to attack due to low cloud and ground smoke which obscured the target markers, when the Master Bomber called off the attack. The final close air support operation in the campaign was on 14 August, when General Montgomery launched Operation Tractable. This was a daylight assault to break through the German Falaise defences, and link up with the American 3rd Army, putting the German 7th Army in isolation.

The seven targeted strong points were all located within 2,000 yards of the Canadian positions, with a combined force of 805 bombers, including 352 Halifaxes. To ensure accuracy, Oboe and visual marking was used, with Master Bomber and deputy controlling all seven targets. The weather was ideal with some crews dropping bombs from 2,000 feet to ensure accuracy, although some Canadian troops were misidentified and bombed inadvertently due to confusion with flares and target markers, killing thirteen. However, by 16 August, the Canadians had broken through to Falaise, allowing the advance to progress, with Bomber Command support no longer required.

While there had been some strategic operations by Bomber Command during the Allied Invasion, the night offensive restarted with a mixed force of just over 1,000 bombers attacking nine enemy night fighter bases in The Netherlands and Belgium on 17 August. With visibility excellent, all targets were successfully hit. In addition to bombing, Halifaxes of 77, 102, 346 and 347 Squadrons transported urgently needed vehicle fuel to Brussels-Melsbroek from 25 September over a period of eight days. In an attempt to reduce German occupancy of Brest, a mixed force of 334 bombers was sent on 25/26 August, but the port was not captured until 18 September, despite a number of attempts. The French ports of Le Havre, Boulogne and Calais were all heavily fortified. After two unsuccessful attacks caused by bad weather on Le Havre, successful bombing was achieved when marked by the PFF on 10 September with no

German defence positions around Calaise being bombed by day on 25 September 1944 by a force of 872 aircraft, including the three Halifaxes photographed from above by a Lancaster. (*Air Historical Branch*)

RAF losses, followed by 105 Halifaxes and 103 Lancasters the next afternoon. The German garrison then surrendered to Allied ground forces. Following the successful capture of Le Havre, Boulogne was the next target with a mixed force of 742 bombers making an attack on 17 September, bringing surrender on 22 September. Calais was attacked between 20 and 28 September, resulting in surrender on 30 September. At the same time, the heavy guns at Cap Gris Nez were put out of action.

With the start of V-1 flying bomb raids on 12/13 June against indiscriminate targets in southeast England, 4 Group Halifaxes targeted the well-concealed launch sites along the French coastline. Although the permanent sites had mostly been destroyed by Allied medium and light bombers slowing the start, using mobile launch platforms, some 250 were launched two nights later. This resulted in V-1 sites gaining tactical priority over any other targets, apart from urgent support of the advancing Allied ground forces. A high level of responsibility fell on Bomber Command, targeting supply sites, permanent launch sites, and the harder prefabricated launchers. By the time heavy bombers were deployed, only the permanent launch sites had been destroyed or abandoned as too vulnerable, resulting in an intensive, but often wasteful campaign, during days and nights. One of the first V-1 sites put out of action was Domleger which was bombed through cloud by a mixed force of over 100 Halifaxes and Lancasters. The weather cleared by 22 June when fifteen 466 Squadron Halifaxes led a 100-strong force on a daylight raid at Siracourt, one of the established sites. The attacking force was met by heavy flak, which shot down one Halifax and damaged another five. With good weather on 23/24 June, a logistics site was bombed near Oisemont by 4 Group Halifaxes and soon after 6 Group Halifaxes dropped on an established site at Bonnetot. Other Halifax targets on the same night were at Noyelle-en-Chausse and Le Grand Rossignol.

With the knowledge of German development of flying bombs, numerous sites in north-west France had been constructed from late 1943. In attempts to disrupt this construction process, RAF and USAAF medium bombers and fighter bombers had attacked them, but with limited success. Where most of the fixed launch sites were abandoned, they were replaced by more mobile launchers which could be camouflaged and hidden in the rural countryside, and were largely undetected by the Allies. When new sites were discovered in May 1944, preparations were in the final stages for the invasion, making it difficult to divert aircraft to the destruction of this new threat. Then, on 13 June 1944, the first four of many of what became known as the V-1 were launched over the Kent countryside, falling indiscriminately when the pulse jet engine ran out of fuel. Therefore, within ten days of the Normandy landings, heavy bombers of Bomber Command and the USAAF were tasked with the destruction of these launch sites and support depots along the Pas de Calais.

With Allied air supremacy during the day, the crews welcomed daylight raids, and there was a significant reduction in losses. The pressure was on to curtail V-1 launches as Allied forces approached the installations, resulting in intensive bombing of often two raids in a day. The offensive against the 'Noball' sites, as the V-1 Weapons were known, started on the night of 16 June, when four sites were attacked by 405 bombers. This included 4 Group units 10, 76, 78, and 640 Squadrons which successfully bombed a bomb supply site at Domleger. In the afternoon of 22 June, ninety-nine

Halifaxes day bombing V-1 sites along the Pas de Calaise 6 July 1944. (*Air Historical Branch*)

4 Group Halifaxes attacked an enormous concrete flying bomb store which was under construction at Siracourt, and due to difficulty identifying the target through broken cloud, bombs were dropped using Gee. Halifax LW116 was shot down by flak, with only four parachutes seen to open.

Despite intensive bombing of the V-1 launch sites, the deadly missiles, known also as 'Doodle Bugs', continued to be directed at London and the home counties, causing severe damage, particularly south of the Thames. By 21 June, 1,000 V-1s had been launched over south-east England, killing 1,769 civilians. In addition to flying bombs, construction had started of massive underground bunkers to launch the next phase of indiscriminate destruction on London and the surrounding areas.

While the V-1s were being launched against south-east England, Germany was also developing new weapons, with the V-2 rocket next. These were 12-ton missiles capable

Halifax B.III as part of a Bomber Command daylight raid on the V-3 Gun emplacement at Mimoyecques in France in mid-June 1944. (*Air Historical Branch*)

of carrying a 1-ton warhead over ranges of up to 200 miles. It arrived vertically, out of low space orbit, with no warning. These weapons were being assembled in vast underground concrete bunkers being built by over 6,000 slave labourers in northern France, which would be impregnable to Allied bombing when completed. The V-3 was a multiple charge long-range gun, capable of firing a continuous barrage of 6-inch shells from its fifty barrels against London. On 27 June 1944, 105 Halifaxes from 4 Group with Lancasters and PFF Mosquitos bombed in daylight the enormous V-3 long-range gun installations at Marquis Mimoyecques located between Calais and Boulogne. That night, 104 more Halifaxes bombed a V-1 launch site near Dieppe. The next morning a V-2 bunker was bombed by 103 Halifaxes near St Omer. It was to be a million-ton concrete dome in a hillside by a quarry. When completed, it would allow the Germans to assemble and launch the rockets without interruption. Although the dome was not damaged, work was disrupted by the destruction of the construction equipment, and severely cratered site. It was destroyed a week later by 617 Squadron using 6-ton 'Tallboy' bombs, led by Wing Commander Leonard Cheshire.

By the end of June, the temporary sites were a priority, but hard to locate, particularly in poor weather and at night, even when marked by Oboe-equipped PFF Mosquitos. The supply dumps for the temporary sites were still targeted, providing more effective results with the first of five attacks on a logistics site at Foret de Nieppe on 28 July, where formations of six Halifaxes were led in by a Mosquito, the final raid being on 6 August. From early August, Bomber Command concentrated on the destruction of potential construction works and supply depots for the V-2 rockets, leaving the V-1 sites to the US 8th Air Force.

While Bomber Command raids on V-1 sites certainly reduced launches to England, a more positive target was the main assembly complex at the Opel works at Russelheim near Mainz. On 9 August, various French targets were bombed in daylight, including V-1 sites and storage depots with the Halifaxes going in at between 8 and 10,000 feet where the flak was intense. A mixed force of 287 Halifaxes and Lancasters was sent on 12/13 August, with fierce night fighter defences and moderate flak which accounted for twenty bomber losses. Damage was limited, but completed by a second raid with the loss of two more Halifaxes. Finally, Allied advances reached the French coastal areas, taking over the V-1 launch sites and Bomber Command raids ceased by 12 September, after an acknowledged successful campaign.

On 18 July, Halifaxes joined Lancasters in the continuing effort to destroy enemy communications, where railway installations were heavily damaged at Vaires, including cutting the main Paris–Meaux line. Ground defences were intense, causing damage to a number of Halifaxes, but only one was lost, and the crew baled out. Railway targets continued with a daylight attack on 6 August at Hazebrouck, followed by a successful attack on 10/11 August at Dijon, then on a railway bridge at Etaples, further paralysing the railway network supplying the retreating German ground forces.

During the period between May and the end of July, when Bomber Command was supporting the Allied advances through France, as well as combating the V weapon menace, there were no strategic attacks on German cities, only attacks on oil

Halifax B.III KW425 Squadron ready for departure on a daylight raid. (*Alan Dowsett*)

installations. The break had allowed the German manufacturing strength to rebuild, which caused some concern. Therefore, the strategic bombing offensive restarted with an attack on Kiel on 23/24 July by a mixed force of 629 aircraft, as the first of thirty major raids on eighteen targets by the end of September. The enemy defences were taken off guard on the first raid for two months, which was successful. Within five nights, there were three raids on the target, but although there was heavy damage, losses were high on the third Lancaster only raid when night fighters destroyed thirty-nine of 494 aircraft in bright moonlight. While the Lancasters were suffering losses, a mixed force of Halifaxes, Lancasters and Mosquitos bombed Hamburg, but with the same clear moonlight enemy night fighters intercepted the bomber formations on their return, shooting down eighteen Halifaxes and four Lancasters. The Halifax units involved included 408, 425, 426, 431, 432 and 433 Squadrons, with 431 Squadron losing five aircraft. Kiel was the target for three more raids, which destroyed major military installations, resulting in no more raids planned on the city for the remainder of the year.

As a trial, a mainly Halifax force bombed Brunswick on 12/13 August using H2S instead of PFF target marking, but little damage was caused to the target with the loss of ten out of 137 Halifaxes. A further seven Halifaxes were lost on the same night while bombing Russelheim using PFF Mosquitos, but most bombs fell in open country.

As Allied forces moved towards German borders, major reinforcements were brought in from the USA to cover the rapidly expanding front line. This progress allowed Bomber Command to return to full control by the Air Ministry, although there was still a requirement to provide tactical support when needed. With Bomber Command strength growing rapidly and expected to increase by 50 per cent at the end of 1944, three major target types were identified. German synthetic oil production was one, with the enemy transport system and the still active industrial centres. The latter was strongly supported by Harris. By September 1944, Allied forces were advancing across France, with Paris liberated and German armies being driven back to the border of Germany. The Soviet Red Army had wiped out sixty-seven German divisions from the east and was rapidly advancing into Germany. The Luftwaffe had lost domination in the air, and with the overrunning of their forward operating control organisation, the night fighter force had collapsed. Although German fighter production was still significant, operations were hampered due to lack of fuel. This allowed the final bomber offensive to commence, moving on from the tactical support for the advancing Allied ground forces.

A directive was issued on 25 September prioritising oil production targets for both Bomber Command by night and the US 8th Air Force by day, with Harris in support, but making sure the RAF targets also included industry. This was the start of the final campaign for Bomber Command in the Second World War. With the dramatically increased strength, came a major increase in bombing capacity, resulting in nearly half the total tonnage dropped by the Command released in the final nine months, with greater accuracy. Despite the increased strength and a reduction in the German night fighter force, there were still strong defences causing significant losses. While some Halifaxes were being used against remaining V-1 installations, oil targets were hit on 20/21 July when 149 Halifaxes bombed Bottrop-Wilhelm, but seven aircraft were lost, although the target was badly damaged. A successful attack was made on the Wanne Eickel site using markers with no aircraft lost, and the Ruhr-based synthetic oil industry was targeted on 18/19 August by 210 Halifaxes on the Sterkrade-Holten factory, with sufficient damage for no further attacks needed until the end of September.

The heaviest raid to date on an oil target was made by 216 Halifaxes on 27 August at the Homberg-Meerbeck plant, and it was also the first major daylight raid over Germany for three years. Making its introduction to combat was the newly reformed 462 Squadron at Driffield on 12 August 1944. The target was heavily damaged, and apart from damage to one Halifax there were no losses. The Bomber Command daylight campaign built up rapidly, with further attacks against Ruhr oil targets from 11 September with losses of eighteen Halifaxes out of a total of 945 which was not excessive. Raids against oil installations continued from late September, but were reduced in effectiveness by poor weather conditions. Also during the first week of September, Bomber Command was called to help defeat a German garrison which continued to hold out in the port of Le Havre. It was bombed five times with nearly 1,000 sorties before the battered forces finally surrendered. On 12 September, in a daylight raid, a force of 119 4 Group Halifaxes went to the oil plant at Buer, with another 106 to Munster. It was a new experience for the crews to penetrate so far into Germany in daylight, with the hazard of enemy fighters, as well as flak. Bombing was from 18,000 feet, visibility was good and the target was destroyed. A further daylight attack was made the next day, when 102 Halifaxes went to the Nordstern oil plant, but the target was obscured by a very thick smoke screen. Many aircraft were damaged by intense flak.

By the third week in September, the Allies had advanced so rapidly, that they were being held back by lack of supplies, particularly fuel, due to non-availability of suitable harbours. To help overcome this problem, Bomber Command were requested to fly urgently needed transport fuel into Belgium. The airfields of 42 Base, including Pocklington, Elvington and Melbourne were supplied by stocks of US Army Jerry cans, which on arrival at Pocklington, were filled and strapped into the Halifax fuselages of 77, 102, 346 and 347 Squadrons and flown to Brussels-Melsbroek. A total of 582 sorties were flown transporting 432,840 gallons of fuel.

When France was being liberated, the German U-boat facilities in French ports were denied to the enemy, with plans made to develop the port of Bergen in Norway as an alternative. Therefore, on 4 October, a mixed force of Halifaxes and Lancasters were sent to disrupt progress. The main force bombed the U-boat pens under construction, while fourteen Halifaxes and six Lancasters attacked moored submarines in the harbour. Although only one Lancaster was lost on this successful raid, there were high civilian casualties caused by two miss-aimed bombs. During October, the weather restricted attacks on oil targets to five by Bomber Command and another four operations by the US 8th Air Force, the RAF concentrating their attacks on installations in the Ruhr. In a group formation on 6 October, 76 Squadron led the attack on Schloven-Buer, while a second force of 126 Halifaxes, escorted by fighters bombed Sterkrade-Holten, with PFF accurately marking the targets. Despite heavy flak the targets were badly damaged, but seven Halifaxes were destroyed and around 70 per cent of the aircraft sustained flak damage. That night, a force of 248 Halifaxes and forty-eight Lancasters were part of a 523 aircraft attack on Dortmund, causing major damage in clear weather, with only five aircraft shot down including two Halifaxes.

The approaches by sea to Antwerp were guarded by the heavily defended island of Walcheren which was below sea level. Lancasters had managed to breach the sea wall, flooding the island, but there were still five major gun emplacements defending the site. On 28 October, an overall force of 277 bombers attacked the guns, with two more attacks over the next two days, allowing a ground assault, leading to the garrison surrender on 3 November.

Immediately after the Walcheren attacks, both Bomber Command and the US 8th Air Force were tasked with softening up the German defences along the River Roer ahead of the Allied ground offensive, but it was delayed due to bad weather until 16 November, when a major attack started. The front-line defences were bombed by the American aircraft, while a mixed force of over 1,000 Halifaxes and Lancasters attacked the heavily fortified towns of Heinsburg, Julich and Duren. The Halifaxes concentrated on hitting Julich, devastating the town with nearly 2,000 tons of bombs, and destroying a bridge over the river.

Meanwhile, the winter offensive had restarted on 6/7 October with an attack on Dortmund, followed by Bremen, Emmeric, Bochum and Duisburg. Duisburg was bombed in a daylight attack on 14 October using over 1,000 bombers, including 474 Halifaxes, which was the largest RAF daylight raid to that date. That night, another 1,000 bombers went back to the city, leaving it burning fiercely with large explosions seen in the docks. Despite the devastation to the city, only twenty-one bombers were lost in the two attacks, mostly having been shot down by the flak. On 15/16 October, a force of 506 bombers bombed Wilhelmshaven, causing severe damage, despite poor visibility.

Bomber Command had reached its peak offensive strength with new bombing and navigation aids, new weapons and the availability of well-trained and experienced crews. The Ruhr was finally effectively neutralised during the last three months of 1944, with 61,000 tons of bombs dropped during over 14,000 sorties and loss rates of less than 1 per cent, with only 136 bombers destroyed. On 23/24 October, Essen was again bombed by a force of 1,055 Halifaxes and Lancasters with the PFF Mosquitos dropping sky markers above the cloud covered target. With much of the combustible material exhausted in many of the regularly bombed German cities, a switch was made from incendiaries to high explosive bombs, creating greater devastation. On 25 October, another return was made to Essen by day, where the Krupp works were destroyed by a mixed force of 771 bombers, reducing the ability to undertake war production.

Cologne was the next target with three attacks over four days starting on 28 October. The first raid was by over 700 bombers in two waves, causing major damage. The second raid was 30/31 October, when jet fighters were encountered, but the target again suffered significant damage with no RAF bomber losses. The third attack continued the devastation of the target. On 16 October, when Bochum was bombed, 346 Squadron lost five French crews out of sixteen aircraft dispatched, as part of an overall loss of twenty-three Halifaxes and five Lancasters from a force of 749 aircraft, mainly from night fighters. Two Halifaxes were lost from 466 Squadron, on what was the last major raid to Bochum. The bombing campaign continued with day and night raids on Hamburg, Oberhausen and Dusseldorf, the latter receiving its last major bombing attack of the war on 2/3 November. On 4/5 November, 705 Halifaxes, Lancasters and Mosquitos bombed Bochum with 3,332 tons of high explosives and incendiaries, causing severe damage to the town centre. The searchlights and flak were daunting and among the twenty-eight bombers shot down, twenty-three were Halifaxes. Bomber Command were kept on the ground for a week towards the end of November due to bad weather, but successful night attacks were made on 38/29 October to Essen with Duisburg the next night. The final heavy raid on Essen was 12/13 December, by a mixed force of 540 bombers causing major damage to the Krupp works.

Bombing of communications centres included rail, road and water routes along a strip to the west of the Rhine bounded by a line through Hamburg, Hanover to Ulm on the east, which continued until the end of the war. Oil targets were also hit during November, with eight daylight and six night attacks, which helped slow supplies of fuel for the German break-out in the Ardennes, which started on 16 December.

Although oil production made a recovery in difficult conditions during October and November, it began a rapid decline in December and January. The airfields at Lohausen and Mulheim were attacked by 338 bombers on Christmas Eve where they were met with determined flak, although the targets were badly damaged. On 26 December, a daylight raid was made on an enemy communications centre at St Vith in Belgium, which had been recaptured during the Ardennes offensive. A force of Halifaxes and Lancasters bombed from 14,000 feet in good visibility. The year was rounded off on 30/31 December with a raid on marshalling yards in Cologne.

With the start of the new year in January 1945, victory for the Allies seemed inevitable, with bomber losses remaining low at less than 1 per cent, the main hazard being mid-air collisions in the crowded skies. At the end of 1944, 462 (RAAF) Squadron transferred from 4 Group to 100 Group for radio countermeasures and bomber support duties. The first operation with 100 Group was on 1 January 1945, when the squadron dropped window and bombs in support of the main force. On the same night, 105 4 Group Halifaxes bombed the Hoech coking plant in Dortmund. The following night PFF Lancasters and Mosquitos marked for 351 Halifaxes from 4 and 6 Groups which destroyed the Farben chemical works at Ludwigshafen and Oppau, with no losses to Halifaxes.

However, a large raid on Hanover on 5 January by 664 bombers, although successful, did cause 4.7 per cent losses, reversing the trend being experienced. Losses to Halifaxes were twenty-three aircraft, plus eight Lancasters. On 6 January, the major rail junction at Hanau was bombed by a combined force from 1, 4, 6 and 8 Groups with moderate damage and at least four Halifaxes from 4 Group were lost. There was then a period of bad weather preventing operations by 4 Group bases in Yorkshire, which included low cloud and snow. Over a period of 24 hours, three attacks were made by 274 bombers on a transport bottle neck at Saarbrucken on 13/14 January. The next night, 100 4 Group Halifaxes with marking by twelve Mosquitos and three Lancasters bombed a fuel storage depot at Dulmen, causing scattered damage and the loss of one 578 Squadron Halifax. Industrial targets continued with Ludwigshaven, Hanover, Hanau and Magdeburg all being bombed, mainly by Halifaxes, led by 76 Squadron on the latter target, with seventeen out of 320 Halifaxes lost. The targets for the month were completed with a raid on 28/29 January on Stuttgart with phase one attacking Hirth jet engine production, and the other phase targeting marshalling yards, with 3 hours between the two attacks. Due to cloud obscuring the target, sky markers were used with bombing scattered. Flak accounted for the loss of four Halifaxes as well as six Lancasters and a Mosquito.

Three types of targets were defined for Bomber Command from January 1945 until the end of the war. These were continuing attacks on war industry, fuel and all forms of transport and communications. With the Allied advances, the majority of targets were in Germany, avoiding collateral damage in occupied countries. Some previously insignificant cities were in the path of planned Allied advances, although they had no industrial significance, one example being Mainz, which was raided on 1/2 February by a force of 293 Halifaxes from both 4 and 6 Group Lancasters and Mosquitos. The PFF marked the partially cloud-covered target with ground markers initially, using sky markers when cloud increased. Defences were light with no RAF bombers lost, but little damage was caused to the target.

The 2nd TAF and USAAF light and medium bombers made a series of attacks on German rail and road targets to deter enemy forces resisting when ground forces began advancing towards Kleve, with a force of around 1,000 artillery guns. In support for this advance by British XXX Corps, Bomber Command bombed both Goch and Kleve on 7/8 February with the loss of two Halifaxes, but the attack had to be called off early by the Master Bomber due to increasing smoke obscuring the target. On 13 February, a maximum effort night raid was planned on the synthetic oil plant at Bohlen near Leipzig, but bad weather caused the bombing to be scattered by the mainly Halifax 368 bomber force, including severe icing. On 20 February, oil production at Rhenania Ossag refinery near Dusseldorf was brought to a standstill by a bomber force including 156 Halifaxes from 4 Group. The accurate marking by PFF resulted in a very concentrated attack, but two each Halifaxes from 158 and 578 Squadrons were lost.

On 21 February, 288 Halifaxes were part of a single attack on Worms and although bombing accuracy was excellent, Bomber Command lost ten Halifaxes and a Lancaster. One of the units taking part was 102 Squadron equipped with the new Halifax B.MK.VIs. A return was made to Mainz on 27 February, when 311 Halifaxes were part of a force of 458 bombers dispatched, which devastated the target without RAF losses. Fuel targets continued to be attacked during February and March, practically eliminating oil production in all its forms by 3 March when a synthetic oil refinery at Kamen was bombed by 201 4 Group Halifaxes. Although there were no losses over the target, Luftwaffe night fighters were waiting over Britain for the returning bombers shooting down seven Halifaxes out of twenty bombers lost and damaging others, although the enemy night fighter force was reduced by this time. This was the last major Luftwaffe operation against RAF bombers over Britain. On 7 March, 4 and 6 Group Halifaxes bombed the Deutsche Erdol refinery at Hemmingstadt with the loss of two 578 Squadron Halifaxes and only one crew member survived.

Two maximum-effort raids were made in early March, the first on Essen comprising 1,079 aircraft; the second on Dortmund the following afternoon, comprising 1,107 aircraft. Some 4,851 tons of bombs were dropped during this raid, the highest tonnage of the war. Only five Lancasters were lost during both operations.

With the result of the war inevitable, Bomber Command began to reduce its strength and 578 Squadron was part of a 345 combined force on 13 March against Wuppertal-Barmen, after which it was withdrawn and disbanded at Burn on 15 April 1945. The target was heavily damaged with no RAF losses. No. 578 Squadron had served well, having flown 2,721 sorties and dropped 9,676 tons of bombs. During the 155 bombing operations, forty aircraft were lost.

Germany was still developing U-boats in late 1944, with the emergence of prefabricated Type XXIs, with bombing starting in November to destroy the facilities in both Hamburg and Bremen, building up in March and April. Luftwaffe jet fighters were encountered in quantity for the first and only time on 31 March during a major raid on Hamburg, shooting down three Halifaxes and five Lancasters in a period of 12 minutes, the Halifaxes coming from 408, 415 and 425 Squadrons. With the Allied crossing of the Rhine, Bomber Command was sent to Sterkrade and Gladbeck, followed the next day by Munster and Osnabruck

The reduction in strategic bombing continued in April, with just twenty-one major raids on day and night operations, mainly on enemy harbours and shipping. One of the few remaining oil targets, the Rhenania Ossag plant at Hamburg was hit during the evening of 4 April with a concentrated attack by 327 bombers from 4, 6 and 8 Groups and on the night of 8 April, U-boat construction yards in Hamburg were bombed through broken cloud cover. Leipzig was a tactical target in the path of advancing ground forces and was bombed on 10 April with little opposition. Two highly successful operations were carried out on 11 April by 129 4 Group Halifaxes on marshalling yards at Nuremburg and the rail centre at Bayreuth, both without loss.

In April 1945, Bomber Command ceased area bombing, as victory was imminent, having been a continuous activity since May 1940. Targets remaining over the final weeks were concentrated on naval installations, any undamaged railway facilities and oil production.

Significant numbers of Halifax Mk.VIs began to reequip 346 and 347 Squadrons, but the squadrons were not operational until 4 April, followed by 158 Squadron which used the new version on a major raid against military installations in Heligoland on 18 April. The force of 332 Halifaxes and 617 Lancasters destroyed the naval base, airfield and town. This was followed on 25 April by 308 Halifaxes, 158 Lancasters and sixteen Mosquitos from 4, 6 and 8 Groups on their last operation of the Second World War to the Frisian Island gun batteries at Wangerooge which controlled the approaches to the ports of Bremen and Wilhelmshaven. Despite heavy flak defences, the attack was devastating.

The last major bombing operation of the Second World War was 2 May on Kiel, with a mixed force of Halifaxes and Lancasters marked by PFF Mosquitos, and although the target was hit accurately in good visibility, seven aircraft were lost, of which five were Halifaxes and two Lancasters, mainly due to mid-air collisions.

On 7 May 1945, the Germans signed an unconditional surrender to bring an end to the war in Europe. As a result, 4 Group was transferred to Transport Command, while 408 and 425 Squadron converted to Lancasters, prior to returning to Canada with six other squadrons. Four squadrons remained with Bomber Command as part of the Armies of Occupation and 426 Squadron transferred to Transport Command with Liberators. With combat operations finished, some of the flights made were known as 'Cook's Tours', where ground crews were flown at low-level over some of the destroyed target cities, to see for themselves the devastation achieved. The two Free French units, 346 and 347 Squadrons remained briefly with Bomber Command, twenty-eight Halifaxes from both squadrons making a flypast over Paris on 18 June before returning to France with their aircraft as a present from the British Government.

8
Signals Intelligence

The principle of signals intelligence was stimulated in 1940 with the need to disrupt German radio navigation beams used to guide their bombers to targets in Britain. This slowly expanded into signals intelligence still active today. The original organisation was the Wireless Intelligence Development Unit, which expanded into full-squadron strength on 10 December 1940 as 109 Squadron at Boscombe Down. It was equipped with Whitleys, Ansons and Wellingtons and moved to Tempsford on 19 January 1942. Over two years, the squadron carried out experiments with radio counter measures and the development of radar. In July 1942, 109 Squadron A Flight became 1473 (Special Duties) Flight on 10 July at Upper Heyford. By September 1943, it was based at Feltwell with two Halifax Mk.IIs on the strength, in addition to Wellingtons and other types. The formation of 100 Group in November 1943 concentrated and coordinated jamming and deception of German defences with 192 Squadron specialising in detecting electronic data of German defences by flying with the RAF bomber streams and recording the characteristics of German radars and radio transmission. No. 1473 Flight finally disbanded at Foulsham on 1 February 1944, when it was absorbed by 192 Squadron. The B and C Flights of 109 Squadron became 1474 (Special Duties) Flight which was formed at Stradishall on 4 July 1942 and also known as 1474 Wireless Interception Flight. The flight was equipped with at least one Halifax Mk.II, DT737, from 9 January and had been redesignated 192 Squadron on 4 January 1943 at Gransden Lodge.

Halifax operations with 192 Squadron started on 22 June with a patrol off the Dutch coast, carrying an eighth crew member, who was referred to as a 'special operator' and operated electronic intelligence systems in the aircraft. The second operation was over the English southwest coastline, in an area search for any enemy shipping communications. Then followed patrols over the Bay of Biscay and the Brest peninsular listening for U-boat communications. Flights were then made over Germany as part of the main bomber stream with Nuremberg and Dusseldorf as the targets. Here, they identified enemy radar and radio signals, while sometimes recording them for later analysis. As the patrols continued to increase, Norway was added to the surveillance areas, with a Halifax and two Wellingtons detached to Lossiemouth, to be closer to the areas of interest.

Halifax Mk.III DT-A 192 Squadron 1945. (*RAF Museum*)

With information obtained from these early intelligence gathering operations, it was possible to develop countermeasures against enemy navigation beams, diverting them off course. The most effective was Mandrel, which could jam German early warning frequencies over enemy territory, helping to protect the bomber force. It was not until 8 November 1943 that all the bomber defensive aids were coordinated by the formation of 100 Group. Instead of referring to the units as Special Duties squadrons, they were referred to as Bomber Support squadrons.

Moving to Feltwell on 4 April 1943, 192 Squadron then went to Foulsham on 25 November, as part of 100 Group, changing its Halifax Mk.IIs for Mk.Vs in July 1943, in addition to operating various marks of Wellingtons and Mosquito Mk.IVs. As well as listening for enemy radio signals, the squadron began a programme of active electronic jamming in support of bombing raids, with more effective Halifax Mk.IIIs arriving in January 1944. Individual squadron aircraft would be sent on specific raids in support of other bombing operations and therefore rarely flew in a collective formation. An example was three Halifaxes on radio/radar evaluation supporting three different raids on railway targets in France and Belgium on 1 May.

Three Halifaxes patrolled between Tonbridge and Yeovil during the night of 5/6 June 1944 using Mandrel, successfully screening the Airborne Forces' approaches to Normandy.

Mandrel was used to create a diversionary force during smaller raids, combined with the use of Window. As the Mandrel-equipped aircraft approached enemy territory, a following small force would pass through the Mandrel aircraft formation and release Window, which on German radar appeared to be a much larger raid. The controllers would then scramble night fighters to counter a ghost raid, causing considerable confusion and delay while the validity of the approaching formation was checked. Many Luftwaffe night fighter bases in France were captured by the advancing invasion ground forces, as were the early warning radar installations along the French coast. Bad weather during the latter part of 1944 was used to cover probing flights, including patrols off the Norwegian coast.

On 8 September 1944, intelligence gathering was increased by the formation of 171 Squadron from C Flight of 199 Squadron at North Creake, operating Halifax Mk.IIIs with Stirlings, until disbanding on 27 July 1945. Mandrel equipment was installed at St Athan in the eight squadron Halifaxes, ready for the first operation on 20 November, with success by three of their aircraft. Meanwhile, during October, 192 Squadron concentrated on attempting to locate intelligence on German rocket weapons by flying off the Dutch coast. During a raid by Lancasters breaching the sea wall at Walcheren, a 192 Squadron Halifax recorded enemy communications. A 192 Squadron Halifax also accompanied a main force raid off the Danish coast recording enemy VHF radio signals and locating the sites of automatic homing systems at coastal watcher stations. While specialising in signals intelligence and jamming, 192 Squadron occasionally participated in Mandrel/Window operations with other Group squadrons. The first was on 9 October, when two aircraft released Window between Heligoland and Wilhelmshaven as a diversion in support of a main Bomber Command raid.

The Special Duties strength in 100 Group was increased by the addition of 462 Squadron which reformed at Driffield on 12 August 1944 with Halifax Mk.IIIs. It joined 100 Group in December with a move to Foulsham on 22 December and finally disbanded on 24 September 1945. The role of the squadron was radar counter measures (RCM), fitted with the latest equipment for jamming enemy radars and radio transmissions. It used ABC (Airborne Cigar) to jam German fighter control frequencies fitted in a large external aerial fairing. While these lengthy modifications were being incorporated, the squadron made its first diversionary sortie on 1 January 1945. With its previous experience as a bomber squadron, it was natural for the Halifaxes to carry two 500lb bombs to add to the overall destruction of targets in Stuttgart. This practice spread to the other Group squadrons. As the bombing campaign was approaching the end, the Australian crews used spoof techniques to entice enemy night fighters into an area where RAF Mosquitos fitted with the new AI Mk.10 radar could destroy them. In February 1945, 199 Squadron joined 100 Group based at North Creake with Halifax Mk.IIIs replacing Stirlings, the squadron disbanding on 29 July 1945.

A new deception plan was developed with the Window force combined with pathfinding target-marking and a spoof master bomber. Halifaxes were part of a main

Above: The personnel of 171 Squadron A Flight in front of Halifax Mk.III at North Creake in 1944. (*RAF Museum*)

Below: Halifax Mk.III EX-E 199 Squadron fitted with H2S in formation with another Halifax Mk.III. (*RAF Museum*)

bomber force on 14/15 January 1945 with an attack on Grevebroich and Dulmen. There was also a wide range of diversionary raids, including 462 Squadron with thirteen Halifaxes, each aircraft carrying Window and a 1,000lb bomb. When bad weather caught out the returning aircraft, a number crashed at their bases, including one Halifax from the Dulmen raid.

On 15 February, the first of the fully modified Halifaxes was delivered to 462 Squadron from St Athan, but there were delays with the remaining aircraft, resulting in the first RCM operation being delayed until 13 March. The ABC interfered with a range of Luftwaffe radio frequencies, and jammed a navigation aid known as Benito, the range being around 50 miles, while other Halifaxes could jam enemy night fighter radars. The long time taken to incorporate these special modifications resulted in only eleven aircraft being equipped by the end of the war. Meanwhile, the squadron continued with spoof attacks on 22 February, dropping both Window and bombs, attracting enemy night fighters to what appeared to be a large raid, followed by cover provided by Mandrel. Then, as the night fighters were returning to their bases, another Window release was made, disrupting any coordination of defences. On one night raid, when 462 Squadron was operating alone, four out of ten Halifaxes were shot down by enemy night fighters, as there were no other diversion raids. On 19 February, a 192 Squadron Halifax was tasked with obtaining data on enemy centimetric

Samlesbury-built Halifax Mk.III RG387 with 199 Squadron at North Creake in 1945. (*RAF Museum*)

radars, and despite suffering an engine failure on the way to the target, continued the mission. During the return flight, the aircraft was attacked by Luftwaffe fighters for 90 minutes, but continued to make a safe landing at Manston, having successfully gained information on the new radars for the first time.

On 10/11 April, 462 Squadron provided three RCM Halifaxes and seven carrying Window in support of a Lancaster and Mosquito attack on Leipzig, the Window bombers turning towards Berlin, attracting night fighters, which were then engaged by Mosquito intruders. On 14/15 April, a return was made to Berlin for the first time in over a year, making the last major bombing operation of the war on the city. The raid was supported by 462 Squadron with twelve Halifaxes, four aircraft on ABC sorties and the remaining aircraft releasing Window. Although losses were light, one ABC aircraft was written off in a forced landing after suffering flak damage.

No. 462 Squadron continued to support Bomber Command main force attacks with one on Pilsen where the squadron put up eleven Halifaxes, six using Window on a spoof raid to Augsburg, two to Schwandorf, and one each to Pilsen and Prague, with one flying an ABC sortie. Two Halifaxes, one from each of 171 and 462 Squadron failed to return, with low losses to the main force. At the end of April, with the end of hostilities fast approaching, none of the 100 Group squadrons operated for ten days.

Then, on 2/3 May, the last major raid of the Second World War was launched by Bomber Command on Kiel, led by 8 Group Mosquitos. A mixed force of 161 Halifaxes, with Mosquitos, Fortresses and Liberators from 100 Group, were sent to a number of targets for a variety of tasks. Out of the four Halifax units, 462 Squadron sent six aircraft to Flensburg dropping Window and four more to Kiel on RCM duties, each aircraft also carried 500lb bombs. The other Foulsham based squadron, 192, sent a total of 14 Halifaxes and five Mosquitos, with six going to Kiel on RCM duties and the remainder releasing Window over the Flensburg area. The two North Creak based squadrons, 171 and 199 Squadrons provided major support, with 171 Squadron using four Mandrel-Window Halifaxes over Flensburg, twelve more on similar operations, plus dropping bombs on Kiel, and two more on similar duties over the Schleswig area. A total of twenty-one Halifaxes were put up by 199 Squadron, five of which carried Mandrel-Window over the North Frisian Islands. Ten more supported the bombing of Kiel on Mandrel-Window duties, with six more on similar duties over Schleswig, each aircraft also dropping a 500lb bomb. Two Halifaxes were lost, probably due to a mid-air collision, with thirteen crew members killed, the last Bomber Command casualties on operations in the war.

Following the German surrender, 100 Group Halifax squadrons continued on routine training, with all four squadrons participating in Exercise Postmortem starting on 25 June, which was to simulate main force raids to check the effectiveness of German raid reporting capability. The exercise continued into early July and confirmed Bomber Command operations were conducted very well. German early warnings were poorly coordinated and unreliable. It was acknowledged the use of Mandrel and Window were both very effective in jamming German radars.

Most of the 100 Group Halifax squadrons began to disband, with 192 Squadron disbanding on 22 August 1945 to become the nucleus of the Central Signals Establishment (CSE) with the Flying and Servicing Wings based at Foulsham, and the HQ at Swanton Morley. A move was then made to the permanent RAF base at Watton during September, with the first of fifteen ex-199, 171 and 462 Squadron Halifaxes arriving from 6 October. At Watton, the CSE was transferred to 60 Group, Fighter Command and by mid-October it had a fleet of twenty-four Halifaxes, plus Fortresses, Mosquitos, Ansons, an Oxford and a Proctor. Although details of the unit's operations were highly restricted, they made considerable advances in both passive and active electronic warfare. Halifax CSE operations ceased by January 1947, with the last aircraft scrapped in March. However, they left a lasting legacy of electronic intelligence gathering from Watton, Wyton and now Waddington, where 51 Squadron operate RC-135W Airseeker R.1s, also known as 'Rivet Joint', gathering data from Russian radars and communications transmissions.

9

Maritime Operations

Britain was supplied with most of its needs by sea during the Second World War, and the German U-boat fleet operating from occupied French ports along the Bay of Biscay coast were threatening vital supplies of food and war materials, mainly coming from North America. More than 6 million tons of Allied merchant shipping was sunk by a fleet of around 400 U-boats, of which only around ten had been confirmed destroyed. While British and American shipyards were beginning to replace the ship losses, there remained an urgent need for more naval escort ships and anti-submarine aircraft. In November 1942 alone, the U-boat 'wolf packs' sank more than 600,000 tons of shipping, mostly in the North Atlantic, beyond the range of the existing RAF maritime aircraft operating from Britain, Iceland or Newfoundland, in what was known as the Atlantic Air Gap. The main area for U-boat detection and destruction was therefore the Bay of Biscay, which they crossed from their bases along the French coast. New detection aids were being developed, including Wellingtons carrying ASV (Air to Surface) radar and a Leigh searchlight for nocturnal operations.

RAF Coastal Command had been formed to protect our ocean routes from 1942, mainly using Sunderland flying boats, with the addition of long-range American Liberators. Even then, the force was too small to have much effect, resulting in the temporary urgent detachment of some Bomber Command Halifax and Lancaster squadrons. On 24 October 1942, both 158 and 405 Halifax squadrons were ordered to provide detachments to RAF Beaulieu, as self-contained units within Coastal Command. Five Halifax Mk.IIs were supplied by 158 Squadron, and a further fifteen from 405 Squadron. Within three days of receiving their orders, three 405 Squadron Halifaxes were on an anti-submarine operation over the Bay of Biscay.

Halifaxes were also responsible for convoy escort duties and anti-shipping strikes in ports and along the enemy coastlines. The crews were therefore generally in action by day, in contrast to their previous role as night bombers. On 2 November, a 405 Squadron crew spotted an enemy submarine on the surface, but it submerged before it could be attacked. There was greater success on 11 November, when a 405 Squadron aircraft spotted two surface ships refuelling a U-boat. Coming down to 900 feet, Pilot Officer College fired the forward machine guns and dropped bombs. While one fell short, the rest hit the targets, and the gunners continued firing, the surface ships raising a white flag in surrender. On 24 November, another U-boat was spotted, but crash dived before an attack. Two days later, another 405 Squadron

Halifax spotted two motor vessels being escorted by a pair of destroyers and started to attack against heavy defensive fire from the destroyers. This made accurate bombing difficult, but the aircraft machine guns were used to advantage. On 27 November, a successful attack by 405 Squadron straddled U-263 with depth charges, causing severe damage. Some nuisance raids were carried out on French ports, including Bordeaux and Gironde, with the small 158 Squadron detachment returning to Bomber Command in December, and 405 Squadron returning to Bomber Command in March 1943.

Meanwhile Coastal Command had used the experience of Halifax operations by forming their own units. The first was 58 Squadron which replaced its Whitleys with Halifax Mk.IIs in December 1942 at Holmsley South and 502 Squadron in February 1943 at the same airfield. Both squadrons were operational by the end of February; the aircraft fitted with the improved ASV Mk.III search radar. A defensive aid code named Boozer was also fitted to warn of detection by enemy radar. Some operational trials were allocated to 502 Squadron, including establishing practical operational capabilities with the aircraft fitted with an additional three 330-gallon long-range fuel tanks. As a result, the aircraft was flown for 14 hours 7 minutes establishing practical operational endurance of 11 hours, allowing safety margins for variations flying conditions and weather diversions. As experience was gained, this endurance was increased.

At the Casablanca conference in January 1943 between Churchill, Roosevelt, and their chiefs of staff, one of the major priorities set was the defeat of the U-boat threat,

Samlesbury-built Halifax GR.II JD376 in April 1945. This aircraft was without guns in the nose or mid-upper turret. (*RAF Museum*)

Halifax GR.II JD376 showing its four blade propellers. It was delivered to 78 Squadron on 23 July 1943, and moved to 1663 HCU on 23 January 1944. It then went to RAE Farnborough on 7 June 1945 and was SOC on 31 December 1946. (*RAF Museum*)

without which there could be no invasion of Western Europe, until the Battle of the Atlantic had been won. Hitler was fully aware of the U-boat effectiveness, promoting Admiral Doenitz to command the entire German Navy, and Albert Speer, the minister in charge of armaments, to give U-boat production the highest priority. The Germans had the strategic advantage of having broken British naval codes and the 'wolf packs' had considerable flexibility of operation for surprise attacks against the slow and poorly manoeuvrable Allied convoys. In contrast to the Germans reading the Allied coded messages, Bletchley Park-based Ultra had broken the German Enigma code and kept track of Doenitz's U-boats at sea. This allowed the Allied convoys to be routed around the positions of the U-boat concentrations, and was the situation when Halifaxes joined Coastal Command. U-Boat weakness included the need to surface to recharge the batteries used for submerged operations, and when submerged its speed reduced to between 5 and 8kt, from surface speed of 12 to 15kt.

When submerged, there was limited visibility for navigating the vast Atlantic Ocean, and locating targets was a challenge. Therefore, the U-boats preferred to operate on the surface as much as possible, only submerging when threatened by aircraft, or ready to attack an unsuspecting target ship. In the Bay of Biscay, where detection by Allied maritime patrols was most common, the U-boats submerged during daylight and surfaced at night. If a submarine detected an approaching aircraft, it would immediately crash dive, and would be deep enough to avoid destruction by depth charges. By just visual means, an aircraft flying at 2,000 feet may be able to see the wake of a surfaced U-boat at 7 miles, but much less at night, and not at all in poor visibility.

With the introduction of ASV Mk.1 in 1942, in ideal conditions, a submarine could be detected up to 20 miles in range, but it was not hampered by poor visibility or darkness. The early ASV had its limitations, including it only faced foreword from under the aircraft, and only gave a very basic indication of the target of whether it was to port or starboard of the beam, and an approximate distance away. When the aircraft was close, the signal disappeared, making blind attacks impossible. However, it was better than having no aid and during 1942 sighting increased encouragingly, reaching 120 in September. The advantage was not held for long. U-boats were fitted with a listening device called 'Metox' which could detect the ASV at a longer range than the approaching aircraft, reducing sightings dramatically in October to fifty-seven.

Shipping losses began to increase at the same time. During the last week of the year, a pack of twenty U-boats attacked a convoy of forty-five ships in the North Atlantic, sinking fourteen without loss. In an Admiralty review in February 1943, it was stated: 'Never before has the enemy displayed such singleness of purpose in utilising his strength against one objective—the interruption of supplies from America to Great Britain. The tempo is quickening and the critical phase of the U-boat war cannot be postponed.'

This was the time when Halifaxes were introduced to maritime duties, fitted with the improved ASV Mk.3, which was Bomber Command's H2S search radar adapted for maritime use, much improved from the Mk.1. It provided all-round search at greater ranges, and also gave more accurate data on range and bearing, as well as very accurate scanning during the attack. With the increase in U-boat losses, the Germans realised a new radar was being used and changed their tactics to remaining submerged at night, when charging their batteries during the day, defence against air attack required additional anti-aircraft guns fitted on the decks. U-boat sightings increased sharply, with more sinkings, but also extra aircraft losses to the submarine quadruple 20mm cannons and also long-range enemy fighters. During May 1943, forty-one U-boats were sunk, of which eight were in the Bay, with Halifaxes participating in five of them.

The initial Halifax maritime war load carried for anti-submarine patrols and convoy escort was six 250lb depth charges. The first success was on 29 March 1943 in poor weather conditions during escorting an approaching convoy. After a thorough search all around the convoy and no contact, the crew was about to break off and return to base, when a surfaced U-boat was spotted 2 miles behind the convoy, preparing to attack. Pilot Officer Davey was approaching from about 10 miles behind the submarine when he started his descent to 50 feet above the waves. With the U-boat crew unaware of the approaching Halifax, Davey was able to straddle the target with depth charges, leaving the ships in the convoy to pick up any survivors. By then, Holmsley South had become closed due to weather, with no available diversions. After 12 hours 14 minutes in the air, the crew were forced to bale out, leaving the

Radlett-built Halifax GR.II HR744 BY-O 58 Squadron fitted with ASV Mk.3 under the fuselage. It was delivered to 58 Squadron on 29 April 1943 and retired to 44 MU on 12 August 1944, where it was SOC on 23 November 1944. (*RAF Museum*)

Halifax to crash near Wivellescombe in Somerset. Among other losses in March were three aircraft, one which failed to return from a convoy escort patrol, another which crashed after take-off and the third in landing at St Eval at night when it hit a B-17 on the ground. As the month came to an end, on 27 March, a U-boat was spotted escorted by two motor vessels with the first stick of depth charges falling short, but the second stick of three straddling U-263. Intense gunfire from the escorts prevented an accurate assessment of damage caused.

U-boat operations ranged far and wide across the Atlantic, attacking vital supply convoys to Britain, but the Bay of Biscay was their operating centre. To reduce the effectiveness of the early ASV surface radars, the U-boats were equipped with a search receiver, but the ASV Mk.III was expected to overcome this. The Luftwaffe also introduced long-range fighters from late 1942, which were a hazard to Coastal Command operations, and not easily overcome. An example was a spirited defence by a 58 Squadron Halifax crew in early April, when they were attacked by a force of seven Ju 88s. During 47 minutes of attempted interceptions, three enemy fighters were driven off by concentrated fire from the Halifax guns, and the remainder broke off the engagement, probably due to shortage of fuel. On return to base, the only damage found on the Halifax was a bullet hole in the tailplane.

A 58 Squadron Halifax GR.II dropping depth charges on U-463 in the Atlantic on 15 May 1943. (*RAF Museum*)

The first success for 58 Squadron was on 7 May when U-663 was sunk by one of the Halifaxes, and four days later U-528 was also sunk in a combined effort with Royal Navy ships. The third success for 58 Squadron was on 15 May when U-463 was sunk, using six depth charges, followed by the Italian submarine *Tazzoli* the next day. On 31 May, after a determined fight, U-563 was left badly damaged, and was finally finished off by a pair of Sunderlands. With supposedly neutral Spanish fishing boats possibly advising the enemy of Allied shipping movements, leaflets were dropped warning that any ships not close inshore would be bombed from 31 May.

In addition to depth charges, 600lb anti-submarine bombs were developed. Maritime Halifaxes used their .303-inch nose-mounted machine guns to good effect against U-boat deck guns, but being only rifle calibre, it was felt a larger gun would be even more effective. The American 0.5-inch machine gun was mounted in the nose of the Halifax Mk.IAs, and after successful trials, over half of 58 Squadron was fitted with the new guns by the beginning of December. Operations were sometimes changed from a single aircraft patrol to a flight of four Halifaxes.

With long duration flights over the sea, it was necessary to establish a maximum safe endurance to maximise maritime operations. Halifax Mk.II HR815 was used by the Coastal Command Development Unit on 25 July, with all the normal operational equipment, full crew and 2,732 gallons of fuel, but with 350lb of armour plate removed, reducing the AUW to 61,570lb. The pilot maintained the lowest possible engine speed of 1,800rpm, allowing a speed of 140 knots, with 2 hours fuel remaining on return to Boscombe Down after 14 hours in the air. This gave a maximum endurance of 16 hours, which resulted in a recommended normal endurance of 13 hours for Halifax Mk.IIs. On a later test from Gibraltar in October, a Halifax flew for 18 hours.

With improved RAF tactics from April, U-boats were no longer able to travel submerged in the Bay of Biscay during the day or on the surface at night. Instead, they had to fight their way out to the Atlantic, and for improved defence were fitted with batteries of twin or four 20mm cannons and sailed in packs for mutual protection. To overcome this disadvantage, Coastal Command combined with special naval escort ships, which helped to counter the new threat. The effectiveness of the new tactics was confirmed when, on 15 June, a Halifax spotted three U-boats, and two damaged by anti-submarine bombs. With the unnamed U-boat circling defensively the Halifax pilot radioed for Royal Navy (RN) assistance, while the rear gunner foiled any attempts at repairing the boats, by firing at the decks of the exposed submarines. With the arrival of five RN warships, the Halifax was able to return to base after nearly 12 hours in the air.

A further confirmation of these new tactics occurred on 30 July, when a 53 Squadron Liberator spotted three U-boats, and called in support, including two 502 Squadron Halifaxes, which were carrying 600lb bombs. These could be dropped from a greater height than depth charges, reducing the hazards for the crew. With heavy fire from the U-boats, one Halifax attacked, but was damaged and dropped the bombs clear of a target, then had to withdraw. The second Halifax dropped three bombs from 3,000 feet seriously damaging U-462. Meanwhile, a Sunderland attacked and sank U-461. The Halifax returned for a second attempt on U-462, causing it to sink, and the remaining U-504 was sunk by the RN warships.

Major unsustainable losses were being made to the U-boat fleet by the RAF and RN, with ninety U-boats lost from May to July and a further sixty from August and October. This compared with the loss of ninety Allied ships in April, reducing to forty in May and only six in June. This resulted in a reversion to the earlier U-boat operation of remaining submerged during the day and only surfacing under cover of darkness. While RAF Coastal Command losses had been only five aircraft from January to July, the increases in Ju 88 formations over the Bay of Biscay resulted in two Halifaxes shot down in mid-August, followed by one ditching in the North Sea after engine failure. Another hit high ground in bad weather, followed by two more lost to Ju 88s, which sometimes flew in packs of up to fourteen aircraft. Fortunately, 502 Squadron was able to claim the sinking of U-221 on 27 September. The tide of the Battle of the Atlantic had turned irreversibly in the Allies' favour, breaking the German first line of defence in the west, in preparation for the invasion of Europe. Both 58 and 502 Squadrons moved to the newly constructed St Davids in early December, bringing them under the same organisation as 517 (Met) Squadron, which was reequipped with Halifax Vs in November 1943 from 1404 Met Flight and moved to nearby Brawdy on 1 February 1944.

Meteorological flights over the sea commenced in 1940, with Coastal Command taking responsibility in 1941, and the units gained squadron status in 1943. Accurate weather forecasting was essential to the success of the Allied bombing campaign against Germany to overcome the limitations of the early navigation and blind flying aids available during the early part of the war. It was also vital from 1943 for the success of the planned invasion of Europe. The accuracy of the forecasting relied totally on collecting weather data from the Western Approaches to Britain from the North Atlantic, from where most of the weather originated. Some information came from surface ships, while more came from regular Coastal Command patrols, but these were at low-level, and secondary to the primary task. It was essential to obtain data from all levels to provide accurate predictions of approaching weather.

The first Halifax unit was 518 Squadron, which formed at Stornoway with Mk.Vs on 6 July 1943. The Met Halifaxes were modified by Cuncliffe Owen at Eastleigh, Southampton, with the nose gun replaced by a navigation table for a meteorological observer. This specially trained crew member was provided with an accurate outside air temperature and humidity gauge with an external sensing probe mounted on the starboard side of the nose. A sophisticated radio altimeter could be compared with the standard barometric altimeter, making it possible to measure sea level pressures. Additional navigation aids included Loran for long-range fixing, Gee, ASV and an accurate American drift meter. To extend the aircraft endurance, additional fuel tanks were fitted in the bomb-bay. On 15 September, 518 Squadron began operations, and a move was made to Tiree ten days later.

To achieve reliable advanced knowledge of the weather to plan major raids across Europe, it was essential to use meteorological flight information way out into the North Atlantic to predict conditions to be expected for operations. The Weather flights were flown from the north of Scotland, down to Gibraltar, with other flights from bases along the east coast of England. These flights were hazardous, as they had to be flown precisely in all weathers, along predetermined routes, with readings taken of barometric pressure, temperature and humidity, complimented by observations of weather conditions, visibility, cloud levels and wind strength and direction. With the vastly increased scale of Bomber Command operations, the Met operations needed to be expanded considerably. Where the early Met readings had been the responsibility of the Halifax navigator, the expansion required the need for skilled meteorological observers with training starting in late 1942, and by the end of the war nearly 100 had

Nose art on Halifax Met.III of 518 Squadron in 1945. (*RAF Museum*)

Radlett-built Halifax Met.III LV788 Y3-R 518 Squadron on a fighter affiliation exercise over Aldergrove with Spitfire Mk.VII MD159. LV788 was delivered to 78 Squadron on 14 January 1944 and passed to 518 Squadron on 25 May 1944. It was SOC on 26 April 1946. (*RAF Museum*)

qualified. This allowed Bomber Command to plan with greater certainty, the strategic campaign against Germany.

The Brawdy-based 517 Squadron operating a triangular pattern and Aldergrove based 518 Squadron flew a single Halifax on a daily straight-and-back course. This latter pattern consisted of flying along 265 degrees a distance of 700 nautical miles, with 50-nautical-mile intervals when steep climbs and descents would be made, crossing each imaginary point at a designated pressure level. Pressure readings were taken at sea level every 100 nautical miles using a radio altimeter, and when 700 nautical miles had been reached, a circular climb was made to around 20,000 feet. It was essential the patterns were flown accurately as defined by the meteorological observer in the crew. With weather conditions often constantly changing, observations were sent to base every half hour. This pattern was flown to reach the 700-nautical-mile point at both midday and midnight. These operations were not without hazards, as all flights had to be made regularly by day and night in all weathers.

An additional triangular flight code named Bismuth was allocated to 518 Squadron with detachments to Tiree, resulting in four flights every day, the apex of the triangle being close to Iceland. At the start, 518 Squadron had nine crews, building up to around twenty-eight crews. Diversions were not uncommon due to weather, and if the forecasted weather was predicted to be bad at base, an alternative departure airfield with better conditions would be selected. Once the results from the aircraft had been received, they were sent to all commands to allow weather predictions to be made for planning Bomber Command raids over Europe. Maintaining very high standards of weather forecasting made it possible for the raids to be more effective.

In September 1943, 520 Squadron became the third Met unit when it was formed in Gibraltar and received its first Halifax Mk.V in February 1944, as part of a mixed fleet of aircraft. The squadron used its Halifaxes to fly similar out and back patrols to 518 Squadron, in addition to the triangular patterns flown by 517 Squadron,

Samlesbury-built Halifax Met.6 RG778 XB-B 224 Squadron over Gibraltar. It was delivered to 1361 Met. Flight on 4 February 1946, passing to 521 Squadron on 16 March 1946, then 518 Squadron on 8 April. It joined 202 Squadron on 4 March 1948, then 224 Squadron on 28 October 1948. It was declared Cat 5 on 7 May 1951 and passed to No. 4 School of Technical Training at St Athan as 6857M. (*RAF Museum*)

Above: Landing accident to Samlesbury-built Halifax Met.6 RG839 at Gibraltar in 1952. (*Handley Page Association*)

Below: Another view of Halifax Met.6 RG839 after crash-landing at Gibraltar in 1952. RG839 was delivered to 224 Met Squadron on 13 December 1958, and was written off in the crash-landing on 13 March 1952. (*Handley Page Association*)

operations continuing until the end of the war. No. 519 Squadron formed at Wick on 7 August 1943, but did not receive Halifax Mk.IIIs until August 1945 at Tain, and finally disbanded at Leuchars on 31 May 1946. The other wartime Met unit was 521 Squadron which formed at Bircham Newton on 22 July 1942, but did not received Halifax Mk.IIIs at Chivenor until December 1945, and disbanded there on 31 March 1946. The final Halifax Met sortie was with Mk.6 RG841 which operated with 224 (Met) Squadron from Gibraltar until August 1946.

To prepare crews for Coastal Command duties, two training units were created in October 1943. At Aldergrove, No. 1674 Conversion Unit was tasked with training crews for the two British based general reconnaissance squadron, complemented by 518 Squadron which trained crews for the specific duties required. Starting on 30 October, sixty crews were trained in five months. Although losses to enemy action were nil, there were losses due to bad weather and technical difficulties. The most critical phase was during take-off and landings, although if the pilot could see the end of the runway, it was considered safe to depart. One challenge was maintaining sufficient fuel levels when forced to make unscheduled diversions, and structural stresses on the airframes due to rough weather caused another challenge. Heavy icing could be experienced as well as violent thunderstorms, which had to be flown right through, if on the aircraft track. As with the long-range bombing sorties over Europe, the early Merlin engines were not ideal for long flights, with high boost and low revolutions required to maintain endurance, followed by the rapid climbs to 20,000 feet. It was not unusual to return to base with one engine failed, and ditching in the North Atlantic was not a survivable option due to low water temperatures. A number of aircraft simply vanished, as if two engines failed on one side, there was no alternative to ditching, and the weather could be so bad that severe icing could bring it down. During 1944, 518 Squadron losses were a high eight aircraft.

With the U-boats sailing across the Bay of Biscay from late 1943, 58 and 502 general reconnaissance squadron Halifaxes were equipped with parachute flares to illuminate the targets. On 2 January 1944, a 58 Squadron Halifax damaged U-445 and three days later another squadron aircraft damaged U-415. The Halifaxes had to fly at around 1,000 feet for the ASH radar to stand a chance of detecting a target, but the radar could often be unreliable. Flares would be dropped at around 2 miles from the target, often flying as low as 200 feet, with the U-boat crew firing at the approaching aircraft. Up to six depth charges or four 600lb bombs could be dropped, but it was often difficult to determine damage. In June, air burst medium case 250lb and 500lb bombs were introduced against deck targets, which were particularly effective in anti-shipping patrols.

By July 1944, 58 and 502 Squadrons were involved in three types of operations. These were anti-submarine in the English Channel and Bay of Biscay mostly at night; anti shipping patrols along the French coast and over the Bay of Biscay; and armed reconnaissance around the Channel Islands and Normandy coast in support of the D-Day landings. From late July into August, the two squadrons were mainly involved over the Bay of Biscay and Brittany coastline on anti-shipping operations, to counter enemy efforts to supply their forces under the cover of darkness. During this time, the last U-boat attacks were recorded with 502 Squadron damaging U-413 on 8 June and destroying U-981 on 12 August.

With the lack of targets, at the end of August, both squadrons moved to Stornaway in the Outer Hebrides for anti-submarine patrols; no targets were detected. In October, the role was changed back to anti-shipping operations covering the area between Norway and Denmark. This disrupted enemy raw material deliveries and troop carriers from Oslo to strengthen the western front against the Allied advances. During the month of October, twenty-seven combat attacks were made with destruction in a number of cases, although others were difficult to confirm in the dark. With the Halifax all-up weight increased to 63,000lb, the bomb load could be increased from five to six 500lb medium blast fragmentation bombs.

The success of the anti-shipping operations forced the Germans to increase their night fighter patrols, but the Halifax crews flew down to 200 feet above the sea, where enemy night fighters had difficulty detecting the aircraft. Attacks against German shipping continued during November with some successes, but with the loss of two 502 Squadron crews, bringing their total combat losses for the year to five aircraft, and four with 58 Squadron. There were greater losses due to accidents. With poor weather in December restricting the normal anti-shipping patrols, the opportunity was taken to attack shipping in harbours along the Norwegian coast.

During February 1945, the more specialised and reliable Halifax GR.III began deliveries to the two squadrons, these aircraft having the bomb load increased to nine 500lb bombs, although the Met.IIIs were not available until March, when they began to replace the Met.Vs. With the end of the war fast approaching, Germany attempted to withdraw troops and equipment from southern Norway, keeping both anti-shipping squadrons busy. During this time, 58 Squadron carried out fifty-five attacks during March, and in April both squadrons managed 101 attacks, the highest to date, and recorded the destruction of at least 5,998 tons of shipping, with four Halifaxes lost. These actions severely limited the import of vital supplies from Scandinavia at a critical time. No. 502 Squadron were congratulated in sinking over an estimated 25,000 tons of shipping since January, with another 50,000 tons damaged. Losses to 58 Squadron included six Halifaxes to enemy action from February to April, with the increased combat patrols.

Both squadrons made their final combat operations on 3 May, with 58 and 502 Squadrons sinking a ship each, followed by the unconditional German surrender on 7 May. Although the aggressive nature of the operations had reduced, there was still a need for Coastal Command, with 58 and 501 Squadrons flying unarmed shipping reconnaissance to identify German ships escaping from Russian held territory. Both squadrons disbanded on 25 May 1945, and although the Halifax was withdrawn from anti-shipping duties in Coastal Command, the type continued in the meteorological role, until replaced by Hastings transports.

In December 1945, 521 Squadron replaced its Fortress IIIs at Chivenor with Halifax Mk.IIIs and was disbanded on 31 March 1946. On 1 October 1946, 518 Squadron was renumbered 202 Squadron when it was reformed at Aldergrove equipped with Halifax GR.6s with Halifax A.9s added in August 1949. The Halifaxes were replaced by Hastings Met.1s in October 1950.

Above: Personnel of 520 Squadron in front of Speke-built Halifax NA223 during a detachment to Gibraltar. It was delivered to 520 Squadron on 3 June 1945 and moved to 518 Squadron on 25 April 1946. It was SOC as scrap on 1 November 1946. (*RAF Museum*)

Below: Samlesbury-built Halifax GR.III NR187 at A&AEE in May 1945. This aircraft was delivered to 102 Squadron on 29 October 1944 and passed to 111 OTU on 28 November 1945. It was SOC as scrap on 13 February 1947. The first GR.III was delivered to 58 Squadron in March 1945 at Stornoway and the squadron disbanded on 25 May 1945. (*RAF Museum*)

Radlett-built Halifax A.9 RT923 Y3-A 202 Squadron after a crash-landing at Aldergrove on 6 September 1949. This aircraft was delivered to 47 Squadron on 13 November 1946 and joined 297 Squadron on 28 July 1947. It was issued to 202 Squadron on 25 August 1949 and was scrapped following the accident. (*RAF Museum*)

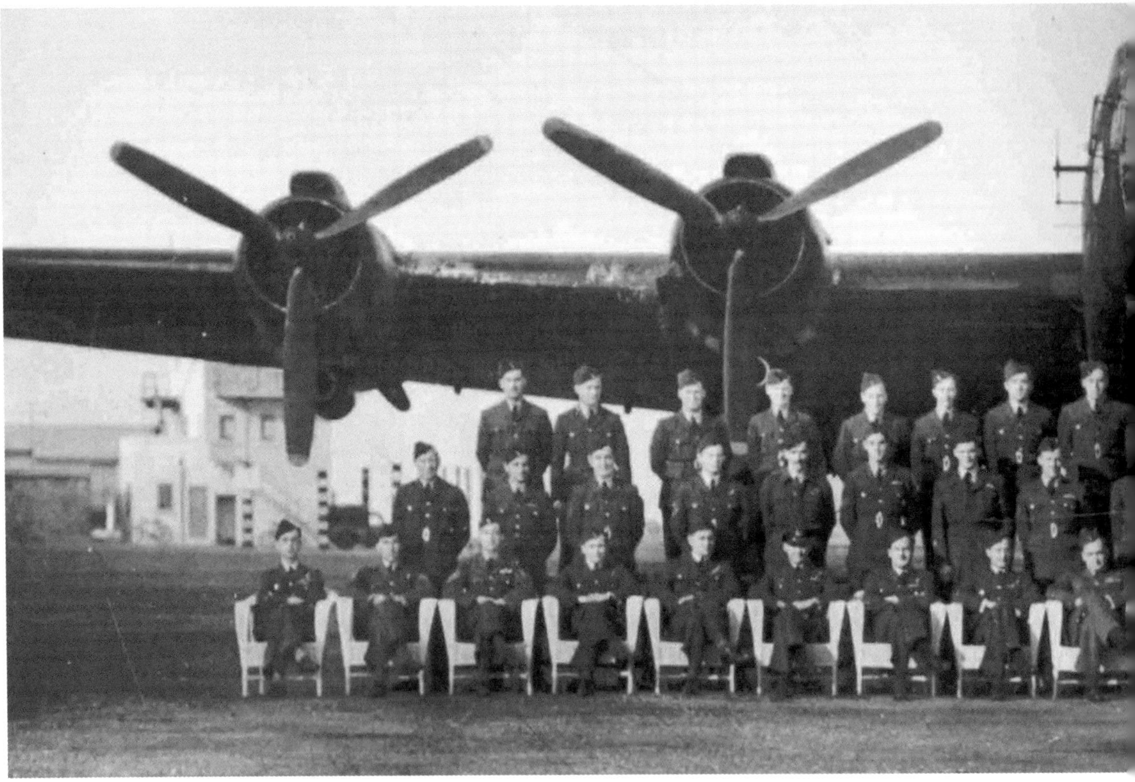

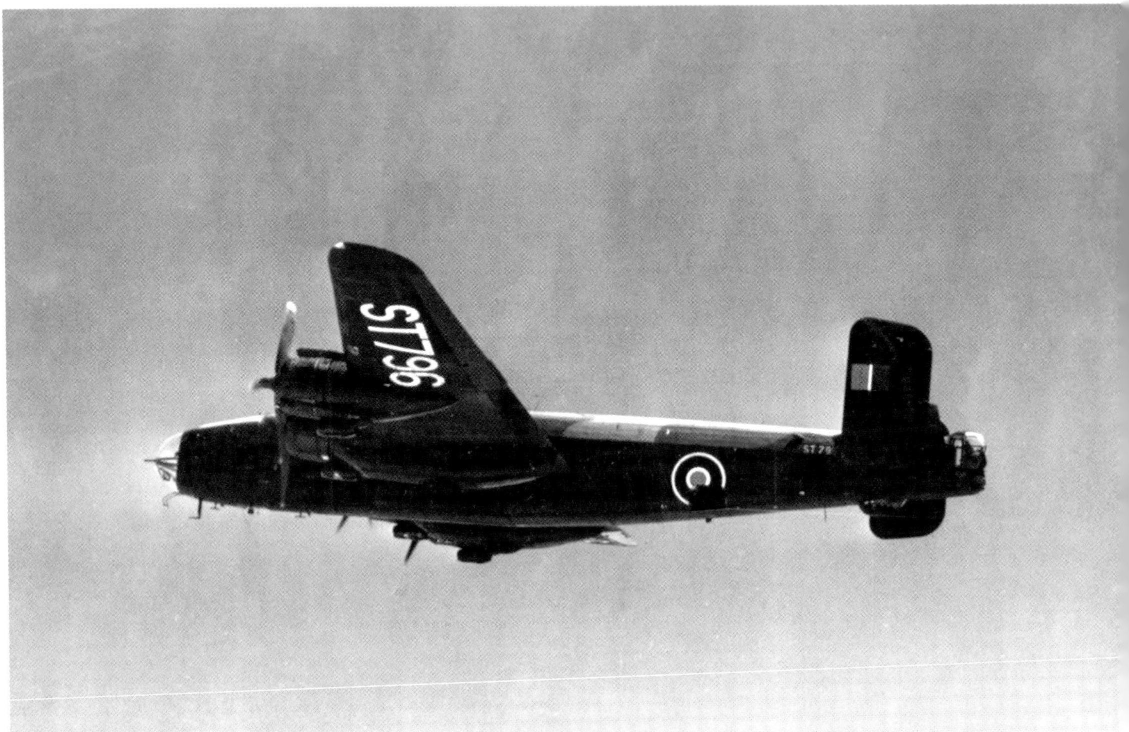
ST796

Above: Samlesbury-built Halifax Met.6 with the personnel from 202 Squadron at Gibraltar in January 1948. (*RAF Museum*)

Opposite: One of the last batch of twenty-five Halifaxes built at Samlesbury, Met.6 ST796 joined the Meteorological Research Flight at Farnborough on 15 September 1950, before going to Aldergrove based 202 Squadron. These flights were not without danger, as thirty-two aircrew members were lost over a five year period.

10

Training

With the high volume of Halifax operations in both Bomber and Coastal Commands, it was essential to create an effective training organisation to convert crews to the aircraft. The Halifaxes were being introduced to service at around the same time as the Stirling and Lancaster heavy four-engine bombers, putting additional strain on the training organisation. The major bomber in service before the entry into service of the new aircraft was the Vickers Wellington, which had allowed crews to become operational, gaining experience which made them suitable for posting to the first heavy bomber squadrons. As already mentioned, 35 Squadron, the first with Halifaxes, were responsible for their own conversion training; but as further squadrons received Halifaxes, it became beyond the capability to train new crews, while still operating in combat. A more formal training system started in a modest way in late 1941 with the formation of 28 Halifax Conversion Flight (HCF) at Leconfield, but in the early stages, the logistical support was lacking, making routine maintenance demanding. New crews came from the Wellington-equipped Operational Training Units (OTUs), with the requirement to convert them to the new bombers at Heavy Conversion Units (HCUs).

The first Halifaxes for 28 HCF were supplied by both 35 and 76 Squadrons in October, while others were allocated after repair from accidents, as they were considered unsuitable for operations. With the need for further expansion, in December 1941, a HCU was formed in each group, with four aircraft allocated to each squadron as a conversion flight. The first was 1652 HCU in 4 Group which formed at Marston Moor on 2 January 1942 with thirty-two Halifaxes and 102 Squadron formed its Conversion Flight five days later. Nos 10, 35 and 76 Squadrons formed their flights within a month, followed by 78 Squadron a month later. The training syllabus consisted of some 20 hours covering all aspects of aircraft operation, providing advanced training to new crews, and they often had the advantage of dual pilot controls.

It would be rare for aircraft allocated to training duties to be new, with existing aircraft allocated from squadrons to training units, as new ones were delivered. This resulted in some very tired well-worn or repaired aircraft being used for training, causing some challenging maintenance problems. These training units were equipped with the early Merlin-powered Mk.I, Mk.II and Mk.V Halifaxes, which, in addition to the known shortcomings, were difficult to maintain by the less experienced ground crews outside in all weathers. Even when the aircraft were serviceable, the performance was unpredictable and to a poor standard. At the HCUs, it was generally accepted training was more hazardous than operations over Germany, especially with low crew experience and bad weather. None of these problems were unique to the Halifax, as the same problems existed in all training units regardless of type. With the aircraft lined up on the airfield for the day's flying, a crew would go to the end of the line, starting pre-flight checks, until they found one which was acceptable, with none normally found ever totally serviceable. A crew could have to check out up to five aircraft, with all their kit, before finding one that was satisfactory, being somewhat weary before they started the flight. A more serious problem could be the proneness of a Merlin to catch fire due to overheating. The extra load on the remaining engines could then cause them to progressively overheat, the results estimated to have caused more casualties than enemy action. Should a crew have an emergency in the air, or just be lost, they were instructed to call what was known as a 'Darkie'. Each aircraft had a 10-mile range transmitter fitted; the signal picked up the nearest Observer Corps post, which would alert the closest suitable airfield to assist. The crews were instructed to make a very precise transmission, repeating every call three times to allow a bearing to be taken for guidance to land as soon as possible.

When 'Bomber' Harris conceived the three thousand-bomber raids, to make up the numbers, OTU and HCU aircraft and crews were added to the front line, often flown by instructors, but also by crews still in training. These operations, while giving first-hand experience, did disrupt the training programme.

In June 1942, conversion flights were formed with 158 and 408 Squadrons with delivery of some totally unsuitable Halifaxes, due to maintenance problems. As Bomber Command expanded during 1942, conversion flights were disbanded and absorbed into the HCUs. It wasn't long before the HCUs began to specialise in training on individual types, with 1667 HCU concentrating on Halifax Mk.Vs with thirty-six aircraft at Faldingworth and later Sandtoft. No. 1656 HCU was formed at Lindholme on 10 October 1942 within 1 Group and by March 1943 had 32 Halifaxes, but by September 1943 shared H2S training between sixteen Halifax IIs and Vs, and sixteen Lancasters. In 4 Group 1658 HCU was formed on 7 October 1942 at Riccall with thirty-two Halifax Mk.I, II, III and V and absorbed the conversion flights from 158 and 10 Squadrons. Also in 4 Group was 1659 HCU (RCAF) which formed at Leeming on 7 October 1942 from 405 and 408 conversion flights to provide crews to 6 (RCAF) Group with sixteen Halifax Mk.I, II and V. It came under the control of 6 Group on 1 January 1943 and moved to Topcliffe in March, with an establishment of thirty-two Halifaxes, increasing to thirty-six aircraft in May 1944. When 6 Group began to convert to Lancasters, 1659 HCU began replacing the Halifaxes from November 1944, with thirty-two Lancasters established by May 1945. No. 1661 HCU in 5 Group briefly operated Halifaxes at Winthorpe in September 1943, but two months later they standardised with Stirlings. On 26 January 1943, 1662, HCU was formed within 1 Group at Blyton and by March was equipped with sixteen Halifax Mk.I, II and V, plus sixteen Lancasters. When the Lancasters were transferred to No. 1 Lancaster

Finishing School in November 1943, the Halifax compliment was increased to thirty-two aircraft. On 2 March 1943, 1663 HCU was formed at Rufforth in 4 Group equipped with thirty-two Halifaxes by the following month, increasing to thirty-six Mk.Vs by May 1944. It disbanded on 28 May 1945. No. 1664 HCU (RCAF) was formed at Croft on 10 May 1943 within 6 Group, and moved to Dishforth on 7 December 1943, with an establishment of thirty-two Halifaxes by April 1944. By August 1944, the total Halifax establishment had increased to thirty-six aircraft, but in November it reequipped with Lancasters, as the RCAF squadrons replaced their Halifaxes.

To provide relevant training for the Airborne Forces squadrons, 1665 HCU was formed at Mepal on 23 April 1943 within 3 Group, and on 1 December 1943 was transferred to 38 Group, moving to Tilstock on 23 January 1944. The main equipment

Early Radlett-built Halifax B.II R9430 19 was with 1658 HCU at Rickall in July 1943. The aircraft was being flown on the No. 3 Merlin only, to determine height loss for an emergency recovery. It was delivered to 10 Conversion Flight on 25 January 1942, and moved to 76 Conversion Flight on 18 March, before going to 1658 HCU. It retained its training role with No. 3 School of Technical Training on 28 February 1945. (*Air Historical Branch*)

Above: Radlett-built Halifax B.II (Special) W7927 TT-R with 1658 HCU after crash-landing at Fairwood Common on 9 April 1944. It was delivered to 102 Squadron on 18 November 1942 and joined 466 Squadron on 6 October 1943. It was allocated to 1658 HCU on 12 March 1944 and following its accident was SOC on 28 April 1944. (*RAF Museum*)

Below: Ground crew with 1663 HCU at Rufforth warming up, before servicing Halifaxes for the training programme. (*Air Historical Branch*)

Halifax B.II in a T.2 hangar with 1663 HCU at Rufforth for maintenance at night. (*Air Historical Branch*)

was Stirlings with Horsa gliders, but there were also seventeen Halifax Mk.IIIs. It moved to Marston Moor in 4 Group in August 1945 to become 1665 (Heavy Transport) Conversion Unit equipped with Halifax A.IIIs, A.Vs and A.VII. It merged with 1332 HTCU at Linton-on-Ouse on 13 July 1946, as part of 4 (Transport) Group. It was then based at Matching, initially equipped with three Halifax A.Mk.VIIs on 1 August 1946, with two more arriving in addition to Stirlings. Two flights were equipped with Halifaxes, and the other with Stirlings. The Halifax strength soon grew to twenty-five A.Mk.III with the Stirlings withdrawn. The unit took part in a number of exercises and training operations, and was disbanded at Wethersfield in January 1946.

With the increasing use of Halifaxes in 6 (RCAF) Group No. 1666 HCU was formed at Dalton on 5 June 1943. A move was made to Wombleton on 21 October 1943, with the first course starting on 5 November with sixteen Halifaxes, increasing to thirty-six aircraft by May 1944. From January 1945, the HCU reequipped with

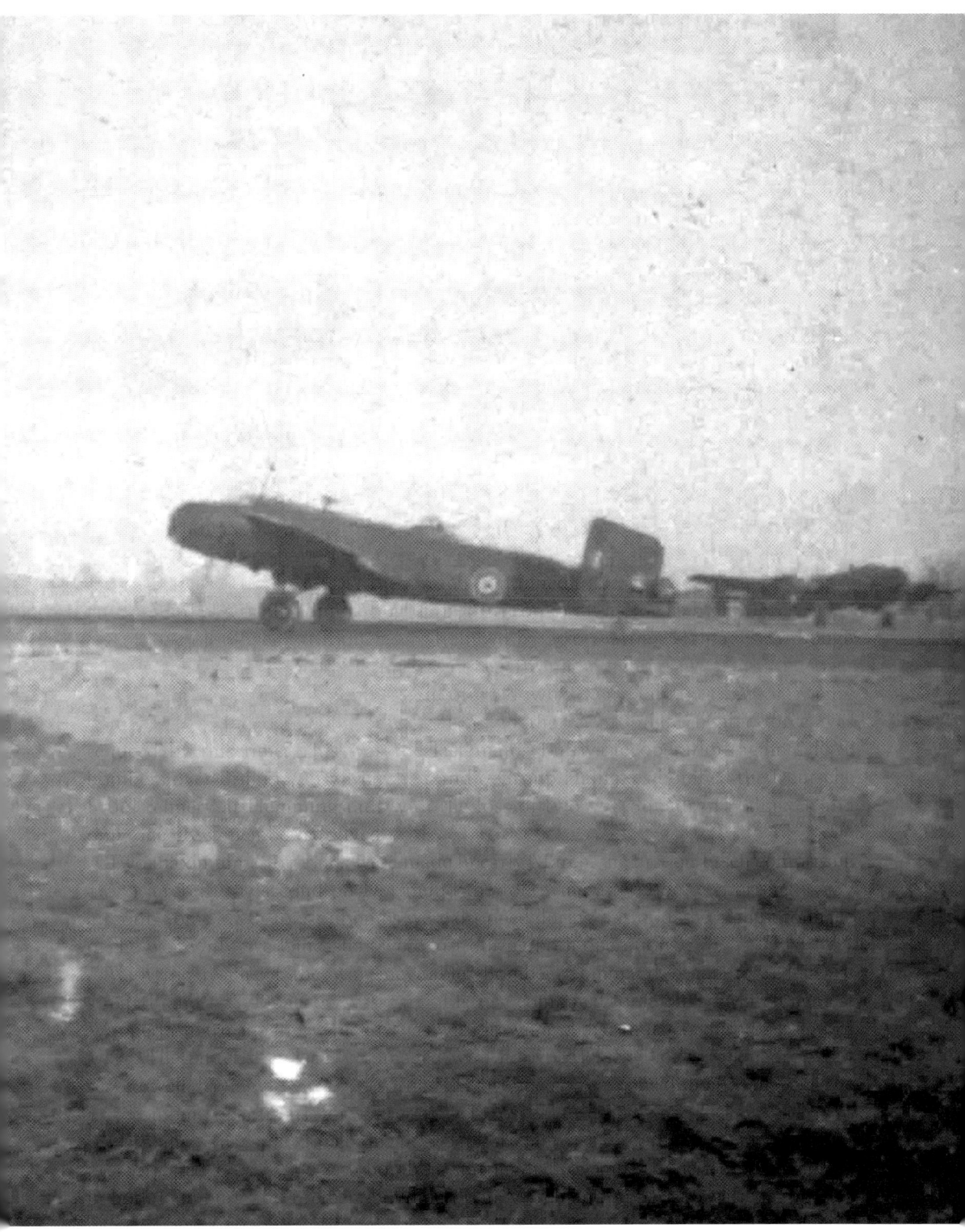

Poor quality shot of Halifax B.II Srs.1 with 1664 HCU at Dishforth in 1944. (*RAF Museum*)

Lancasters. No. 1667 HCU was formed at Lindholme in 1 Group on 1 June 1943, with two flights, one equipped with Halifax Mk.IIs and Vs, the other with Lancasters. Moving to Faldingworth and then Sandtoft by May 1944, the establishment had increased to thirty-six Halifax Mk.Vs and it was disbanded on 9 November 1945. No. 1668 HCU was formed at Balderton in 5 Group on 15 August 1943 with sixteen each of Halifax Mk.IIs and Lancasters, but became No. 5 Lancaster Finishing School in November 1943 at Syerston. The final bomber heavy training unit was 1669 HCU which formed at Langar on 15 August 1944 with thirty-six Halifax II and Vs. By November 1944, it had converted to Lancaster flight training. On 10 October 1943, 1674 HCU formed at Aldergrove within 17 Group, to train crews for long-range patrol squadrons in Coastal Command with Halifax Mk.II and Vs, in addition to Fortresses and Liberators. On 18 January 1944, Halifax Met flying training started at Longtown until July 1944, when a return was made to Aldergrove. Each course included 45 hours flight training over a period of three weeks. The HCU disbanded at Lossiemouth on 30 November 1945.

Flight training was not without its hazards. It was not helped by the poor condition of some of the aircraft. As a result, a large number of aircrew casualties during the war occurred during training, with the urgency of getting crews on to operations to replace combat losses. It was not only poor serviceability, but also bad weather which caused accidents with inexperienced crews, either hitting high ground in cloud, or during local airfield flying. While some aircraft were written off after only a short period, others managed to survive the rigours of training for a considerable time. One example was B.Mk.I L9534, which was originally delivered to 76 Squadron on 15 June 1941. It moved to 28 Halifax Conversion Flight, before being used by 1652 and 1659 HCUs, finally being withdrawn on 20 September 1945.

Typical monthly flying times at the HCUs were often over 2,000 hours, and even when a Halifax was withdrawn from flying training, some were adapted for ground training in crew procedures. By the end of 1944, the training courses had been increased to five weeks, starting with one week in ground school followed by four weeks flying training. Total training flight hours had been increased to 41 hours, with about ten crews during the summer months, reducing to seven in the winter.

Another specialist training unit was the Pathfinder Force Navigation Training Unit which was formed on 10 April 1943 at Gransden Lodge for 8 Group. Initial equipment was eight Lancasters, four Stirlings and four Halifax Mk.IIs, eventually growing to nine Halifax and nine Lancasters by September 1943. The Halifaxes were mainly ex-35 Squadron aircraft equipped with H2S. A move was made to Warboys in March 1944, by which time the Halifaxes had been withdrawn, as Lancasters had been standardised with 8 Group path finding heavy bomber operations.

Towards the end of 1944, improved Halifax B.Mk.IIIs began to join the HCUs training programme, flying alongside the earlier Mk.Is and IIs. With the possibility of the war coming to an end, the HCUs went through a major reorganisation in November 1944 with the formation of No. 7 (Bomber HCU) to manage all Bomber Command HCUs. With Lancasters becoming the primary RAF heavy bomber, many of the Halifaxes were withdrawn from the HCUs, but some continued into mid-1945, with 1652 HCU finally disbanding on 25 June.

For overseas postings, crews were usually type trained before departure, but with Halifaxes arriving in the Middle East, there was a need for the formation of No. 2 Middle East Training School at Aqir in Palestine. Three Halifaxes were allocated, although one was soon lost on 8 December 1942 when it had to ditch due to an engine fire. The other two survived until March 1944, by which time the training requirement no longer existed.

The 1385 (Heavy Transport Support) Conversion Unit (HTSCU) was formed at Wethersfield on 1 April 1946 for training skills in supply and heavy equipment dropping and some glider towing. Five Halifax A.VIIs were delivered and after four courses had been completed, the unit was amalgamated with 1333 Transport Support Conversion Unit (TSCU) at Syerston in early July. By May 1947, it was renumbered 1332 HTCU and was disbanded on 5 January 1948.

The Empire Air Navigation School (EANS), which formed at Shawbury on 28 October 1944, was to have been equipped with twenty Lancasters, but in January 1945, it was decided to supply eighteen Halifax B.Mk.IIIs, with two Lancasters, the

One of the last Halifaxes, was Samlesbury-built Mk.VI ST814 SG-FB with the Empire Air Navigation School in India 1946/47. All armament was been removed with the turrets faired over, but H2S was retained as a navigation aid. The aircraft was delivered to the EANS on 29 November 1946, and went to Cranwell on 27 September 1948. After going to 29 MU on 5 August 1949, it was sold to the Lancashire Aircraft Corporation on 2 February 1951. (*RAF Museum*)

first four Halifaxes arriving on 6 February. The staff pilots were soon trained with the first navigation course departing for Gibraltar with three aircraft on 28 March. Destinations were as far afield as Malta, Italy and Iceland. One particularly long-range flight was to South East Asia in Halifax Mk.III NA279, which departed on 15 June 1945 and returned to Shawbury on 28 July, the aircraft operated by 3 Flight being used for the long flights. No. 1 Flight with nineteen Mk.IIIs specialised in advanced navigation training. Other long-distance flights were made, one of which was to India and Burma in January 1946, when the aircraft performed well throughout the trip. Flights were also made to the Middle East, around the Mediterranean and to Africa demonstrating the latest navigation aids and evaluating new techniques. These flights were able to increase the knowledge of the school's experienced staff navigators operating in hot climates. The EANS received a final Halifax 6 ST814 named *Sirius* in November 1946 which was used for liaison flights to Iceland and the Mediterranean, and although most of the school's Halifaxes were disposed of in August 1947, *Sirius* was not withdrawn to 45 MU until January 1948.

Also established at Debden on 7 March 1946 was the Empire Radio School (ERS), as the main RAF unit for air radio training, with the first of two Halifax B.6s delivered in June fitted out as a flying classroom. The second aircraft, RG815, named *Mercury*, was sent to Canada for cold weather trials at temperatures down to -35 degrees C. The ERS retired most of its Halifaxes during August 1947, but in February 1948, Mk.6 ST806 was delivered from 29 MU and *Sirius* followed in June, both aircraft being finally withdrawn in September.

The final Halifax training duties were with No. 1 Parachute Training School at Upper Heyford which used a few Mk.9s from January 1950, until the last one was retired in April 1953, bringing a final end to RAF Halifax operations.

11

Cargo Halifax and Halton

The large capacity of the Halifax fuselage made it suitable for the carriage of both passengers and freight without any major structural modifications, following experience of the SOE supply dropping operations. The first modification to carry cargo was made by 144 MU at Maison Blanch in North Africa, where some ex 148, 178 and 462 Halifax IIs were modified as freighters to carry spare engines, and even a Spitfire fuselage externally, below the bomb-bay between sheet metal side plates. The first of four conversions were made in March 1944, achieving a high utilisation, with the capacity in the fuselage to carry passengers.

In Britain, four Halifax Mk.IIIs were allocated to 246 Squadron, which reformed at Lyneham on 11 October 1944, with the title Halifax Development Flight, which became C Flight of the squadron. To establish the best accommodation for long-range passenger operations, a trial flight was made to Cairo in December, rapidly followed by a special flight to India. Regular Halifax services were started on 17 January 1945, flying from Lyneham to Cairo via Istres and two more Halifaxes were soon delivered. One of these was configured to carry twelve passengers on an experimental trooping flight to Karachi, but instead of passengers, 4,000lb of freight was substituted and the seats stowed to make room. On 12 March, operations were transferred from Lyneham to Merryfield for 187 Squadron, which had been formed on 1 February 1945 with a planned strength of twenty-five Halifax C.Mk.IIIs, but it converted to Dakotas in March.

Meanwhile, 96 Squadron became the second Halifax transport unit which reformed at Leconfield on 21 December 1944, and shared the airfield with 640 Squadron Halifax bombers, to combine technical support at a base planned to become part of Transport Command. Crews were mainly Australian tour expired personnel, and only a few of the planned twenty-five Halifax C.Mk.IIIs were delivered, which had been converting from B.Mk.IIIs with all bomber operational equipment removed. For passenger carrying, eight seats were fitted in the rear fuselage, with another six in the centre section. The interior could be configured for nine stretcher patients, or with a bare interior freight could be carried. With the arrival of the first four Halifaxes on 7 and 8 January, training started, and on 2 February, the squadron personnel were told the unit would be moved to the Middle East to replace 267 Squadron. Then, in mid-March, both 96 and 187 Squadrons reequipped with Dakotas, with the Halifaxes going into storage at 29 MU at High Ercall where they were sold for scrap.

Speke-built Halifax C.III NA195 in April 1945. (*RAF Museum*)

The Halifax Development Flight continued to operate on cargo duties to the Middle East until the end of March, and disbanded on 3 April 1945.

With Germany defeated in May 1945, most of the Bomber Command Halifaxes were surplus to requirements, while surviving Lancasters were earmarked for the 'Tiger Force' to be used in the offensive against Japan. Some of the surplus Halifax squadrons were allocated to interim transport duties, pending re-equipping with more suitable transport aircraft. Among these units were squadrons in 4 Group, which became part of RAF Transport Command on 7 May 1945 under the command of Air Vice-Marshal H. S. P. Walmsley. The redesignated group was organised into three groups, 42 Base with 102 Squadron at Pocklington, 346 and 347 Squadrons at Elvington and 77 Squadron at Full Sutton. 43 Base consisted of 466 (RAAF) Squadron at Driffield, 51 Squadron at Leconfield and 158 Squadron at Lisset. The third was 44 Base with 76 Squadron based at Holme-on-Spalding Moor, 78 Squadron at Breighton and 10 Squadron at Melbourne. While the emergency runway at Carnaby was retained, Snaith and Burn were put under care and maintenance. No. 640 Squadron was not included and therefore disbanded at Leconfield on 7 May 1945. The squadron had flown 2,423 Halifax sorties, but lost forty aircraft. It had also won the 4 Group Bombing Trophy a record five times.

The plan was for the squadrons to maintain currency with their Halifaxes, pending re-equipment with more suitable transport. Both 51 and 158 Squadrons were to convert to Stirling Vs; 10, 76, 77 and 78 Squadrons to Dakota IVs and both 102 and 466 Squadrons to Liberators. With the future of Free French 346 and 347 Squadrons undecided, they retained their Halifaxes and remained under the control of 4 Group. Throughout the remainder of May and into June, the crews continued on cross country flights, and the 'Cooks Tours' of groups of twelve ground personnel, to see the devastation caused by the bombers. The new aircraft began to reequip the squadrons in June, the Group taking over responsibility for conversion training in Transport Command, a contrast to its wartime role as pioneering night bombing within Bomber Command.

On 1 June, 4 Group absorbed stations and units from 44 Group consisting of three OTUs and other heavy bomber training units. These were 105 OTU at Bramcote with satellites at Nuneaton and Bitteswell, 108 OTU at Wymeswold with a satellite at Castle Donington and 109 OTU at Crosby-on-Eden. They also took over the Lancaster Finishing School at Ossington, the Heavy Conversion Unit at Rickall and the Bomb Disposal Wing HQ at Doncaster.

The first Stirling V transport version was delivered to 51 Squadron at Leconfield in June 1945, the aircraft carrying five crew and up to forty passengers with all armament removed and faired over. Also, in May, 158 Squadron received its Stirlings, with training including the Cooks Tours, followed by a flight to Castel Benito and long-distance training flights to India, via St Mawgan in July and August. Halifaxes were replaced by Dakotas with 10, 76, 77, and 78 Squadrons from May to August. No. 102 Squadron retained Halifaxes until October 1945 and moved to Bassingbourn on 8 September, where it was equipped with Liberators. No. 466 Squadron retained their Halifaxes until August 1945 and after also moving to Bassingbourn, it took Liberators on charge in October. The two Free French squadrons spent time dumping surplus bomb stocks in the North Sea, and were used on transport duties until transferred to the French Air Force, and from late October they departed Elvington for new bases in France. The surplus Halifaxes were never used on RAF transport duties, but having been used for crew currency, they were then flown to MUs and scrapped.

However, this was not the end of the Halifax in the transport role. Halifax B.Mk.VI TW783 was being tested at Boscombe Down at an increased all up weight of 68,000lb under all flight conditions, and the resulting modifications were incorporated in LV838, which was the prototype of the C.Mk.VI, with all operational equipment removed. The bomb doors were replaced by a 272-cubic-foot cargo pannier, below what was the bomb-bay, which was almost identical to the bulged bomb door configuration developed to carry 4,000 and 8,000lb bombs. Handling characteristics changed little from the B.Mk.VI. Cold weather trials were conducted by the Bristol Aeroplane Company with B.Mk.VI RG814 in Canada in the winter of 1945/46 at Churchill, Manitoba, the aircraft not returning to Filton until September 1947.

In addition to C.Mk.VI with LV838, B.Mk.VI PP225 was modified more drastically, including the removal of all gun turrets and adjustments to the flying controls, it was

Above: Prototype Halifax C.VI LV838 in June 1945. (*RAF Museum*)

Below: Halifax C.VI March 1945 with guns in the mid-upper and tail turrets. (*RAF Museum*)

delivered to Boscombe Down on 4 April, in what was to be the C.Mk.VIII prototype. Handling assessments were made at weights of 50,000lb and 68,000lb, but it was found strengthened elevators were required to maintain effective control in a dive. The first production C.VIII was delivered to the Air Transport Tactical Development Unit at Ringway on 9 June 1945 for service and handling trials, which continued for the remainder of the year, although minor accidents kept it out of action on repairs for some of the time.

Above: Radlett-built Halifax C.VIII PP219 in light camouflage finish. Delivered to 301 Squadron on 17 January 1946, it was delivered to 29 MU on 13 December 1946 and sold to Air Technology Ltd at Aylesbury on 17 September 1947. (*RAF Museum*)

Below: Halifax C.VIII PP245 fitted with under fuselage pannier and running engines. It was delivered to BOAC on 23 April 1945 until 6 July when it went to 44 MU. It was sold to London Aero at Elstree on 11 April 1947. (*RAF Museum*)

Above: Dark camouflage Halifax C.VIII. (*RAF Museum*)

Below: Halifax C.VIII PP285 fitted with under fuselage pannier and in natural metal finish. (*RAF Museum*)

With testing proving successful, 301(Polish) Squadron reequipped with Halifax C.Mk.VIII in January 1946 at Chedburgh, replacing its Warwicks. Following training, with eighteen aircraft allocated, the squadron was to fly cargo operations to Oslo, Istres, Naples and Athens starting on 15 March. With only a few of the aircraft delivered, the squadron never became fully operational on the type, as the first C.VIIIs did not arrive until May and all flying ceased on 21 November. The squadron

Above: Halifax C.VIII PP310 fitted with passenger windows, entry door and under fuselage pannier. It was operated by English Electric and Short & Harland from 30 April 1946 (*Alan Dowsett*)

Below: Halifax C.VIII PP326 configured for cargo, fitted with an under fuselage pannier. It was delivered to YARD on 6 July 1945 and loaned to BOAC on 29 October, until going to 29 MU on 4 June 1947, from where it was sold on 29 September 1948. (*Alan Dowsett*)

Above: Halifax C.VIII Sky Train *Vington* fitted with post-war treaded main wheel tyres. (*Handley Page Association*)

Opposite: The Gaewar of Baroda with his wife, son and son's nanny ready to depart Radlett on 16 November 1946 for India in Halifax G-AGZP. (*Alan Dowsett*)

disbanded on 18 December the same year. Also at Chedburgh was 304 (Polish) Squadron which began to exchange its Warwicks for Halifax C.VIIIs in May 1946, but aircraft deliveries were slow, and the Polish crews were repatriated to Poland, the remaining crews continuing training. As with 301 Squadron, it was disbanded on 18 December, ending C.Mk.VIIIs RAF brief operations. All air transport duties were then allocated to 38 Group Halifax squadrons.

The surplus Halifax C.VIIIs were therefore available for civil use, and the first to be privately owned was as corporate aircraft by Maharajah Gaekwar of Baroda who used the aircraft as a transport from India to his racehorse stables at Newmarket. Collected from 29 MU, it was granted a certificate of airworthiness (C of A) on 20 March 1946 as G-AGZP. A B.Mk.III was bought by an ex-ATA pilot to fly his family and other Australians back home and registered G-AGXA on 16 May. After flying to Australia with basic seating in the cabin, the aircraft was reregistered VH-BDT, but only made one trip to Singapore and back, and was later scrapped. Another Mk.III, NA684 was registered as G-AJPG for the College of Aeronautics at Cranfield.

Above: The luxury cabin in Halifax G-AGZP. (*Alan Dowsett*)

Below: Nose art on Halifax G-AGZP. (*Alan Dowsett*)

Before use with the Lancashire Aircraft Corporation (LAC), Halifax G-AGZP was originally ordered by the RAF as PP336. It was sold to British American on 26 February 1946 before going to LAC. (*Alan Dowsett*)

While waiting for the delayed delivery of Avro Tudors to BOAC, as a stop gap, the airline ordered twelve Halifaxes for the West Africa services. Following structural modifications by Handley Page, fourteen C.Mk.VIIIs were reconfigured by Short Brothers in Belfast with ten passenger seats in a furnished cabin with all the amenities and a window for each occupant. Passenger entry was through a large door on the starboard side of the rear fuselage, with toilet in the rear and galley forward. Passenger baggage was carried in the nose and cargo in the underside pannier. On delivery to BOAC from July, the name Halton was given to the type, and the first example was G-AHDU *Falkirk*.

By September, the first six aircraft were delivered to BOAC, allowing a limited service to commence in September, but a hydraulic fault grounded the fleet within six weeks. The aircraft returned to HP for modification and fitting de-icing equipment. In the interim, eight RAF Halifaxes were loaned to the airline for the period of the modifications. In addition to replacing Dakotas on the West African services, Haltons were also flown to India and Ceylon, and the final six aircraft were delivered by August.

With the withdrawal of practically unused C.Mk.VIIIs in storage, HP acquired a batch of aircraft to sell in 1946. Six were sold to Elstree based London Aero and

Above: The first Halton for BOAC was G-AHDU 'Falkirk'. (*Alan Dowsett*)

Below: BOAC Halton G-AHDU was fitted with a pannier for passengers' baggage and additional cargo. (*Alan Dowsett*)

Above: BOAC Halton G-AHDU flying over Cairo. (*Alan Dowsett*)

Below: Passenger cabin with ten forward facing seats in the BOAC Haltons. (*Alan Dowsett*)

BOAC Halton *Falmouth* at a destination in India. (*Alan Dowsett*)

Motor Services (LAMS) for conversion to passenger operations, and operated from Stansted. With a successful commercial introduction, a further ten C.VIIIs were ordered, although one of the original aircraft was lost in an accident, and another used for spares. With an overall shortage of spares, two of the new batch were also cannibalised. The LAMS fleet, and other operators were used for charter cargo flying often carrying up to 500 tons of soft fruit a month by the middle of 1947. The LAMS fleet would travel all over Europe, North Africa and the Middle East, operating like merchant ships from and to varied destinations. The aircraft had the all-up weight of 68,000lb and could carry a load of up to seven tons at a very competitive cost, and it allowed perishable fruit to be delivered rapidly and fresh, without it being spoilt. With plans for expansion, the possibilities were investigated of establishing bases in Australia and South Africa, but following a proving flight, no further progress was made.

BOAC started a London to Karachi service with Haltons in July 1947, followed by a Trans-Sahara London to Lagos route on 1 September, with six flights a week on the latter route until the interim Haltons were withdrawn in May 1948, and offered for sale.

LAMS Halifax preparing for departure on 9 June 1947. (*Handley Page Association*)

LAMS Halifax Mk.8 departure for Australia on 9 June 1947. (*Alan Dowsett*)

Meanwhile, Halifax operators had continued to increase in Britain and overseas, with surplus Halifax Mk.VIs available, although these were mostly bought by the Lancashire Aircraft Corporation (LAC) for use as spares. By 1948, the boom was declining with the possibility of many of the independent operators going out of business. Then, on Monday 28 June 1948, the Berlin Air Lift commenced, following the closing of the land borders by Russia. While the RAF and USAF undertook the supply of essential goods into the city by air, it became obvious further support was required, with the invitation for British charter operators to support the air lift. With the offer made on 1 August, the first Halifaxes in a force of twelve aircraft made the initial supply sortie on 4 August with Bond Air Services, and as the airlift grew, Halifaxes of Eagle Aviation and Skyflights were in service. With their stock of Halifaxes, LAC put into service six freighters and six fuel tankers, becoming the largest fleet operating on the airlift. While the six cargo freighters were already operating with LAC, the six tankers were modified from standard RAF aircraft with special modifications for civil flying.

With the increase of civilian flights into Wunsdorf, a number of other airfields came into use, including Fuhlsbuttel, Tegel and Schleswigland. With the urgent need for fuel,

Above: Lancashire Aircraft Corporation Halifax Mk.8 G-AGZP was ordered by the RAF as PP336. (*Alan Dowsett*)

Below: A poor quality photo of Halifax Mk.8 G-AKGZ operated on the Berlin Air Lift. (*RAF Museum*)

Above: A Westminster Airways Halifax Mk.8 after a wheels up landing at Scheswigland during the Berlin Air Lift. (*Handley Page Association*)

Below: World Air Freight Halifax Mk.8 after crash-landing at Gatow in October 1946 during the Berlin Air Lift. (*RAF Museum*)

many more Halifaxes were converted making use of a 1,350 gallon tank replacing the belly pannier. Three 250 gallon tanks were also fitted inside the fuselage, with the entire load delivered under pressure in 14 minutes. As winter flying started, the load was kept down to 1,500 gallons of fuel oil, to allow the aircraft to carry sufficient fuel for diversions. During the summer months, operations were daylight only, but with the shorter winter days, a 24-hour programme was started. The intensive operations round the clock resulted in the loss of nine aircraft, sometimes only through damage which could not be repaired due to lack of spares. A number of the Halifax crews on the airlift had been flying for Bomber Command during the war in an effort to destroy Berlin, and were now helping to sustain it. Maintenance support was provided at the main destinations, where additional aircrew were stationed to cover the 24-hour operations. All major LAC scheduled overhauls and C of A renewals were done at Bovingdon.

Operations were intensive, the civil operators flying a total of 22,576 hours in 4,653 cargo trips and 3,509 carrying fuel. This was equivalent to 311 tons every day. The achievements by LAC included twenty-six round trips to Berlin over 14 hours, and for one week, a Halifax was flying for over 96 hours, while another aircraft flew an average of 48 hours every week over a period of five months. A total of forty-one Halifaxes had been deployed by seven operators.

On 11/12 May 1949, after 318 days, the Berlin blockade came to an end. Soon after the civil operators were withdrawn and with the closure of Schleswigland on 12 July LAC, BAAS, Scottish Airlines and Westminster Airways closed down operations. Fuhlsbuttel closed just over a month later with the withdrawal of BAS, Eagle Airways and World Air Freight, and on 16 August, all civil operations ceased.

During the Berlin airlift, Halifaxes continued other charter operations, including in April a 6-ton, 17-foot ship's propeller shaft, which was supported under an 8,000lb

With the end of the Berlin Air Lift, most Halifaxes were redundant with the wings and engines removed from G-AHWN. (*Handley Page Association*)

Above: Waiting the scrap man, Halifax G-AILO still largely complete. (*Handley Page Association*)

Below: Lancashire Aircraft Corporation Halifax Mk.8 G-AKEC took part in the *Daily Express* Air Race in 1950. (*Handley Page Association*)

British American Halifax Mk.8 G-AIAR used for cargo carrying. (*Handley Page Association*)

bomb beam, with a similar load three months later. There was also a disaster relief flight to Palestine in January 1947 carrying 180,000 blankets. However, there was insufficient charter work to sustain commercial operations, particularly as lower operating cost aircraft were becoming available. From the middle of 1948, Halifax engine costs had increased dramatically. At the start of the airlift, engines could be obtained very cheaply, but by 1949, the original surplus had been used up, and a reconditioned engine was costing up to £1,200. With an increase in passenger charters overall, it was uneconomic to make conversions with high operating costs for a small passenger load. Some were not worth the C of A renewal, although a few were being kept available in case of an increase in demand.

With the end of operations obvious, many of the survivors were ferried to Squares Gate, Bovingdon, Southend or Woolsington for scrapping. Halifax G-AKEC was flown by LAC in September 1950 in the *Daily Express* air race from Hurn Airport, achieving 24th position at an average speed of 267mph. Eagle Aviation continued to fly G-AIAP until it was destroyed in a crash at Calcutta on 20 November, and LAC operated G-AJZY until it crashed at Great Missenden on 8 March 1951, bringing civil Halifax charted operations to a violent end.

12
Flight Lieutenant Douglas F. Newham DFC

Doug Newham joined the RAF in August 1941 and after initial basic training, was posted to No. 2 Air Observers School (AOS) at Millom, Cumbria for training as an air observer flying in Ansons and Bothas, but the AOS closed after a number of accidents to the totally unsuitable Bothas. He then did elementary ground school training before continuing his flight training at Jurby and was posted to 19 OTU at Kinloss for final air observer training and joining a crew on Whitleys with the rank of sergeant. Doug served on his first combat unit, 156 Squadron at Warboys from 5 September to 22 October 1942 as Air Observer (Navigation) in Wellington B.IIIs concentrating on Gee training, specialising in early pathfinder target marking. With the formation of the PFF in August 1942, within 8 Group with experienced crews of ten operations or over, Doug was posted to 150 Squadron based at Kirmington, where he had the same duties still on Wellington B.IIIs. It was from here where he had his first combat mission on 15 November, when he was navigator on a 'gardening' mine operation off La Rochelle. He flew on two more operations before the squadron was detached to Blida in Algeria as part of the Northwest African Strategic Air Force on 18 December 1942 until 23 April 1943, when his operations reached twenty-eight. Doug maintains the detachment to North Africa probably saved his life, as the defences were lighter than in North Europe from Britain.

After returning to Britain and serving as ground school navigation instructor with 10 OTU at Abingdon, he was detached to the Central Navigation School at Cranage on a Staff Navigator's Course from 13 September to 22 November 1943, being commissioned as a Pilot Officer from 12 October. He then returned to 10 OTU as a navigation instructor, with promotion to Flying Officer from 12 April 1944. On completion of the Staff Navigator's Course, there was a mandatory minimum one year on staff or instruction duties. On completion of his ground tour, Doug was posted to 10 Squadron on 10 November 1944 at Melbourne as Squadron Navigation Leader with the rank of Flight Lieutenant. To achieve familiarisation with H2S in Halifax B.IIIs, he went to 4 OTU at Acaster Malbis from 10 to 24 November, in preparation for assuming the role of Squadron Navigation Leader. He was limited to one or two combat operations a month, but was disciplined for exceeding that number. He flew a total of twelve operations with 10 Squadron with the last on 25 March 1945, bringing his over total to forty, of which there are some details below mainly in his own words:

RAF Melbourne

The task of Navigation Leader to a crowd of some forty or fifty navigators was itself initially a bit daunting. I was fine on all the theory, but although I had done my best to keep up to date with new navigation aids, instruments and techniques, I was nevertheless somewhat out of practice on the sheer practical side. Still, it was a marvellous challenge, it was back on a heavy bomber squadron, and I would try and make a go of it!

In the event it took little time to become thoroughly familiar with the aircraft and the new instruments, and aids that we never had in our earlier Whitley and Wellington aircraft. The administrative duties of Nav. Leader were within my capabilities, as I had co-operation from others already on the squadron, I was new to the task of monitoring navigation standards and of trying to promote new and better ways of navigation so as to stay on track, on time and alive!

Apparently, the idea was for me to operate comparatively infrequently, spending most of my time on the administration duties, monitoring, training and pre-ops briefing. In consequence, I was not allocated to a particular crew and only managed to secure a trip if one of the other navigators became sick, or was withdrawn from his crew due to injury. This was more than a little frustrating, and a bit lonesome without particular comradeship of my regular crew.

Happily, on one occasion I was asked to operate with one of the flight commanders, Squadron Leader Bill Alan, to Mainz, his regular navigator being sick. Bill had already been awarded the DFC for performance on his first tour of operations. He was a somewhat dour Scot, but had established for himself a reputation as an excellent flight commander. Bill rarely put himself on the operational list if he felt that it was an 'easy' target, was when he used his less experienced crews. On the other hand if it appeared might be a bit fraught, a long distance, difficult or heavily defended target, bad weather or full moon (which meant night fighters could be particularly nasty), then Bill's name would be on the crew list. Knowing crews would comment that this was indicative that it was likely to be a rough trip. On more than one occasion, when a relatively 'easy target' was changed late in the day (due to adverse weather or some urgently tactical need) to one that was more 'dicey', Bill would take an inexperienced crew off the operational list, and substitute himself at short notice.

The trip to Mainz went well, and our pilot/navigator cooperation and mutual confidence seemed natural and relaxed. Our only problem was an engine defect about an hour short of target, which necessitated shutting down one of the engines. Having got that far, the crew all agreed with Bill that the situation did not justify jettisoning our bombs, aborting the trip and returning to base, so we carried on, with three engines. This meant we arrived over the target a bit later and lower than planned.

A few nights later the target was Bonn and again Bill asked me to join his crew, his navigator by then in hospital. This trip was somewhat more dramatic. When I switched on my H2S ground mapping radar sometime after we crossed the French coast, I found it was giving no response. This was not really serious, but made navigation somewhat more difficult, as I had to rely on another radio navigation aid (Gee) which was being heavily jammed by German counter measures. Nevertheless, we arrived over target as planned, but due to an electrical defect, the bombs did not release. There were emergency manual releases, but these necessitated someone going into the fuselage area above the bomb-bays, and actuating a series of manual cable toggles. Rex, our Rhodesian bomb aimer was more familiar with the location and operation of these toggles than I was, so when we went around the target again, I guided Bill in, using the bomb site and at the appropriate time told Rex via the intercom to pull the release toggles. In the event we had to go round the target two more times before we had released our full bomb load.

By this time the rest of the aircraft on this raid were already on their way home. On each circuit we got a little lower in order to avoid the undivided attention of the numerous searchlights and anti-aircraft fire. We finally ended up at less than 12,000 feet. It was quite noisy and bumpy set of fireworks they directed at us! To add to my interest, we had just got ourselves over the North Sea when my one remaining radio navigation aid (Gee) decided it had had enough, and went unserviceable. Fortunately the old traditional methods of navigation were not too deeply buried in the grey matter and we arrived back at Melbourne without further ado, but quite late.

Somehow or other this operation, and the problems experienced, seemed to cement our crew relationships and Bill asked me if I would join his crew on a permanent basis. I was happy to do this, and we flew together until we were forcibly parted by Group HQ in early 1945, never to see each other again.

There were three occasions in this period when I operated some extra trips with other crews, to Bill's mild annoyance (once due to another navigator being taken off a trip at the last minute due to illness, once when trying to found out why a particular navigator was having really serious problems and getting himself virtually lost over Germany, and once when we had a short notice operation and a navigator was in York with his girlfriend), but I think under Bill Allan, we were a good and efficient crew, and I enjoyed my time as his navigator. After Bill and I had been separated, the crew received a number of awards. Bill was given the DSO to add to his DFC, and a number of DFCs and DFMs went to the rest of us, included my DFC.

The only brick structures on Melbourne Airfield were the control tower and station guard room. All the other buildings were either prefabricated wooden huts covered in camouflage painted roofing felt and lined with plaster board, or corrugated metal Nissen huts of various sizes. There was a small hangar (corrugated sheeting on a metal framework) which could accommodate a couple of aircraft for engine changes or major repairs. All minor and semi major maintenance work and repairs were carried out in the open where the aircraft were parked on concrete pads, dispersed around the perimeter of the field. Well-deserved tribute has often been given to the loyalty and dedication of the ground crews, the fitters and riggers, armourers, electricians and radar mechanics who carried out this work, in the open in all weathers, has often been referred to in books about the bomber offensive. They were a marvellous crowd!

Great comradeship developed between aircrew and their ground crew. One never departed on an operation without one's ground crew being there on the pad to see their aircraft was fully okay and to wish you well. The departure point, at the end of the runway, was never without its knot of ground crew, cooks, clerks, drivers and WAAFs to wave you off. And on your return from a raid your ground crew would always be at the parking spot to see if their baby had performed as it should. They often berated us when we brought their pride and joy back damaged with flak or fighter shells, not because meant repair work, but because the pride in their aircraft. They often used to say it was THEIR aircraft, not ours, they only let us use it.

Subject to aircraft serviceability permitting, any 'alcoholic thrash' at the 'Bomber Arms' (Blacksmith Arms) on a night's stand down from operations would very often result in a combined group of aircrew and their ground crew (officers, NCOs and airmen ground engineers all together as a team) with good natured rivalry with other similar teams.

Our own personal living quarters were widely dispersed around the local countryside, anything up to about a mile from the airfield. Again, it was a mixture of prefabricated huts or Nissen huts, perhaps just two or three together, tucked into hedges, copses or under trees. The whole idea of dispersal of aircraft and buildings was to minimise the possible effects of air attack. Heating inside these huts consisted of a small cast iron stove with metal chimney. A small quantity of coal dust was delivered infrequently, and the scrounging of wooden boxes, broken furniture, fallen branches and anything combustible was the norm. Even so, it was difficult, if not impossible in the winter, to keep your room warm anything better than mildly damp. You could often see a sheet of water beneath the floorboards. I purchased an electric boiling ring and wired it up to the mains, which was absolutely forbidden. My batman never said a word and stood it on a couple of bricks under my bed. At least I had a slightly warm bed to creep into when I came back from a freezing 6 or 8 hours over Germany.

We nearly all had bicycles loaned by the RAF. You cycled from your billet to the mess for breakfast, then to the office or Ops Room, back to the mess for lunch, back to bed for a few hours' attempted sleep if you were operating that night, and back to the Ops Room before 'going to work'. No one had any lights and there were often dozens of aircrew on all the local lanes to the airfield. The local policeman was very tolerant; indeed, the police and publicans were more than patient and understanding when road signs, pub signs, and almost anything moveable disappeared as trophies from a boozy steam letting thrash on a stand down night. The police would come round and either collect their property, or ask us to replace any pub signs.

Unlike most of the mass of similar dispersed airfields in Yorkshire, Lincolnshire and East Anglia, we only had one squadron of aircraft at Melbourne. Most airfields had two squadrons with twice the number of aircraft, but as Melbourne was equipped with FIDO, a system for dispersing fog, there was only room for one squadron to allow room for mass diversions in poor weather. The FIDO installation consisted of a series of horizontal pipes running along both sides of the main runway. These pipes, in sections of 100 feet or so, were about 18 inches above the ground, then doubled back underneath themselves. The lower length of pipework had a series of holes drilled along its upper surface. When there was really thick fog, petrol was pumped through the pipes and ignited where it sprayed out of the perforations in the lower pipe. To start with, the petrol burnt with black smoky flames, but before long, when it got the upper length of the pipe hot, the fuel vapourised and the fuel burnt with a clean roaring flame some four feet high. The end result was a line of roaring fire either side of the runway, clearing the fog from its immediate vicinity. It was relatively effective, but not without serious difficulties. In thick fog, you could see your way on the approach until suddenly burst out into this devil's inferno, there was very rough turbulence necessitating a higher landing speed and tricky handling for the pilot. It also demanded that you approach dead in line with the runway. Generally you could see the glow of FIDO from above the fog, but this was of little use in getting correctly lined up. I devised a system using the radio navigation aid Gee by which I could direct the pilot, right or left, and with the distance to go information as well, straight down the runway. All this had to be done at low-level down to less than 100 feet, and required great accuracy in setting up the Gee receiver, and even greater confidence by the pilot in his navigator, in case he was directed into the ground, or the local church tower. Fortunately Bill Allan and I worked this technique to a fine art. Some others wouldn't even try it except in good visibility and then chickened out of using it for real. It was also exceptionally expensive to operate and used up much valuable fuel, although it was worth-while if it saved a crew and aircraft.

A Job of Work
It was February/March 1945, still with 10 Squadron. Spring couldn't be far away and the war appeared to be progressing towards a satisfactory conclusion in Europe. The Allied forces were forging ahead and at last facing Germany on her own doorstep. A fair measure of air supremacy had been achieved, at least over Western Germany, and we were going on fairly large raids penetrating well into Germany in daylight. On 24 February, we had gone on a 600 aircraft raid against the German oil refinery complex at Kamen. 10 Squadron had been selected to lead the raid and it was therefore not unexpected that my pilot, Bill Allan, would be selected to take the lead aircraft of the whole attack. Nevertheless, it was a bit of a strain on the self-confidence to find myself as the lead navigator. I remember that as we were crossing the Channel, Bill called me to the astrodome to look behind. I found it very daunting to look back at all of them tagging along behind us. Some 600 four engine bombers looked like a big following! I rapidly went back to my nav. table, concentrated on the job and tried to forget everybody else. Still, it all went well, Group HQ were happy with the job and commented favourably on some of my personal 'tricks of the trade.'

On 2 March, we were again on a daylight raid to Cologne, with Allied troops close to the west bank of the Rhine. I remember we took our station commander, Group Captain Larry Ling with us 'for the ride.' This occasion we were to be about mid-way through the raid. It was I believe, relatively successful, and from our point of view fairly uneventful and a short trip of only 6 hours. However, I do remember that it was quite spectacular as we approached from the south, amidst several hundred bombers. As we got near, Rex our bomb aimer, got busy in his office in the Perspex nose of the aircraft with his bomb release switch gear and his bomb site. He stretched out on the floor over the bomb site which of course meant I couldn't get much of a look see. I went back and stood next to Bill. Ahead the sky was crowded with aircraft and literally hundreds upon hundreds of heavy flak. Of course, the smoke from the bursts hung around for some time, so it looked much more impenetrable than in fact it was, nevertheless I remember a couple of aircraft, one quite near, that were smitten, one loosing height in a turn with smoke pouring from an engine, and another that must have had a real wallop such that it virtually came apart at the seams.

We were more fortunate, just a few thumps and rattles nearby. Sometimes you could smell the acrid smoke as you went through a nearby burst. However, that was only the scenery; the more vital task was to keep a sharp eye upwards, as the pilot kept his attention on accurate flying to the bomb aimer's commands. All around were other aircraft edging their way into the correct position to release their bombs and the last thing we wanted was to receive somebody else's load through our roof. Again, I remember warning Bill to try and edge out of the way of a Lancaster, which couldn't have been more than 20 feet above us, with his bomb doors open and I was looking up into a bomb-bay full of everything but the kitchen sink, umpteen tons of bombs ready to be released. In the meantime poor old Rex was trying to get his sights steady on the aiming point and couldn't see why we were edging a bit away. The Lanc. dropped his load harmlessly beyond our wing tip!

A few days later, 5 March, I had another busy day! By mid-morning, we were already into the planning and pre-briefing activity in readiness for raid to Chemnitz that evening/night. Because it was likely to be a longish trip, penetrating fairly deep into Germany, which meant the German fighters would have time to get well organised, I didn't find it surprising that Bill Allan put us on the operational list for this trip. The pre-ops briefing revealed that this raid was intended to destroy much of the road and rail communications by which the Germans were still withdrawing troops from the Russian front. The more we could delay the withdrawal, the more they could be mauled by the Russians, furthermore any delay would hinder the redeployment of German troops from the Eastern to the Western front, where the Allied troops were planning for the crossing of the Rhine.

The briefing went with the usual thoroughness. It was a complex picture overall, with another raid and 'spoof' sorties taking place elsewhere in Northern Germany, as well as mining the Baltic, all coordinated in a manner designed to confuse German defences and fighter organisations. From my own point of view my prime concern was on routeing, timing, heights, weather, wind and temperature, radar countermeasures, marker flares and target marking, radio and visual beacons in the UK etc. Nevertheless, as one of the few persons in the crew who could have easy reference to written notes whilst in flight, the navigator took on the role of recorder of all relevant briefing information, and at times to remind his colleagues of pertinent points and to answer their queries if at any time they called for a recap on details. For obvious reasons none of the other crew members could use a reading light when approaching the target at night.

After the main briefing I went, with the other navigators, to the Navigation hut to get down to preparing my own charts and flight plan. The first task was to plot the route turning points, altitude change points, and target on my chart. Then you joined these up, measured the direction and distances for each leg, and drew up your flight plan leg by leg, extracted the relevant wind and temperature from the page of weather forecast. Next, using a handheld vector calculator and circular slide-rule, you calculated the airspeed, drift, true heading, magnetic heading, ground speed and time for each leg. It was my own personal practice, and one I suggested to newcomers, to write crucial reminders all along the track on my chart, including when I could switch on my H2S, when we were to start using window, and the colours and times of target marker flares. I would also plot the route on the Gee lattice charts, extracting critical readings that would help me to avoid overshooting turning points. After the usual pre-flight meal I collected a precious bar of chocolate and a hefty corned beef sandwich. Then I collected the small escape kit: the bulky parachute harness, detachable parachute pack and yellow inflatable life jacket, known as a 'Mae West.' If, as this trip, it was going to be long, high and cold, wear suitable flying gear as protection. On your head went your flying helmet and detachable oxygen mask, which had an inbuilt microphone and earphones, which was plugged into the intercom system.

When ready to go we assembled with our crew mates, and travelled out to our aircraft, Halifax B.Mk.III 'O', in three-ton trucks with canvas tops, one truck serving two or three adjacent aircraft, and were usually driven by WAAFs. The aircraft would be standing there ready to go. The fuel would already have been loaded and the covers removed from the engines and wheels. The bomb doors would be hanging down open, with 10 to 12 tons of high explosive and incendiary bombs all in their racks with arming devices held safe. Inevitably, our ever-faithful ground crew would be putting a last bit of effort into cleaning to perfection the Perspex windows of the gun turrets or pilot's glass windscreen and windows. A small petrol generator would be providing electrical power to the aircraft by which essential systems could be checked.

Once at the aircraft with generally about half an hour to spare, each crew member had their own particular area to check. The pilot and flight engineer would do their walk round the aircraft, chatting to the ground crew. The gunners would check out their turrets and rounds of 0.303-inch ammunition. The wireless operator would be checking his radios for normal operation. As the navigator, I would climb aboard and stow my gear around and under the map table. I was frequently subject to air sickness, so I took an empty ammo tin if required.

Once all the checks had been completed, the crew would gather outside and if the weather allowed lounge around on the grass under the wing chatting to the ground crew. As the take-off time approached the crew would climb aboard and shut the lower hatch. From that moment forward, it was a strict working discipline which prevailed with checks made of the intercom. All crew general communication ceased during engine start up, following which the radio operator and navigator would check radios and radar gear, while the flight engineer would be checking systems operation and the gunners making sure their guns could be elevated and turned around. Then, when the engine oil and cylinder head temperatures were up to the required temperatures, the skipper would run up each engine to max power against the brakes and check that both magnetos on each engine were performing okay.

Finally, the pilot would query a last 'okay everybody', and each crew member would respond. The skipper would then signal to the ground crew to remove the chocks, allowing the brakes to be released and we would lumber out of our dispersal along the taxi track.

Out on the airfield, near the take-off point, a queue of aircraft ready to depart would form. Edging towards the take-off point, it would be turned on to the runway and with brakes on the engines would again be checked at full power. Maintaining strict radio silence, which could be a signal to the enemy that a raid was about to start, a green Aldis light was flashed from the runway controller in his caravan clearing the bomber ready for departure. In the event of an accident after take-off, the navigator, radio operator and bomb aimer would be wedged in behind the main spar, before returning to their positions once airborne after the take-off when the pilot would be telling the flight engineer when to retract the wheels and flaps.

As soon as we were airborne the pilot would be climbing away and turning the aircraft on to a predetermined course, which I would have previously given him. This would normally be out to the west over the edge of York city. I would, by then, be calculating how long we should stay on this course before turning round in a tear drop pattern to bring us back over the airfield at precisely the time that I wanted to set course for the target, and to allow some twenty aircraft to form up in formation. On the raid to Chemintz we were airborne at 16.55hrs and were climbing slowly under a layer of cloud, when there were warning calls from the pilot, bomb aimer and mid-upper gunner who saw another Halifax in a shallow dive, not more than a couple of hundred yards ahead, and plough down into a row of houses. The aircraft disintegrated, with wings and tail unit being torn off and the whole thing enveloped in fire as it ripped through the street. Then, whilst still in our tear drop pattern and back overhead Melbourne, we saw two more Halifax aircraft descend through the cloud and crash into fields. What a disturbing start to a night's work!

The 10 Squadron crews were concerned that they may be under attack by long-range enemy night fighters, catching the bombers after take-off when they were most vulnerable, despite radio silence. However, it was found out later that there had been four or five Halifaxes from heavy conversion training units that had crashed that afternoon due to mechanical, handling or icing problems. The 10 Squadron crews were unaware and therefore remained on high alert.

From overhead Melbourne we set course for Reading, a frequent routeing down to the English south coast, climbing to between 4–5,000 feet. It was at this time I settled into my routine for the next eight hours, all the time checking position and progress. Passing over the south coast over Beachy Head, thence climbing into the dark, with the other aircraft lost to view, and the temperature began to drop. As the French coast was being approached, thin fingers of searchlights could be seen, followed by flak when a bomber was illuminated. The navigator's work was to fix air position, log, calculate, recheck, adjust course continuously over and over again. About every 30 or 40 minutes we changed direction, first heading towards one potential target, then just before getting there turning away on a zig zag as if heading to another deeper into Germany. In between these changes in direction we also made changes in height, slowly climbing, perhaps only 2,000 feet at a time. The essence was to make the night fighter controller's job as difficult as we could. Once we got into the areas where there were heavy flak belts, or where night fighter activity could be expected, we started throwing out 'window'. It would start with one small bundle every minute, increasing as we got near the target or into heavily defended areas. The type of window designed to confuse ground-based radar was different from that used against night fighter radar. One type was about an inch wide and 18 inches long, the other type was thin shredded strips about 10 inches long.

As we got deeper into the continent the effect of the German jamming transmissions would seriously mask the little blips on the face of my Gee tube, and the aircraft would gradually fly out of range of the beacon's transmissions. Before we got to that state, I would switch on my H2S ground mapping radar, but this was delayed for as long as possible as it was found that the German night fighters could in fact home-in on to the transmissions from our equipment. As we crawled on in the dark, searchlights of the main defensive belts around large cities were continually groping for us, and often there would be some poor guy coned by literally dozens of lights with flak twinkling all around him.

My concern was not only to time our arrival at the target precisely correct, but also to stay on the designated track. The objective here was, from a time point of view, to afford maximum concentration of aircraft over the target, thereby sharing the flak between all of us, rather than it being concentrated on to relatively few aircraft. Correct timing also resulted in the planned sequence of bomb loads, for example the first wave of aircraft with incendiaries to start massive fires, followed by a second wave with high explosives to keep the fire fighters in the shelters and prevent them from tackling the blaze, followed by a third wave with more incendiaries and a final wave with more high explosives and delayed action bombs. Brutal and carefully planned. Insofar as adherence to track was concerned, the idea was that if we all discharged window to disrupt enemy radar defences, the greater the concentration of window, and the more impossible would it be for the radar to detect and hence predict the flak against a single aircraft.

Eventually we were getting close to Chemintz, and Rex was in the nose of the aircraft setting up his bomb selector panel, to release the bombs in a close sequence. He also had to setup his bomb sight with corrected altitude, airspeed and wind, all of which required a few minutes calculations on my part. Just ahead the pathfinder illuminators were going in, dropping long skeins of parachute flares to illuminate the target area, followed by the markers whose job it was to identify the precise aiming point. Then mark it by dropping brilliantly coloured ground marker flares on it. Then came those of us in the first wave of the Main Force bombers. There was broken cloud below and I can still recall Rex calling out that he had an excellent view of the target indicator ground flares, he called for bomb doors to be opened and went straight into the routine 'Right—steady—left/left—steady—steady—right a little—steady—steady—Bombs Gone!'

Below the area was one of smoke, erupting flashes and fires, huge explosions of 4,000lb and 8,000lb high explosives opening up like pink pansies, explosions that were scattered fairly closely around the markers. Nevertheless, even at this stage of the raid the smoke and eruptions would soon mask the ground marker flares and another group of pathfinder markers and recenterers had the job of ensuring that subsequent waves of aircraft were provided with the best possible aiming point. Below, and silhouetted against the inferno, other aircraft at lower altitude could be seen. At our own altitude, and somewhat above, more aircraft were visible in the reflected light from below. Dozens of searchlights were groping for individual targets, and all around were the flashes and more persistent smoke puffs from exploding flak.

But, having released our bombs, we were not immediately at liberty to do anything other than continue on a straight and steady course. At the tail end of our stick of bombs we had also dropped a 3 feet × 5 inches cylinder containing a brilliant magnesium 'photo flash'. This was less streamlined than the bombs, so lagged behind them in their fall, and exploded in a brilliant flash just as the bombs hit the ground, illuminating the area of actual impact. At this instant the automatic camera located near my feet wound to a new piece of film and hopefully recorded a photograph of where our bombs had actually fallen, permitting a subsequent analysis of our bombing accuracy and likely target damage assessment.

Having checked that the lights on his control panel showed all the bombs had left their racks, the bomb aimer was again lying down, looking below his bomb sight at the target. Once he identified that our photo-flash had exploded, we were free to depart. Down went the nose and after a few prescribed miles on the same heading, round we came on to a new course—westward. We now followed yet another detailed routing plan, as precise as that on the outward flight. Generally about 20 minutes on any one leg, before changing height or direction. By now, there was no doubt in the German minds about where we were! We had just plastered Chemintz with thousands of pounds of explosives and incendiaries and were heading home to the UK. All the night fighters of the Third Reich were now being concentrated to intercept us, and every pair of eyes was alert to spot them. Whilst I was concentrating on fix after fix, to find the latest wind, to give alterations of course to stay as near to track as possible, and to avoid overshooting the next turning point, the flight engineer was still poking bundles of window down the chute. The bomb aimer squeezed past my position and was back peering out of the right-hand windscreen, another pair of eyes looking for the fighters. The two gunners, keeping their eyes away from the mass of fires on the ground behind us, systematically moved their power operated gun turrets as they searched and re-searched the surrounding area, periodically one or other of them would ask the pilot to drop the wing first one side, then the other so that they could look into the blind spot aft and below.

Although we had descended two or three thousand feet, it was still bitterly cold in the aircraft, particularly when we were slowly losing height, when the engines were throttled back a little and only cold air came through the flexible 'hot air pipe' which I would otherwise stuff up the front of my battle dress jacket, or down the front of my neck.

Sometime later came:

'Rear gunner to mid-upper. Can you see that chap on the rear starboard quarter, slightly up, coming in towards us?'

'Mid to rear. I see him.'

'Christ! He's coming in fast. Rear gunner to pilot. Corkscrew starboard. Corkscrew starboard. Now!'

We go into a violent evasive manoeuvre. Diving down in a hard right-hand turn, followed by a sharp turn to the left, and pulling up hard, climbing up left then swinging down again hard right and down again. ... A corkscrew!

'Rear gunner. He's coming in as if he was tied on with a piece of rope, despite the corkscrew. There was the background clatter as eight machine guns belt out their fury as we twist and turn.

'Got the bastard!! We got the bastard! He's going straight up!!'

'Christ! He got close.'

'Funny, looked a bit like a V-1 with a jet out of the back. We must have hit his gyro.'

'Pilot to gunners. Okay lads. Good work! Back to normal everybody.'

On we thrashed our way. Gunners continually alert for fighters, bomb aimer and pilot look out for a possible collision risk with another bomber. Pilot continually flying to the correct height, speed and course that I kept giving him, engineer checking on fuel and engine performance, wireless operator listening out for periodic broadcasts from HQ or keeping an eye on 'Fishpond', a cathode ray tube display that took its input from the H2S radar, giving a somewhat unreliable warning of enemy fighters.

Somewhere over West Germany and approaching the Low Countries, we started experiencing engine problems—fluctuating oil temperatures, first on just one engine, then on two and finally on three. This was a problem that was not too uncommon on our Hercules radial engines, a snag seemed to be confined to conditions of sustained periods of flight at very cold air temperatures. There ensued a lengthy exchange of technicalities between pilot and flight engineer, as they tried different combinations of engine revs, boost and cowl settings in order to resolve the problem. What worked on one engine didn't work on another. Then, having got an engine stabilised, it all started up again and there was a risk of having to shut the affected engine/s down due to overheating and/or loss of oil pressure. There was a degree of seriousness in the situation since, although we could cope without too much trauma with one engine shut down, it would become a different story if we had to shut down two, and a real emergency if we were left with only one.

The final outcome was a decision to divert to the nearest emergency airfield in the UK. By this time one engine had been shut down as a precaution against serious engine damage, due to oil starvation, and a second engine was approaching a similar state.

There were three such emergency fields, all on coast—Woodbridge in East Essex, Carnaby in East Yorkshire and Manston in East Kent. They were each pretty massive airfields, very long runways and very wide, three times the width of normal runways, with runway lights marking it out into distinct landing lanes. One lane was for real emergencies, no wheels, no radio, just get the thing down somehow, even if it tore apart on doing so. Bulldozers and ambulances were standing by to get to the crew, often with dead or injured aboard and then to bulldoze the remains off the strip to make room for the next aircraft. The middle strip was for a normal, wheels-down landings, but with no brakes and/or flaps, invariably aiming to put it down near the runway threshold and followed by a long and fast landing run, and try not to swerve off the central strip. The last (right-hand) lane was for aircraft that had full landing capability, but were going into that field because of desperately injured crew members where the longer flight to their own base might have been fatal, or mechanical snags (such as we were experiencing) or bad weather at one's own base.

Each of these fields had a cone of three searchlights as markers, and Manston and Woodbridge could often be seen on a clear night from over the enemy coast. Nice though it was, in a way, to see the lights of the UK from afar, it was not a sight we generally welcomed. This was because it was, of course, associated with clear conditions for hunting by Jerry night fighters that sometimes followed us back to the UK, picking off the tired and unwary who relaxed on the sight of home. Even more vulnerable were the crews with engine problems who were unable to keep up and lost the protection of the mutual bomber stream, and could be picked off with greater ease by enemy night fighters.

So it was that somewhere in the vicinity of Southern Belgium we left our designated route back to Melbourne and I gave Bill the course for Manston, avoiding major cities and known concentrations of anti-aircraft defences. Finally we were in radio contact with Manston, briefly told them our problems, and in our turn got the clearance to land. Other aircraft, less fortunate than we, were being put down in less reliable states of airworthiness, engines shut down, or badly shot up and damaged. We landed and were marshalled by a Jeep to a parking area, although we were picked up by a pick-up truck at low priority, due to more urgent situations. Eventually we ended up briefing the ground engineers of our problem, and the requirement for an inspection of the suspect engines, and full tanks of oil for our subsequent departure. We had a debrief by the intelligence staff, we satisfied ourselves that Melbourne had been told of our diversion, a quick meal of bacon and eggs with thick wads of bread, and lashings of tea. We washed our filthy hands and faces, before tumbling on to beds in Nissen hut dormitories to cover ourselves with a blanket over our clothes and fell, or tried to fall into an exhausted sleep for a few hours.

It hadn't been a particularly long trip, 8 hours and 5 minutes from take-off to landing. We had taken off from Melbourne at 16.55hrs, and landed at Manston at exactly 01.00hrs, but I had been busy in the office, or in the Ops. Room, or at briefing from about 07.30hrs. Anyway, after about 4 hours of cold and uncomfortable 'rest', we dragged ourselves together, made our way to get some breakfast, collected a weather forecast for Melbourne, got a truck out to the aircraft, checked it over, and found no engine damage, the oil replenished, and everything reasonably okay. We organised some fuelling, got started up, clearance for take-off, and got up into the skies again for the 1 hour 25 minutes back home.

When we got there, we went through a more thorough de-briefing. The gunners told the story of the strange craft that had attacked us. We learned that ours was not the first such report over previous days. The belief was that the thing was indeed a modified V-1, taken aloft piggy-back fashion on a Ju 88 or Me 110 into the vicinity of the bomber stream, the pulse jet engine started up and then the thing was released from its parent aircraft to home itself, either by its own radar or an acoustic device, on to one of the bombers and explode on impact.

By that time, it was lunch time. Back at my hut for a more thorough wash and clean up, smelling of sweat, engine fumes, hydraulic fluid, machine gun cordite. Then back on the bicycle to the office and Ops. Room, ready to brief the navigators who were due out on a different trip that night. Bed, when it came, with clean sheets and surrounding silence, was welcome indeed. But next day the job of work resumed as normal.

Doug operated four more combat missions, and flew a final Halifax air test on 26 March, bringing his overall total flying time to 298.05 hours.

On 7 May 1945, 10 Squadron transferred to Transport Command and started conversion to C 47 Dakota aircraft, in preparation for service in Asia. He retained his duties as Squadron Navigation Leader, and VE Day was on 8 May 1945. Before deployment to Asia, VJ Day was declared on 15 August 1945 and 10 Squadron was sent to India. From 9 May 1946, Doug began the demobilisation, with 21 August 1946 his last day in the RAF, after which he joined BOAC as a ground operations officer, and retired in 1982.

13

Friday the 13th Restoration

It all started with Halifax GR.Mk.II HR792 which, when serving with 58 Squadron at Stornoway, crashed on 13 January 1945 while being flown on circuit and landing practice. The pilot inadvertently retracted the undercarriage too early and the aircraft came to rest on farmland near the airfield, fortunately without any loss of life. The 25-foot rear fuselage section, from aft of the wing main spar to forward of the tailplane, survived as a hen coop with a farmer on the Isle of Lewis. The owner, Farmer MacKenzie was contacted in 1984 and agreed to donate this unique piece of Halifax to what was to become the Yorkshire Air Museum (YAM) at the Second World War Bomber Command base at Elvington in Yorkshire.

Contact was then made via RAF Finningley, resulting in a visit to Stornoway where RAF Chinooks were exercising and as part of a training exercise, it was hoped it might be possible to lift the fuselage section to a more accessible location on the airfield, from where it could be transported by road to Elvington. At the same time, four Merlin engine wrecks from another Halifax crash on Lewis in 1945 had been offered, which the RAF were also willing to recover. A difficulty was that all the relics were embedded in peat and would have to be freed before the Chinook lift. Local ATC cadets came to the rescue and the parts were moved to Stornoway Airfield where the fuselage section was supported in a tubular steel cradle due to its fragile condition. Transport was then organised with free carriage on the Caledonian MacBrayne ferry where the load was carried to Glasgow for road transport to Yorkshire.

The Halifax was built at Radlett in 1943 as B.Mk.II HR792 in Bomber Command camouflage, but was modified and transferred to Coastal Command as a GR.Mk. II, which was overall white. However, after 40 years in the open, the white paint had faded away, leaving the original camouflage underneath. With no suitable accommodation available at Elvington, an empty garage was offered at Dishforth, allowing restoration work to commence by the YAM volunteers at weekends. Work progressed cleaning away the peat and stripping the badly corroded lower fuselage frames, with no idea how, or who could restore the section properly.

Once the identity of the fuselage section had been established, it was possible to trace some of its history and it was established that ATA pilot Lettice Curtis had delivered HR792 from Radlett after its conversion to a GR.II, to Coastal Command in 1943, and its service with 58 Squadron was confirmed. With the ultimate fate of the fuselage section still in doubt, contact was made with the general manager at British

The rear fuselage section of Halifax HR792 as recovered. (*Yorkshire Air Museum*)

Aerospace at Brough, who agreed to a restoration by the apprentices as training in forming and shaping aluminium parts.

With a need for drawings, ex-Handley Page designer, Harry Frazer-Mitchell was contacted, and was able to access a complete set of drawings which had been donated to the Imperial War Museum at Duxford. This resulted in identifying the drawings required by the Brough apprentices to replace the scrap under fuselage structure. The detail work took some 18 months to complete and the beautifully restored fuselage section, complete with a mid-upper gun turret was delivered to Elvington for a welcome ceremony on 20 May 1987. The gun turret had been in use as garden cloche and had also been completely restored.

By this time, the rear fuselage restoration project had grown into a complete Halifax restoration. The next stage was to locate a wing centre section on which were mounted the stub wings, inner engines and main undercarriage. It was then realised this area was practically identical to the Hastings transport, although the wingspan of the outer section had been extended. There was a redundant Hastings, TG536, with the Fire Training School at Catterick, which was about to be destroyed in a fire fighting training exercise. With an urgent approach to the Ministry of Defence, it was released to YAM for a modest fee. The major task of separating and dismantling

The restored rear fuselage of Halifax HR792 complete with middle-upper gun turret. (*Yorkshire Air Museum*)

the Hastings was achieved and the assemblies moved by road with a police escort to Elvington, with the 110-foot wings cut into two 55-foot sections to fit in the only building available. During the restoration, it was found the outer wings were badly corroded, requiring the start of the search for replacements. Then it was discovered there was a set of two outer Hastings wings in boxes, which had never been used, located at a scrap dealer in the south of England. The necessary several thousand pounds was raised and the wings delivered to Elvington.

The next challenge was to acquire a tail section. BAe at Brough were again approached and with a full set of drawings available, agreed to ask the apprentices to manufacture a new rear fuselage, fins and rudders with the work beginning in 1986, and the tailplane was built by YAM volunteers at Elvington. A rear turret in poor condition was acquired from the Cotswold Aircraft Recovery Group which was restored locally by the Jefferson brothers over a period of 18 months, delivering the turret complete with four 0.303-inch machine guns and new Perspex in fully operating condition.

With so much progress being made, the next challenge was the undercarriage. The original substantial main undercarriage were legs cast from heavy manganese, which were not available, but the oleo legs existed. The high level of local publicity generated, particularly through the apprentice work at Brough, attracted the interest of a local foundry. The loan of an undercarriage leg from the RAF Museum was used as a pattern from which moulds could be made of a structure 5 feet high and 4 feet across. John Wilkinson cast the legs with s steel frame strengthening to take the weight

The wings of Hastings TG536 being prepared for restoration. (*Yorkshire Air Museum*)

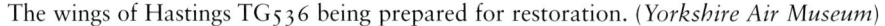

The restored rear gun turret on display before being assembled to the complete Halifax. (*Yorkshire Air Museum*)

of the aircraft, and delivered the units to Elvington. Sadly, John died soon after, as he had been selling his company and planned to become a YAM volunteer.

Although the original fuselage section had come from a Merlin-powered Halifax Mk.II, the Hastings wing sections had been powered by Bristol Hercules radial engines which would fit the Hastings wings and engine mounts. This made the restoration logically into a Mk.III. Through the close contact with the associations of 346 and 347 Free French Air Force Squadrons, who had operated Halifaxes from Elvington in the Second World War, the squadron associations began negotiations with the French Air Force, resulting in four immaculate Hercules engines delivered to Elvington on 20 August 1987 by C-160 Transall.

With so many major assemblies, the major missing item was the front fuselage, which accommodated the pilot, navigator, flight engineer, wireless operator and bomb aimer in a 25-foot section forward of the main wing spar. Despite the Imperial War Museum (IWM) at Lambeth having a Halifax nose section, they would not make it available. Undaunted, and having access to all the drawings, Dick Chandler—a YAM trustee and ex-pilot from Brough, offered to get together some skilled aerospace retirees to form a team to build the nose from scratch at Elvington. A team of eight retirees created the new nose and front fuselage on Thursdays, while on Tuesdays another team worked on engine nacelles and bomb doors. Following nearly three years' work, the front section was close to completion in early 1996.

A relatively small, but vital item, was the tail wheel, and although one had been retrieved from the Outer Hebrides, it went missing from the restorer's home. Luckily, with the help of the French connection, another tail wheel assembly from 466 Squadron (RAAF), HX271, which had crashed in France, had been recovered by the local farmer, and was donated to the Halifax project.

Large and potentially difficult parts to find were the four bulky hydromatic variable pitch propellers and hubs. With the great luck on the project continuing, a call came from some RAF personnel in Germany, who reported some German civilians had been excavating the wreckage of 432 (RCAF) Squadron Halifax, and the hub sub-assemblies were made available for the project. To keep the weight down of the overall structure, some main parts of which were over 50 years old, a dozen new propeller blades were made in fibreglass, looking as good as the originals.

Start of building the main fuselage from scratch with the frame structure. (*Yorkshire Air Museum*)

To complete the aircraft exterior, wheels and tyres were required, which were similar on all Second World War four engine heavy bombers. During the war, the tyres were smooth without treads, but after the war the tyres had treads, although they were all difficult to locate. The RAF Museum at Hendon kindly loaned a set of smooth tyres, but their age precluded them being able to support the weight of the aircraft, resulting in the aircraft being supported on axle stands. However, a set of treaded tyres were located at the Brooklands Museum at Weybridge, which can be used when the aircraft is being moved around.

The YAM had amassed a large collection of interior fittings, but for the initial roll-out benefit to the surviving Halifax veterans, it was just a shell. The next generation of volunteers had the task of fitting all these parts, including instrumentation, to make the aircraft as representative as possible for future generations, with work still continuing.

The Halifax was externally complete for a christening ceremony on Friday 13 August 1993 with 3,000 visitors present. The ceremony was performed by the station commanders of RAF Leeming and RAF Linton-on-Ouse, Group Captains Philip Roser and Tom Eeles. The name *Friday the 13th* derived from 158 Squadron Halifax B.Mk. III LV907 based at RAF Lissett, which made its first combat operation on 30 March 1944 to Nuremburg. By October, it had completed eighty operations, when it had a major service. On completion, it returned to service with the squadron and achieved its hundredth operation on 22 January 1945 to Gelsenkirchen, having been flown by more than two crews. After achieving the century, its pilot Flight Lieutenant stated: 'We always feel absolutely confident in her. She flies right and always gets us there.' LV907's last operation was her 128th, on 25 April 1945 to Wangerooge on 4 Group's final attack on an enemy target in the war. This aircraft, which survived, despite the many bad luck markings on the nose, was exhibited in Oxford Street London in 1945, but was not earmarked for preservation, and scrapped with all the other Halifaxes.

To house and preserve this fine exhibit, there was a need for a suitable hangar where the aircraft could be assembled and put on display. A fundraising campaign was started and a stored Second World War T.2 hangar was located dismantled at Popham, having been recovered from RAF Keevil. The structure was purchased and moved to Elvington, where it was cleaned and erection began during the winter of 1994/1995. The main construction was funded by a Heritage Lottery Fund grant of £135,000, to which was added funds from Canadian and UK based YAM supporters and patrons, plus £20,000 from the Science Museum PRISM Fund. Assembly of the 220 × 120-foot hangar continued during the winter of 1995/1996 and was completed by the early summer of 1996. It has been designated the Canadian Memorial Hangar in memory of the many RCAF aircrew who served in Halifaxes during the Second World War.

The aircraft is a lasting memorial to all those young men from Britain, the Commonwealth and Allied Air Forces who paid the ultimate price. It is also in memory of those aircrew who bravely faced the enemy over Germany, night after night and survived, and who have only been recognised in recent years. They should be able to take pride in having operated the Halifax, the most versatile heavy bomber in the war. The Elvington Halifax is the only complete example preserved in Europe as a fine example of the aircraft and crews' contribution to Allied victory in the Second World War, 1939–1945.

Above: Halifax B.III 'LV907 NP-F 158 Squadron' was officially rolled out at Elvington on Friday 13 September 1996 as a complete airframe, but without much interior detail. (*Newark Air Museum*)

Below: Halifax B.III 'LV907 NP-F 158 Squadron' inside the RCAF Memorial Hangar. (*Philip Birtles*)

Appendix I

Halifax Production

Mark	Factory	Number	Serials
Prototypes	Radlett	2	L7244, L7255.
B.Mk.I	Radlett	84	L9485-L9534, L9560-L9584, L9600-L9608.
B.Mk.II	Samlesbury	200	V9976-V9994, W1002-W1021, W1035-W1067, W1090-W1117, W1141-W1190, W1211-W1253, W1270-W1276.
B.Mk.II	Radlett	200	W7650-W7679, W7695-W7720, W7745-W7784, W7801-W7826, W7844-W7887, W7906-W7939.
B.Mk.II	Leavesden	200	BB189-BB223, BB236-BB285, BB300-BB344, BB357-BB391, BB412-BB446.
B.Mk.II	Speke	12	DG219-DG230.
B.Mk.V	Speke	138	DG231-DG253, DG270-DG317, DG338-DG363, DG384-DG424.
B & GR.Mk.II	Samlesbury	250	DT481-DT526, DT539-DT588, DT612-DT649, DT665-DT705, DT720-DT752, DT767-DT808.
B.Mk.V	Speke	100	EB127-EB160, EB178-EB220, EB239-EB258, EB274-EB276.
B & GR.Mk.II	Radlett	250	HR654-HR699, HR711-HR758, HR773-HR819, HR832-HR880, HR905-HR952, HR977-HR988.
B & GR.Mk.II	Radlett	49	HX147-HX191, HX222-HX225.
B & GR.Mk.III	Radlett	101	HX226-HX247, HX265-HX296, HX311-HX357.

Mark	Factory	Number	Serials
B & GR.Mk.II	Samlesbury	350	JB781-JB806, JB834-JB875, JB892-JB931, JB956-JB974, JD105-JD128, JD143-JD180, JD198-JD218, JD244-JD278, JD296-JD333, JD361-JD386, JD405-JD421, JD453-JD476.
B & GR.Mk.II	Leavesden	250	JN882-JN926, JN941-JN978, JP107-JP137, JP159-JP207, JP220-JP259, JP275-JP301, JP319-JP338.
B & Met. Mk.V	Ringway	96	LK626-LK667, LK680-LK711, LK725-LK746.
B.Mk.III	Ringway	104	LK747-LK766, LK779-LK812, LK826-LK850, LK863-LK887.
B, A & Met. Mk.V	Speke	420	LK890-LK932, LK945-LK976, LK988-LK999, LL112-LL153, LL167-LL198, LL213-LL258, LL270-LL312, LL325-LL367, LL380-LL423, LL437-LL469, LL481-LL521, LL534-LL542.
B & A.Mk.III	Speke	60	LL543-LL559, LL573-LL615.
B.Mk.III	Radlett	225	LV771-LV799, LV813-LV842, LV857-LV883, LV898-LV923, LV935-LV973, LV985-LV999, LW113-LW143, LW157-LW179, LW191-LW195.
B.Mk.VII	Radlett	15	LW196-LW210.
B.Mk.II	Samlesbury	100	LW223-LW246, LW259-LW301, LW313-LW345.
B & A.Mk.III	Samlesbury	260	LW346-LW348, LW361-LW397, LW412-LW446, LW459-LW481, LW495-LW522, LW537-LW559, LW572-LW598, LW613-LW658, LW671-LW696, LW713-LW724.
B.Mk.III	Leavesden	180	MZ282-MZ321, MZ334-MZ378, MZ390-MZ435, MZ447-MZ495.
B.Mk.III	Samlesbury	360	MZ500-MZ544, MZ556-MZ604, MZ617-MZ660, MZ672-MZ717, MZ730-MZ775, MZ787-MZ831, MZ844-MZ883, MZ895-MZ939.
B, A & Met. Mk.III	Speke	219	MZ945-MZ989, NA102-NA150, NA162-NA205, NA218-NA263, NA275-NA309.

Appendix I: Halifax Production

Mark	Factory	Number	Serials
A.Mk.VII	Speke	121	NA310-NA320, NA336-NA380, NA392-NA431, NA444-NA468.
B & A.Mk.III	Ringway	180	NA492-NA531, NA543-NA587, NA599-NA644, NA656-NA704.
B.Mk.VII	Radlett	117	NP681-NP723, NP736-NP781, NP793-NP820.
B.Mk.VI	Radlett	83	NP821-NP836, NP849-NP895, NP908-NP927.
B.Mk.III	Samlesbury	200	NP930-NP976, NP988-NP999, NR113-NR156, NR169-NR211, NR225-NR258, NR271-NR290.
B.Mk.III	Ringway	41	PN167-PN207.
B & A.Mk.VII	Ringway	90	PN208, PN223-PN267, PN285-PN327, PN343
B.Mk.III	Leavesden	80	PN365-PN406, PN423-PN460.
B.Mk.VI	Radlett	60	PP165-PP187, PP2203-PP216, TW774-TW796 (PP142-PP164 renumbered).
C.Mk.VIII	Radlett	100	PP217-PP247, PP259-PP296, PP308-PP338.
A.Mk.VII	Radlett	40	PP339-PP350, PP362-PP389.
B & Met. Mk.III	Samlesbury	80	RG345-RG390, RG413-RG446.
B.Mk.VII	Samlesbury	20	RG447-RG458, RG472-RG479.
B.Mk.VII	Samlesbury	300	RG480-RG513, RG527-RG568, RG583-RG625, RG639-RG679, RG693-RG736, RG749-RG790, RG813-RG853, RG867-RG879.
A.Mk.VII	Radlett	5	RT753-RT757.
A.Mk.IX	Radlett	145	RT758-RT799, RT814-RT856, RT868-RT908, RT920-RT938.
B & Met. Mk.VI	Samlesbury	25	ST794-ST818.

Final total manufacture was 6,178 Halifaxes, with over 900 more cancelled at the end of the war.

Appendix II

Halifax Units

Squadrons and Flights

Unit	Code	Formed/Base	Mk/Dates	Disbanded/Reequipped
10 Squadron	ZA	Leeming 8.7.40	B.Mk.I 12.41-8.42 B.Mk.II 12.41-3.44 B.Mk.III 3.44-8.45	Melbourne 5.45
35 Squadron	TL	Boscombe Down 7.11.40	B.Mk.I 11.40-2.42 B.Mk.II 1.42-3.44 B.Mk.III 12.43-3.44	Graveley 3.44
47 Squadron	MOHD	Qastina 1.9.46	A.MK.VI 9.46-9.48 A.Mk.IX 9.46-9.48	Dishforth 14.9.48
51 Squadron	MH	Snaith 11.42	B.Mk.II 11.42-1.44 B.Mk.III 1.44-6.45	Leconfield 5.45
58 Squadron	BY	Holmsley South 2.12.42	GR.Mk.II 12.42-3.45 GR.Mk.III 3.45-5.45	Stornoway 25.5.45
76 Squadron	MP	Linton-on-Ouse 1.5.41	B.Mk.I 4.41-12.42 B.Mk.V 2.43-7.44 B.Mk.III 1.44-5.45 B.Mk.VI 2.45-10.45	Holme-on-Spalding Moor 5.45
77 Squadron	KN	Elvington 5.10.42	B.Mk.V 11.44-12.44 B.Mk.III 5.44-3.45 B.Mk.VI 3.45-8.45	Full Sutton 8.45
78 Squadron	EY	Croft 20.10.41	B.Mk.II 3.42-1.44 B.Mk.III 1.44-4.45 B.Mk.VI 4.45-7.45	Breighton 7.45
96 Squadron	6H	Leconfield 21.12.44	B.Mk.III 12.44-3.45	Leconfield 4.45
102 Squadron	DY	Dalton 15.11.41	B.Mk.II 12.41-5.44 B.Mk.III 5.44-9.45 B.Mk.VI 7.45-9.45	Bassingbourn 8.9.45

Appendix II: Halifax Units

Unit	Code	Formed/Base	Mk/Dates	Disbanded/Reequipped
113 Squadron	MOHC	Aqir 1.9.46	C.Mk.VIII 9.46-12.46 A.Mk.IX 9.46-4.47	Aqir 1.4.47
138 Squadron	NF	Newmarket 25.8.41	B.Mk.I 10.41-12.42 B.Mk.II 10.42-8.44	Tempsford 8.44
147 Squadron	5F	Croydon 1.9.44	C.Mk.VII 1945-9.46	Croydon 15.9.46
148 Squadron	FS	Gambut 14.3.43	B.Mk.II 3.43-11.44 B.Mk.V 8.44-6.45	Brindisi 5.45
158 Squadron	NP	East Moor 6.6.42	B.Mk.II 6.42-1.44 B.Mk.III 1.44-6.45 B.Mk.VI 4.45-7.45	Lisset 5.45
161 Squadron	JR	Tempsford 8.4.42	B.Mk.V 11.42-10.44	Tempsford 10.44
171 Squadron	6Y	North Creake 7.9.44	B.Mk.III 9.44-7.45	North Creake 27.7.45
178 Squadron		Hosc Raui 4.3.43	B.Mk.II 5.43-10.43	Hosc Raui 9.43
187 Squadron	PU	Merryfield 1.2.45	C.Mk.III 2.45-10.45	Merryfield 3.45
190 Squadron	G5, L9, 6S	Great Dunmow 14.10.44	A.Mk.III 5.45-12.45 A.Mk.VII 5.45-12.45	Great Dunmow 21.1.45
192 Squadron	DT	Gransden Lodge 4.1.43	B.Mk.II 1.43-3.45 B.Mk.V 8.43-11.43 B.Mk.III 3.44-8.45	Foulsham 22.8.45
199 Squadron	EX	North Creake 1.5.44	B.Mk.III 2.45-7.45	North Creake 29.7.45
202 Squadron	Y3	Aldergrove 1.10.46	Met.Mk.VI 10.46-5.51 A.Mk.IX 8.49-1951	Aldergrove 12.50
224 Squadron	XB	Aldergrove 1.3.48	Met.Mk.VI 5.48-3.52	Gibraltar 3.52
246 Squadron	VU	Lyneham 11.10.44	B.Mk.III 11.44-2.45	Holmsley South 3.45
295 Squadron	8E, 8Z	Tarrant Rushton 21.1.46 Fairford 10.9.47	A/B.Mk.V 2.43-11.43 A.Mk.VII 2.46-3.46 A.Mk.IX 9.47-10.48	Tarrant Rushton 1.4.46 Fairford 1.11.48
296 Squadron	7C, 9W	Brize Norton 14.3.44	A.Mk.V 9.44-3.45 Mk.III 1.45-1.46 A.MkVIII 12.45-1.46	Earls Colne 23.1.46

Unit	Code	Formed/Base	Mk/Dates	Disbanded/Reequipped
297 Squadron	L5, P5	Earls Colne 30.9.44 Tarrant Rushton 1.4.46	Mk.III 10.44-3.46 A.Mk.V 10.44-12.44 A.Mk.IX 1.47-10.48	Earls Colne 1.4.46 Fairford 10.48
298 Squadron	8A, O6, 8T	Tarrant Rushton 4.11.43	B.Mk.V 11.43-8.45 Mk.III 10.44-8.45 A.Mk.VII 8.45-12.46	Mauripur 21.12.46
301 Squadron	GR	Brindisi 7.11.44	B.Mk.II 11.44-3.45 B.Mk.V 11.44-3.45 C.Mk.VIII 1.46-12.46	Chedburgh 18.12.46
304 Squadron	QD	Chedburgh 6.9.45	C.Mk.VIII 5.46-12.46	Chedburgh 18.12.46
346 Squadron	H7	Elvington 15.5.44	B.Mk.V 5.44-6.44 B.Mk.III 6.44-4.45 B.Mk.VI 3.45-11.45	Bordeaux 15.11.45
347 Squadron	L8	Elvington 20.6.44	B.Mk.V 6.44-7.44 B.Mk.III 7.44-4.45 B.Mk.VI 3.45-11.45	Bordeaux 15.11.45
405 Squadron	LQ	Pocklington 20.6.41	B.Mk.II 4.42-9.43	Gransden Lodge 9.43
408 Squadron	EQ	Leeming 14.9.42	B.Mk.II 12.42-8.43 B.Mk.V 8.42-12.42 B.Mk.III 7.44-2.45 A.Mk.VII 2.45-5.45	Linton-on-Ouse 10.43
415 Squadron	6U	East Moor 26.7.44	B.Mk.III 7.44-5.45 A.Mk.VII 2.45-5.45	East Moor 15.5.45
419 Squadron	VR	Croft 1.10.42	B.Mk.II 11.42- 4.44	Middleton St George 4.44
420 Squadron	PT	Tholthorpe 12/12/43	B.Mk.III 12.43-5.45	Tholthorpe 5.45
424 Squadron	QB	Skipton-on-Swale 6.11.43	B.Mk.III 12.43-1.45	Skipton-on-Swale 1.45
425 Squadron	KW	Tholthorpe 10.12.43	B.Mk.III 12.43-5.45	Tholthorpe 5.45
426 Squadron	OW	Linton-on-Ouse 18.6.43	B.Mk.III 4.44-5.45 A.Mk.VII 6.44-5.45	Linton-on-Ouse 3.45
427 Squadron	ZL	Leeming 5.5.43	B.Mk.V 5.43-2.44 B.Mk.III 1.44-3.45	Leeming 3.45

Unit	Code	Formed/Base	Mk/Dates	Disbanded/Reequipped
428 Squadron	NA	Middleton St George 4.6.43	B.Mk.II 11.43-6.44 B.Mk.V 6.43-6.44	Middleton St George 6.44
429 Squadron	AL	Leeming 13.8.43	B.Mk.II 8.43-1.44 B.Mk.V 11.43-3.44 B.Mk.III 3.44-3.45	Leeming 3.45
431 Squadron	SE	Tholthorpe 15.7.43	B.Mk.V 7.43-10.44 B.Mk.III 3.44-10.44	Croft 10.44
432 Squadron	QO	East Moor 19.9.43	B.Mk.III 2.44-5.45 B.Mk.VII 6.44-5.45	East Moor 15.5.45
433 Squadron	BM	Skipton-on-Swale 25.9.43	B.Mk.III 11.43-2.45	Skipton-on-Swale 1.45
434 Squadron	WL	Tholthorpe 15.6.43	B.Mk.V 6.43-5.44 B.Mk.III 5.44-12.44	Croft 12.44
460 Squadron	UV	Breighton 4.1.42	B.Mk.II 8.42-10.42	Breighton 10.42
462 Squadron	Z5	Fayid 7.9.42 Driffield 12.8.44	B.Mk.II 9.42-3.44 B.Mk.III 8.44-9.45	El Adem 15.2.44 Foulsham 24.9.45
466 Squadron	HD	Leconfield 22.12.42	B.Mk.II 9.43-11.43 B.Mk.III 10.43-5.45 B.Mk.VI 2.45-5.45	Bassingbourn 6.9.45
502 Squadron	YG, V9	St Eval 22.2.42	GR.Mk.II 1.43-5.45 GR.Mk.III 2.45-5.45	Stornoway 25.5.45
517 Squadron	X9	St Davids 25.11.43	Met.Mk.V 11.43-6.46 Met.Mk.III 2.45-6.46 Met.Mk.VI 2.45-6.46	Chivenor 21.6.46
518 Squadron	Y3	Stornoway 6.7.43	Met.Mk.V 7.43-8.45 Met.Mk.III 3.45-10.46 Met.Mk.VI 3.46-10.46	Aldergrove 1.10.46
519 Squadron	Z9	Tain 17.8.45	Met.Mk.III 8.45-5.46	Leuchars 31.5.46
520 Squadron	2M	Gibraltar 20.9.43	Met.Mk.V 2.44-6.45 Met.Mk.III 4.45-4.46	Gibraltar 25.4.46
521 Squadron	5O	Chivenor 3.11.45	Met.Mk.III 12.45-4.46 Met.Mk.VI 12.45-4.46	Chivenor 31.3.46
578 Squadron	LK	Snaith 14.1.44	B.Mk.III 1.44-4.45	Burn 15.4.45

Unit	Code	Formed/Base	Mk/Dates	Disbanded/Reequipped
614 Squadron	Letter	El Adem 15.2.44	B.Mk.II 3.44-3.45	Amendola 3.45
620 Squadron	D4, QS	Great Dunmow 18.10.44	A.Mk.VII 5.45-9.46 A.Mk.IX 8.46-9.46	Aqir 1.9.46
624 Squadron	Letter	Blida 22.9.43	B.Mk.II 9.43-9.44 B.Mk.V 9.43-2.44	Blida 15.2.44
640 Squadron	C8	Leconfield 7.1.44	B.Mk.III 1.44-3.45 B.Mk.VI 3.45-5.45	Leconfield 7.5.45
644 Squadron	2P, 9U	Tarrant Rushton 23.2.44	A.Mk.V 3.44-12.44 Mk.III 12.44-11.45 A.Mk.VII 3.45-9.46	Qastina 1.9.46
1341 Flight	Letter	Digri 5.45	B.Mk.III 3.45-10.45 A.Mk.VII 1945-10.45	Digri 13.5.45
1575 Flight	Letter	Tempsford 28.5.43	B.Mk.V 5.43-8.43	Maison Blanche 22.9.43
1577 Flight	Letter	Llandow 9.8.43	B.Mk.V 8.43-1945 B.Mk.III 11.44-5.46	Dhamial 1.6.46
1586 Flight	GR	Derna 3.11.43	B.Mk.II 10.44-11.44	Brindisi 7.11.44

Training Units

Unit	Code	Formed/Base	Dates	Disbanded
1654 HCU	JF, UG	Swinderby 19.5.42	B.Mk.II/V 9.43-2.44	Wigsley, 1.9.45
1656 HCU	BL, EK	Lindholme 10.10.42	B.Mk.I/V 2.43-12.44	Lindholme 10.11.45
1658 HCU	TT, ZB	Rickall 7.10.42	B.Mk.I/II/III/V 10.42-4.45	Rickall 13.4.45
1659 HCU	FD, RV	Leeming 7.10.42	B.Mk.I/II/III/V 10.42-5.45	Topcliffe 10.9.45
1660 HCU	TV, YW	Swinderby 22.10.42	B.Mk.V 10.42-11.43	Swinderby 11.11.46
1661 HCU	GP, KB	Waddington 9.11.42	B.Mk.II/V 2.43-9.43	Winthorpe 24.8.45
1662 HCU	KF/SV	Blyton 26.1.43	B.Mk.I/II/V 1.43-4.45	Blyton 6.4.45
1663 HCU	OO, SV	Rufforth 2.3.43	B.Mk.II/III/V 4.43-5.45	Rufforth 28.5.45

Appendix II: Halifax Units

Unit	Code	Formed/Base	Dates	Disbanded
1664 HCU	DH, ZU	Croft 10.5.43	B.Mk.II/III/V 9.43-11.44	Dishforth 6.4.45
1665 HCU	NY, OG	Mepal 23.4.43	A.Mk.III/ AMk.V, A.Mk. VII 1.44-2.45	Linton-on-Ouse 13.7.46
1666 HCU	ND, QY	Dalton 5.6.43	B.Mk.II/III/V 11.43-1.45	Dalton 3.8.45
1667 HCU	GG, KR	Lindholme 1.6.43	B.Mk.II/V 6.43-11.44	Sandtoft 9.11.45
1668 HCU	CE	Balderton 15.8.43	B.Mk.II 9.43-11.43	Balderton 21.11.43
1669 HCU	L6, 6F	Langar 15.8.44	B.Mk.III/V	Langar 16.3.45
1674 HCU	Letter	Aldergrove 10.10.43	B.Mk.II/V 10.43-7.44	Lossiemouth 30.11.45
1331 HTCU		Syerston 15.12.46	A.VII 12.46-1.48	Syerston 5.1.48
1332 HTCU	YY	Dishforth 7.11.45	C.VI 8.44-1.48	Dishforth 5.1.48
1333 TSTU		Syerston 6.7.46	A.IX 3.45-1.48	North Luffenham 5.1.48
1383 TSCU	GY	Crosby-on-Eden 1.8.45	A.VII 8.45-8.46	Crosby-on-Eden 6.8.46
1385 HTSCU		Wethersfield 1.4.46	A.III 4.46-7.46	Syerston 3.7.46
21 HGCU	FEO-FET	Brize Norton 20.10.44	A.III/VII 2.46-12.47	North Luffenham 3.12.47
22 HGCU		Keevil 15.10.44	A.III 10.44-11.45	Blakehill Farm 15.11.45
Halifax Development Flight		Holmsley South 15.11.44	A.III 11.44-3.45	Merryfield 31.3.45
AFTDU		Tarrant Rushden 1.12.43	A.Mk.V 12.43-1.44	Netheravon 14.1.44
BCIS	IK	Finningley 5.12.44	B.Mk.III/V 12.44-7.47	Scampton 15.6.47
EANS	FGC-FGE	Shawbury 28.10.44	B.Mk.II/III 1.45-6.49	Shawbury 31.7.49
ORTU	OX	Thruxton 9.12.43	A.III/VII 5.44-1.46	Wethersfield 1.4.46

Unit	Code	Formed/Base	Dates	Disbanded
1 (C) OTU	Letter	Silloth 1.4.40	GR.II 3.43-10.43	Silloth 19.10.43
PFNTU	QF	Gransden Lodge 10.4.43	B.Mk.II 4.43-5.45	Warboys 12.44

HCU: Heavy Conversion Unit

HTCU: Heavy Transport Conversion Unit

TSTU: Transport Support Training Unit

TSCU: Transport Support Conversion Unit

HTSCU: Heavy Transport Support Conversion Unit

HGCU: Heavy Glider Conversion Unit

AFTDU: Airborne Forces Tactical Development Unit

BCIS: Bomber Command Instructors School

EANS: Empire Air Navigation School

ORTU: Operational Refresher Training Unit

1 (C) OTU: 1 (Coastal) Operational Training Unit

PFNTU: Pathfinder Force Navigation Training Unit

Halifaxes also operated with a number of the establishments, and other training and development Units.

Appendix III

Halifax Specification

Dimensions

Wingspan: 98 feet 8 inches, 103 feet 8 inches in late Mk.III
Overall length: 71 feet 7 inches
Height (tail down): 20 feet 9 inches.

Performance

Mark	Max Weight	Engines	Service Ceiling	Max. Speed	Range
B.Mk.I Srs 1	55,000lb	1,130hp Merlin X	18,000ft	262mph @ 18,000ft	1,000 miles
B.Mk.I Srs 2	60,000lb	1,130hp Merlin X	18,000ft	262mph @ 18,000ft	1,000 miles
B.Mk.I Srs 3	60,000lb	1,220hp Merlin XX	18,000ft	262mph @18,000ft	1,000 miles
B.Mk.II Srs 1	60,000lb	1,220hp Merlin XX	22,000ft	261mph @22,000ft	830 miles
B.Mk.II Srs 1A	60,000lb	1,480hp Merlin 22	21,000ft	253mph @ 19,000ft	830 miles
B.Mk.III	65,000lb	1,675hp Hercules XVI	20,000ft	231mph @ 13,500ft	1,020 miles
A.Mk.III	65,000lb	1,675hp Hercules XVI	20,000ft	289mph @ 13,500ft	1,020 miles
C.Mk.III	65,000lb	1,675hp Hercules XVI	23,000ft	309mph @ 19,500ft	1,020 miles
B.Mk.V Srs 1	61,500lb	1,220hp Merlin XX	22,000ft	261mph @ 19,500ft	
B.Mk.V Srs 2	61,500lb	1,480hp Merlin 22	21,000ft	253mph @ 19,000ft	

Mark	Max Weight	Engines	Service Ceiling	Max. Speed	Range
B.Mk.VI	65,000lb/ 68,000lb	1,680hp/1,800hp Hercules 100	22,000ft	309mph @ 19,500ft	1,450 miles
B.Mk.VII	65,000lb	1,675hp Hercules XVI	20,000ft	281mph @ 13,500ft	
A.Mk.VII	65,000lb	1,675hp Hercules XVI	20,000ft	289mph @ 13,500ft	
C.Mk.VII	65,000lb	1,675hp Hercules XVI	20,000ft	293mph @ 13,500ft	
C.Mk.VIII	65,000lb	1,800hp Hercules 100	25,000ft	322mph @ 19,500ft	
A.Mk.IX	65,000lb	1,675hp Hercules XVI	20,000ft	289mph @ 13,500ft	

Armament

B.MK.I
Guns: 2 × 0.303in. nose turret, 2 × 0.303in. beam guns, 4 × 0.303in. tail turret.
Bombs: 13,000lb—2 × 2,000lb + 6 × 1,000lb in fuselage +6 × 500lb in wings.
Or: 4 × 2,000lb or 9 × 500lb in fuselage.

B.Mk.II Srs 1
Guns: Beam guns replaced by 2 × 0.303in. dorsal turret
Bombs: Same as Mk.I.

B.Mk.II Srs 1 (Special)
Guns: No nose turret or initially dorsal turret, tail turret as before.
Bombs: Same as Mk.I.

B.Mk.II Srs 1A
Guns: 1 × 0.303in. in nose, dorsal and tail guns same as (Special)
Bombs: Same as Mk.I with fuselage alternatives of 1 × 8,000lb, 2 × 4,000lb bombs, or 2 × 1,500lb mines.

GR & Met.Mk.II Srs 1A, 1B, GR & Met Mk,III
Guns: Same as B.Mk.II Srs 1A
Depth charges: 8 × 250lb added to bomb load.

GR.Mk.III
Bombs   9 × 500lb in fuselage.

A.Mk.III, A.Mk.V & A.MkVII
Guns: Tail turret only.

B, GR. & Met.Mk.V:
Guns: Same as B.Mk.II
Bombs: Same as B.Mk.II

B.Mk.VI & B.Mk.VII
Guns: Same as B.Mk.III, later aircraft introduced 2 × 0.5in. tail turret
Bombs: Reduced to 12,000lb maximum + 4 × 500lb in wings. All fuselage alternatives available.

A.Mk.IX
Guns: 2 × 0.5in. tail turret.

Appendix IV

Preserved Halifaxes

With the end of the Second World War, there was little interest in preserving RAF combat aircraft used during the war, even significant examples. Most were just scrapped and melted down for the metal required in a Britain recovering from an economy devastated by the challenges of war. It was not until the 1960s that an interest began to awaken, by which time many complete types had been lost, including Halifaxes.

The loss and recovery of Halifax B.Mk.II W1048 during an attack on *Tirpitz* has been covered in Chapter 4, and Chapter 13 details the restoration of Halifax B.Mk.III LV907 *Friday the 13th* starting with a rear fuselage of GR.Mk.II HR792 in use as a hen coop on Stornoway.

The other significant survivor was A.Mk.VII NA337, which like W1048, was raised from a lake in Norway. The last surviving Halifax was A.Mk.VII PN323, which was moved to Radlett in 1950 and fitted with a single fin for radio trials, where it remained until 1961, when it was finally scrapped. The nose and forward fuselage were saved for the Staverton based Skyfame Museum in 1965. When the Museum closed in 1979, this Halifax relic was acquired by the Imperial War Museum, where it was exhibited as a walk-through attraction. The nose section was moved in 2012 to Duxford where it is stored on public display.

As mentioned in Chapter 4, Halifax B.Mk.II W1048 had crash-landed on ice-covered Lake Hoklingen during the night of 27/28 April 1942, following an attack on *Tirpitz*. After the crew escaped, it sank through the ice, where it remained until 30 June 1973. After going through the ice, the aircraft sank 92 feet to the mud-covered lakebed in total darkness, preserving the Halifax at 4 degrees centigrade until it was raised.

The wreck was first investigated by local Norwegian divers, who were following up on a rumour that an aircraft had crashed into the lake in the Second World War. They began investigating using grapnel hooks, sending a diver to take a closer look. The Halifax was found to be essentially complete by a team from RAF Wyton, fortunately without any bombs on board. By locating the surviving aircrew members, it was established that no human remains were within the wreck, otherwise it would be declared a war grave and would remain undisturbed.

The main challenge was to raise it to the surface of the lake, which was land-locked, making it impossible to bring in a floating crane. The lift team consist of RAF Strike

Halifax Mk.VII PN323 at Radlett used for radio trials, until scrapped and the front fuselage sent to Staverton. (*Handley Page Association*)

Command personnel with civilian specialist diving advice, and the assistance of Norwegian amateur divers. The RAF team arrived in mid-June 1973 and assembled a working platform over the Halifax site, with the divers becoming accustomed to diving in the cold dark water.

The first task was to expose the wing to fuselage bolts and heavy cables looped around for the lift, with great care for the starboard wing which had suffered fire damage during the crash-landing. The outer wing attachment was so fragile it broke off during the lift. Eighty empty oil drums, with a capacity of 40 gallons were loaned, which were required for the buoyant lift when filled with air. This would allow the hulk to be moved to a shallow area, where it could be pulled out of the water, the drums allowing a gradual lift capability. To release the nose buried in mud, drums were attached to the tail, allowing the nose to be carefully eased out without suction damage.

A typical diving crew consisted of two divers, who would be briefed on the state of the aircraft, and what was required during the dive. As the divers pulled themselves down a rope to the Halifax, 12 feet down all light was gone in the brown stained water. With the light of four car headlamps, the air feed from a full drum would be attached to an empty one, and then position the next drum for air filling by the next pair of divers. The aircraft eventually came clear of the lakebed and was free to push on the wing tip. It was also possible to enter the aircraft and inspect the condition with a powerful torch. A survey of the banks of Lake Hoklingen located a gently sloping area about 2 miles from the wreck, with an access road, and 80 yards out the water was about 12 feet deep, dropping away abruptly to a 50- or 60-foot depth. An ideal place for the recovery. To protect the aircraft underside, a wooden sledge was made to fix in the open bomb-bay when it was dragged up over the mud, which had steel matting laid on the ground.

Ready for the lift to start, the raft over the Halifax was moved to one side, with surface marker buoys fixed at the aircraft extremities along the lifting ropes to indicate lift progress, while there were indicators on the lakebed to ensure nothing was left below. Remarkably the aircraft came to the surface with air bubbles, having risen slowly from the depths. The aircraft condition was good with no additional damage and much of the original paint still there. It was then towed to the shallow approaches of the beaching area. The concern about fuel leakage made the beaching of the aircraft urgent, as the lake was used as a freshwater reservoir. The move to the beaching site took about 3 hours, where the aircraft was secured for overnight.

The next morning, the bomb-bay skid was pushed into place under the fuselage where it was secured ready for two tractors dug in a ditch on the far side of the track, ready to winch up using a wire tow line. The drums under the tail were punctured to release the air and allow the nose to rise, with the slow pull to start. Once on to dry land it was ready to be dismantled and removed, taking three days to achieve. More than 950 gallons of fuel and 158,000 rounds of 0.303-inch ammunition were recovered for destruction. Included in the wreck were documents, personal items and equipment. After 3 weeks of dismantling by 71 MU engineers, the aircraft was shipped to Britain for preparation to go on display at the RAF Museum at Hendon.

When the first attempts were made at restoration, the surviving structure was found to be very fragile, resulting in a conservation plan, with restoration limited to the nose turret, throttle box, and pilot's and engineer's panels. The Halifax was delivered to Hendon in 1982, and installed in the new Bomber Command Museum, where it has been placed in its unrestored condition, protected by a coat of red inhibitor, as a tribute to the RAF bomber crews in the Second World War.

In 1982, another Halifax was located under water, this time 770 feet down on the bed of Lake Mjosa in Norway. It was identified as A.Mk.VII NA337 of 644 (RCAF) Squadron, which was shot down on 23 April 1945 while dropping supplies to the Norwegian resistance. Of the six crew, only the rear gunner survived, while the rest

Halifax B.II W1048 emerging from Lake Hoklingen in Norway in June 1973. (*Handley Page Association*)

of the crew died of exposure in the icy water. The wreck was offered to the Halifax Aircraft Association in February 1994 for recovery and restoration in Canada.

Salvage rights were granted by the Norwegian government in July 1994, allowing fund raising to start. A Norwegian diving and salvage company, DACON Subsea of Oslo, were successful in tendering for the raising of the wreck, using a specially designed steel lifting frame called 'Moby Grip' which was intended to hook over the inboard wing leading edge ready for lifting in a nose down attitude. The floating control room was moored over the aircraft location equipped with a Remote Operating Vehicle (ROV) fitted with video cameras, manipulating arm and gripping device. The first part raised was a 17-foot section of the rear fuselage with gun turret, which had broken off the remainder of the aircraft, which came up on 15 August 1995. By the end of the month, the team were ready to begin raising the remainder of the fuselage and wing. On 5 September, the aircraft was freed from the mud and over 12 hours was successfully raised and moved to the safety of shallow water, ready for lifting on to dry land.

Twelve men—a volunteer military maintenance team from Canada—disassembled the aircraft and put the sections in crates for storage at Gardermoen Air Force Base near Oslo. From here, it was flown in a RCAF Hercules to the National Air Force Museum of Canada at Trenton, Ontario on 12 December 1995. Then started a 10 year restoration by 100 volunteers taking some 350,000 man hours, ready for the official unveiling on 5 November 2005 in memory of the many Canadian air and ground crew who flew in Halifaxes during the Second World War.

Halifax B.Mk.II HR871 operated by 405 (RCAF) Squadron crashed in the Baltic off the coast of Sweden during the night of 2/3 August 1943. The aircraft had been on a raid to Hamburg and was struck by lightning causing two engines to fail. The crew were able to safely bail out of the aircraft, and the wreckage was located in May 2015. Fundraising continues for this demanding salvage operation, where the wreck is badly damaged and immersed in sea water. Some advanced restoration was started using the wing parts from two scrapped Hastings transports in Malta in 2011.

Halifax B.II W1048 on the surface of Lake Hoklingen in Norway with the outer starboard wing and No. 4 Merlin still on the lake bottom. (*Handley Page Association*)

Appendix IV: Preserved Halifaxes

Halifax B.II W1048 conserved in its original condition, as the surviving structure was too fragile to restore. (*Handley Page Association*)

Further Reading

Barnes, C. H., *Handley Page Aircraft Since 1907* (Putnam, 1976)
Bingham, V., *Halifax: Second to None* (Airlife, 1986)
Birch, D., *Rolls-Royce and the Halifax* (Rolls-Royce Heritage Trust, 2014)
Blanchett, C., *From Hull, Hell and Halifax* (Midland Publishing, 2006)
Buttler, T., *Halifax* (Warpaint, 2006)
Ellis, K., *Testing to the Limits* (Crecy, 2015)
Falconer, J., *Handley Page Halifax* (Haynes, 2016)
Jefford, C. G. (Wing Commander), *RAF Squadrons* (Airlife, 1988)
Mason, T., *The Secret Years: Flight Testing at Boscombe Down 1935–1945* (Crecy, 2010)
Merrick, K. A., *The Handley Page Halifax* (Aston Publications, 1990)
Rapier, B. J., *Halifax at War* (Ian Allan, 1987)
Robertson, B., *Halifax Special* (Ian Allan, 1990)
Robinson, I., *The Unbeaten Warrior Returns* (Yorkshire Air Museum, 1996)
Robinson, I., *Home is the Halifax* (Grub Street, 2010)
Sturtivant, R., Hamlin, J., & Halley, J., *RAF Flying Training & Support Units* (Air-Britain, 1997)